CULTURAL PSYCHOTHERAPY

Working with Culture in the Clinical Encounter

Karen M. Seeley, Ph.D.

JASON ARONSON INC.
Northvale, New Jersey
London

This book was set in 11 pt. Berkeley by Alpha Graphics of Pittsfield, NH and printed and bound by Book-mart Press, Inc. of North Bergen, NJ.

Library of Congress Cataloging-in-Publication Data
Seeley, Karen M.
    Cultural psychotherapy : working with culture in the clinical encounter /
Karen M. Seeley
    p.   cm.
    Includes bibliographical references and index.
    ISBN 0-7657-0224-X
    1. Cultural psychiatry.   2. Psychotherapy—Cross-cultural studies.
3. Ethnopsychology
    I. Title.
    RC455.4.E8S44   1999
    616.89'14—DC21   99-17469

Printed in the United States of America on acid-free paper. For information and catalog write to Jason Aronson Inc., 230 Livingston Street, Northvale, NJ 07647-1726, or visit our website: www.aronson.com

To my parents,

Aileen and Robert Seeley

To my children,

Hayley, Brigitte, and Tyler

And to my husband,

Brink

Contents

Acknowledgments

I owe thanks to many people for their assistance at various points in the preparation of this book. The cooperation of the subjects of this research was essential. For their participation in a series of intensive interviews with me, interviews in which they openly reflected upon their intercultural psychotherapies, they have my enduring gratitude. Although I do not report here on my own clinical work, I want to acknowledge my patients of diverse backgrounds, whose cases have significantly informed my thinking about cultural phenomena in psychotherapy.

I am intellectually indebted to my former professors, Marshall Segall of Syracuse University and Robert A. LeVine of Harvard University, for their commitments to interdisciplinary psychologies. My training as a therapist began at the New York University School of Social Work, where it was enriched by the supervision of Barbara Greenstein during my internship in Gouverneur Hospital's Parent Infant Therapeutic Program. My training continued at the University of Michigan Psychological Clinic under my supervisors Barbara Cain and Jeffrey Urist, both of whom made important contributions to my clinical work. Research preliminary to this project was carried out with the support of Robert Hatcher, Director of the University of Michigan Psychological Clinic, and was funded by the International Institute and by the Office of the Vice President for Research at the University of Michigan.

My dissertation committee helped shape and refine this research. I thank Frederick Erickson and Howard Stevenson, anthropologist and psychologist, respectively, of the University of Pennsylvania's Graduate School of Education, and Jeffrey Seinfeld, of the New York University School of Social Work, for their critical responses to this work. Susan Agrest, Sema Gurun, and Judy Roth read earlier drafts of the manuscript; Janaki Bakhle, Webb Keane, and Monique Stark helped me think through particular interpretive problems. Their comments and suggestions have greatly enhanced this book. I give special thanks to Alan Roland, a pioneer in intercultural psychoanalytic treatments, for his careful readings of my sections on psychoanalysis. I also thank the staff at Barnard College Mental Health Services for their ongoing intellectual stimulation and collegial support.

My greatest debts are owed to the members of my family, who generously tolerated my distractions and patiently suffered my absences while I devoted myself to writing this book. I especially thank Hayley, whose "Certificate of Hope" buoyed me in dark moments, Brigitte, whose luxuriant naps in her first three years of life gave me hours to sit and write, and Tyler, whose unfolding musical talents were a source of inspiration to me. Most of all I am indebted to Brinkley Messick. Had I not been provided his intellectual engagement, constant encouragement, and loving kindness, this book would not have been written.

Introduction

Contemporary psychotherapists increasingly find themselves treating patients whose cultural backgrounds differ from their own. In these intercultural treatments, therapists work with foreign patients who are temporary residents, refugees, or immigrants, or with patients who, as the children of immigrants, were raised in bilingual and bicultural environments. As more and more such patients seek mental health treatment, there is a growing demand for cultural approaches to psychotherapy. These are approaches that recognize the existence of important psychological differences across cultures, that conceptualize cultures as constitutive of human psychologies, that acknowledge the particular cultural subjectivities involved in therapeutic encounters, and that encourage clinical explorations of cultural material. Despite the clear demand for such cultural orientations, however, they have yet to materialize.

In this book, I examine the conditions of and the possibilities for a cultural psychotherapy. I argue that the standard models of psychotherapy are rooted in Western and universalizing psychological assumptions, and I suggest specific theoretical and technical revisions that create spaces within these models for considerations of other cultural notions of psychic being and functioning. I also argue that by selectively drawing on cultural anthropology's comparative perspectives on human behavior and consciousness, and by adapting some of its ethnographic and linguistic methods for use in clinical investigations, psychotherapists can become more analytically attuned to the lives and minds of their patients from other cultural backgrounds.

In addition, in my view, a cultural psychotherapy must be informed by the experiences and evaluations of foreign and ethnic patients who have undergone intercultural clinical treatments. In *Cultural Psychotherapy*, I analyze a set of extensive interviews that I conducted with six foreign and ethnic patients who were treated by American psychotherapists. I am aware that presenting patients' assessments of their treatments, especially in the absence of corroborating information from their therapists, poses certain questions. Throughout the clinical literature therapists' voices prevail, while patients' voices are conspicuous by virtue of their absence. Yet to dismiss patients' evaluations of their treatments is to lose information that is critical to the field in general, and especially so to the development of a cultural psychotherapy.

Therapists may not realize the extent to which their foreign and ethnic patients' subjectivities, idioms of distress, and treatment expectations are culturally inflected, may not understand the ways in which the interpersonal dynamics of clinical encounters are culturally shaped, and may be unaware that many such patients refrain from introducing significant cultural material into their psychotherapies. The patient interviews analyzed here draw attention to these and other cultural dimensions of clinical encounters, and raise specific questions regarding the benefits and limitations of Western psychotherapies in treating non-Western patients.

ORGANIZATION OF THE BOOK

This book is divided into two parts. Part I examines the fundamental theoretical issues of intercultural psychotherapies. After considering the legacy of Freud, Chapter 1 critically examines the Western cultural assumptions that underlie the standard models of psychodynamic psychotherapy, and that, in the perspective of this book, limit their utility in treating patients from other cultures. Chapter 1 suggests a number of ways in which these standard models of psychotherapy might be adapted to incorporate cultural approaches to clinical material.

Chapter 2 turns to selected bodies of anthropological research that are relevant to intercultural psychotherapies. Here, anthropological understandings of culture, selfhood, emotion, child development, and language are examined. Illustrating the wide cross-cultural variation within each of these topics, Chapter 2 argues that such research may benefit psychotherapists by allowing them to better grasp the cultural nature of the material that their foreign and ethnic patients present in treatment.

Part II shifts to the sphere of clinical practice and considers intercultural treatments from the patient's point of view. Extensive interviews with six foreign and ethnic patients who underwent psychotherapy with American therapists provide specific examples of such patients' understandings of, and reactions to, their intercultural psychological treatments. Each of Chapters 3 through 8 focuses on a particular patient's experiences of his or her psychotherapy. These chapters highlight the particularities of intercultural treatment dynamics, even as they place in question the utility of Western psychotherapies in the treatment of patients from other cultures.

Part III, providing the proposed foundations for a contemporary cultural psychotherapy, synthesizes the theoretical issues discussed in Part I with issues raised by the interview material analyzed in Part II. It identifies both the specific and the common themes of the six intercultural psychotherapy cases presented in Part II, and reviews their theoretical and technical implications for intercultural treatments.

Part I

Taking Culture into Account

Introduction:
Culture and the Clinic

FREUD'S LEGACY

An essential feature of Freudian theory is its identification of an intergenerational conflict in which the son struggles to replace his father as the object of his mother's passions. Indeed, Freud (1940) characterized this conflict, which he called the Oedipus complex, as "the central experience of the years of childhood" (p. 48). While Freud explained the ensuing father–son rivalry as the natural result of the child's covetous longings for his father's wife, it is possible to interpret these oedipal strivings, to which Freud attributed a murderous intensity, less literally. They might be understood, for example, as representing the younger generation's wish to displace its elders in order to assume their positions of authority and control. When conceptualized in this way, oedipal desires, which are usually notorious for their destructive capacities, acquire an adaptive dimension in that they ensure the transmission of power from one generation to the next and guarantee social continuity.

As the creator of psychoanalysis, Freud was the patriarch of an intellectual tradition—indeed, some of his followers considered him their spiritual father (Sutherland 1989). In this paternal role, Freud manifested an ambivalence about the younger generation of analysts who would succeed him. To be sure, he often welcomed their contributions, revising his science in light of their discoveries (Grosskurth 1987). But he also manifested the oedipal father's fear of usurpation, concerned that those who disputed his teachings threatened his authority, and that their growing power foreshadowed the decline of his.

The wish to shield psychoanalytic theory from critical reaction and to preserve its central tenets was not Freud's alone. Many of those who were among the succeeding generation of psychoanalysts, as if choosing not to enact the oedipal drama, refrained from altering this new science in ways that might have marked it as their own. Instead, they protected the work of their spiritual father with a fervor characteristic of the intellectual climate of turn-of-the-century Vienna. Lacan (1977) observed that psychoanalysts, "terrified" of exposing themselves to "the fresh air of criticism" (p. 37), defended disciplinary tenets with something resembling religious zeal. Bettelheim (1990) also noted the devotional character of early psychoanalysts, representing Freud's followers as disciples who considered it their duty to spread his message throughout the world. Theoretical divergences and technical innovations were commonly received not in the impersonal jargon of the scientific tradition to which psychoanalysis claimed to belong, but in the emotionally charged language of intimate relationships. Melanie Klein's ideas, for example, were characterized as betrayals of classical psychoanalysis (Greenberg and Mitchell 1983).

Indeed, those who openly broke with psychoanalysis's "sacred texts" risked suffering not only the wrath of the patriarch, but the ostracism of those who competed for his legitimation as well. Under threat of "excommunication" (Crapanzano 1992), psychoanalytic theoreticians who privately rejected Freud's theory of the instincts continued to incorporate as much of classical drive theory as possible into their novel theoretical formulations.

While it is true that such feverish loyalty to the work of the master did not bring theoretical innovation in psychoanalysis to an absolute halt, it successfully delimited the theory's scope, excluding areas of inquiry and points of view considered irrelevant or antithetical to psychoanalytic tenets. Moreover, once Freudian theory attained the paradigmatic status of a Kuhnian science, its boundaries became more definite and more rigid (Kuhn 1962). Practitioners found it increasingly difficult to admit information and to investigate problems that fell outside of its parameters. Supporters of psychoanalysis refused to seriously consider opposition to the discipline. Instead, they subjected negative reactions to the very frames of analysis that critics had challenged. Psychoanalytic research, rather than openly questioning disciplinary concepts, principles, and conventions, served instead to reformulate and to defend the existing body of theory.

Not only were such conservative positions transmitted from one generation of psychoanalysts to the next, but they influenced the shape of clinical psychology and of other mental health professions as well, interfering with the development of psychotherapeutic theory and research in a variety of areas. Indeed, in many aspects of psychological treatment, Freudian perspectives remain firmly in place. Of central interest in this book are the ways in which Freudian theory's emphasis on the timeless and universal features of the human mind, on intrapsychic reality, and on the culturally decontextualized individual patient has turned clinical attention away from the investigation of cultural variation in human behavior and consciousness, and has clouded the fact that persons are profoundly embedded in cultural groups.

It is not that Freud was uninterested in the relationship between human psychology and culture. His writings on other cultures, however, were influenced by the social evolutionary theory ascendant in his time. Such theory claimed that every civilization would progress through a fixed sequence of development, beginning with the primitive and culminating in the modern—that is, the Western. Applying these ideas to his universalizing conceptions of human mind, Freud claimed that the psychic processes of the members of preliterate societies resembled the primitive mental operations of the neurotic Viennese patients he treated (Freud 1913).

Although social evolutionary theory has long since receded in influence, universalizing models of mind and development continue to influence mainstream psychology's theories of behavior and consciousness. Supporters of these ideas, however, currently find themselves in an intellectual climate in which all such master narratives (Levy 1994) have fallen from favor, and in which universalism is variously criticized as being ethnocentric and Eurocentric.

Indeed, the critique of psychology as a monocultural science (Kennedy et al. 1984) is increasingly expressed. There is growing awareness that although psychology attempts to make timeless and universal claims about human behavior and consciousness, it is rooted in specific social, cultural, and historical circumstances; that although psychology aims to be value free, it is embedded in Western ideals of the individual, of the family, and of the mind; and that although psychology wishes to be the authoritative voice on human behavior and consciousness, it typically studies a narrow segment of the human population.

While charges of monoculturalism most frequently have been aimed at general psychology, every field of practice involved in the delivery of mental health services has become the target of similar complaints. Some contend that the standard models of psychological treatment are actually European ethnopsychologies (Roland 1988, Sampson 1988). By explicitly demonstrating their foundations in the worldviews, norms, and values of the West, these critics argue that the theory and practice of psychotherapy are relevant only to extremely circumscribed Western cultural milieus, and lack transcultural relevance.

Despite this emerging cultural critique of psychological treatment, to which this book contributes, the contemporary theory and practice of psychotherapy are among Freud's most enduring legacies. To emphasize the role that classical psychoanalysis continues to play in the everyday practice of psychotherapy is not to minimize the ways in which contemporary conceptions of psychological treatment differ from Freud's. Over the past several decades, many elements of clinical theory and practice have been adapted to better fit the changing circumstances and pressures of modern life in the West. The theories and techniques that clinicians currently employ in psychological treatments take into account relational patterns as well as biological drives, normal individual development as well as psychopathology, the self as well as the object, interpersonal as well as intrapsychic reality, and analytic subjectivity as well as objectivity. Even as they embrace such theoretical revisions, however, significant numbers of psychotherapists continue to incorporate Freudian psychoanalysis's universalizing perspectives into their clinical work. In consequence, they fail to attribute psychic significance to their patients' cultural formations. Rather, they take their patients' "basic feelings and conflicts" as their primary subjects and disregard the "superficial" influences of culture (Ticho 1971, p. 313).

Thus Freud's cultural decontextualization of the patient remains a persistent feature of contemporary clinical theory and practice. By providing psychotherapists with a rationale for overlooking the particular cultural dimensions of their foreign and ethnic patients' psychologies, Freud's legacy continues to compromise the psychotherapeutic treatment of patients from other cultures and ethnic groups. Given the newly global character of the psychological clinic, it is a legacy with profound implications for contemporary psychotherapy.

GENEALOGIES OF PSYCHOTHERAPY

To enter into a discussion of contemporary psychotherapy is to confront, from the outset, a disunified field of practice. How is it possible to represent a field that is so internally diverse? The practitioners of psychotherapy have such distinctive professional formations—in social work, in clinical psychology, in counseling psychology, in psychiatry, and in psychoanalysis—that to address the field as a whole often more closely resembles speaking across disciplines than within one. Intradisciplinary disunity is also a consequence of the widely varying theoretical orientations of contemporary psychotherapists. The therapeutic models clinicians currently embrace range from the cognitive-behavioral to the humanistic, and from the Jungian to the existential; many clinicians conduct eclectic psychotherapies that combine a variety of treatment approaches. Such variations in clinical theory and practice make charting the contours and the contents of the field of psychotherapy famously difficult. They also make it necessary to specify what I will be talking about when I refer to the standard models of psychotherapy.

For the purposes of this book, the standard models of psychotherapy refer to treatment approaches that are based on the assumptions that patients' unconscious motivations shape their overt behaviors, and that patients' past experiences affect their present functioning. Such approaches frequently focus on patients' developmental histories, past and present relational experiences, central conflicts, and mechanisms of defense. Clinicians who use these approaches commonly incorporate the principles of transference, countertransference, and resistance into their clinical work, although they may employ revised versions of these principles that differ from classical formulations. They provide their patients with attuned and attentive listening, and they offer them interpretations, insight, and opportunities to work through troubling personal and relational matters. They seek to reduce their patients' symptoms, to enhance their self-knowledge, and to remove the psychological obstacles that prevent them from living satisfying lives.

As the above discussion suggests, these approaches to clinical treatment are rooted in psychoanalysis (Schafer 1992, Wallerstein 1995). Some are anchored in Freudian psychoanalysis's theory of the mind, while others are firmly attached to psychoanalytic theories of the ego, of objects, of the self, or of interpersonal relationships. Clearly, the standard models of psychoanalysis provide more than the tools of such treatment approaches; instead, by providing their principal theoretical assumptions and methods, and by defining their field of practice, they contribute their essential character. Therefore, for the purposes of this book, I will speak of the standard models of psychoanalysis as constituting the standard models of psychotherapy as well.

THE GLOBAL CLINIC

Like many other professional fields, late twentieth-century psychotherapy has been marked by advancing globalization. The combination of growing transnational diasporas, new forms of international shuttle migration, and domestic demographic shifts has, increasingly, turned psychotherapeutic treatment into an international and multicultural endeavor. In this rapidly diversifying sociocultural climate, intercultural contact has become commonplace in the clinical consulting room. With a frequency unimagined even a decade ago, psychotherapists in public and private mental health settings alike are asked to treat both foreign and ethnic patients.

As psychotherapy's clientele has become more culturally diverse, the limitations of its standard theories and methods have grown more apparent. Despite the rising demand for intercultural psychotherapies, the theoretical and practical requirements of such treatments are poorly understood, as are the challenges they pose to conventional clinical practice. The standard models of psychotherapy offer universalizing conceptions of human behavior and mind. As a rule, they disregard the cultural dimensions of human psychological functioning, and they neglect to examine the ways in which significant cultural differences between patient and psychotherapist affect the progress and outcomes of psychological treatment. Further, as a result of their universalistic orientations, the standard models of psychotherapy discourage clinicians from exploring cultural variations in human psychologies. Clearly, there is a pressing need to develop a cultural psychotherapy that would better serve the foreign and ethnic patients who increasingly seek psychological help; yet many psychotherapists continue to employ standard models of psychotherapy in the treatment of such patients. In consequence, psychological treatment remains, largely, a universalizing and Western project.

My interest in developing a cultural psychotherapy is not simply academic; rather, it is grounded in my experience as a psychotherapist. In my clinical practice over the past several years, I have worked with patients from a wide array of national and ethnic origins. Yet neither my formal clinical training nor clinical supervision nor case conference exchanges with colleagues adequately prepared me to perform intercultural psychological treatments. Seeking to effectively treat patients of varied cultural backgrounds, I realized that the standard models of psychotherapeutic theory and practice required significant critical revision to more fully address the demands of the newly global psychological clinic.

Cultural Psychotherapy critically examines the lack of fit I have perceived between universalizing psychotherapeutic models and the therapeutic requirements of culturally diverse psychotherapeutic patients, and proposes culturally enriched approaches to psychological treatment. Primarily addressed to psychotherapists who practice in international and multicultural clinical settings, and who have sensed the need for culturally informed treatment approaches, this book explores the theoretical and practical requisites of a cultural psychotherapy. By extending forms of cultural inquiry into the clinical domain, *Cultural Psychotherapy* attempts to provide clinicians with new ways of enlarging their theories and methods for use in intercultural treatments, with new ways of conceptualizing the psychologies of their foreign and ethnic patients, and with new ways of understanding intercultural treatment relationships.

CASE VIGNETTES

Jennifer

Jennifer came to her first psychotherapy session in a highly agitated state. Skittish and slight, wearing immaculate sneakers, jeans, and a baseball cap turned backward over her short dark hair, 22-year-old Jennifer was expecting a visit from her parents later that day, and she was worried. In defiance of their orders, she had continued to date a man of whom they disapproved. Jennifer feared that her parents had learned of her deceptions, and that, as in the past, they would physically harm her. When I asked Jennifer how I could help her, she told me that she needed to develop strategies for coping with their abuse.

Jennifer's self-presentation underwent radical shifts as she told her story. At times, she appeared helpless and frightened in the face of her parents' authority and control, and she seemed to suggest that she deserved their punishment. Describing herself as incapable of confronting her parents, she claimed that she had no choice but to accept the decisions that they made for her future. But then suddenly Jennifer would pull herself up, declare her autonomy, and assert her intention to distance herself from her parents.

As Jennifer spoke, I wondered what to make of her sudden shifts in self. How was I to understand the fact that she was of two distinct minds about her independence? What was I to make of her ambivalence toward her parents' abuse and control of her? And how might she differently experience my interventions as she moved from one self state to the other?

Toward the end of that first hour, another factor entered the clinical picture. Jennifer informed me that her parents were Pakistani. They had immigrated to the United States from the city of Karachi as teenagers, and had raised Jennifer and her brothers in a traditional Muslim home. Although Jennifer was currently attending college and living on campus, her parents expected that she would return home after her graduation and that she would live with them until the day she married. Just as Jennifer's Americanized appearance concealed her Pakistani heritage, her flawless English disguised the fact that her first language was Urdu, and that this remained the language of her relationship with her parents.

With this information, new clinical questions arose. How might Jennifer's varying self-presentation be related to her bicultural identity? How might her experiences of living in two distinct cultural worlds—and of having a native language other than English—affect her participation in psychotherapy?

Tina

Tina, a 25-year-old Chinese-American, sought a psychological consultation at the urging of a colleague who had noticed her deepening despondency. In our initial meeting, Tina, who had a successful career in banking, complained of feeling unmotivated at work and uninterested in life. She found herself unable to concentrate in the office, and she had begun to take frequent sick days and to fantasize about quitting her job. Tina stated that she had gone into banking at her parents' insistence, but that she disliked her work and strongly wished to change professions. She worried, however, that her parents would react badly if she decided to leave her field. At the end of the consultation, Tina recalled that a dispute about careers between her older sister and her parents had precipitated her sister's suicide.

Tina's sister had committed suicide at the age of 29; Tina had been 20 at the time. As Tina approached the age at which her sister had taken her life, she found herself flooded by family memories. A third-generation Chinese-American, Tina had grown up in the West Coast Chinese community where her parents still lived. Her sister's suicide had left Tina without a sibling and had made her her parents' only child. Tina currently lived alone and had few social contacts. She had nowhere to turn for help, yet she was reluctant to enter psychotherapy. As she told me, her sister had been in treatment after graduating from college, and in her parents' view it had exacerbated the conflicts between them.

After Tina left the room, I was unsure of how to evaluate her predicament and her condition. What might it mean to Tina to be the sole surviving child of a Chinese-American family? Might her sense of familial obligation differ from mine, and from that of my mainstream American patients? Should I assume that Tina's sister had suffered from depression, and that Tina, too, might be depressed—or might depression be much differently configured among Chinese-Americans? How might I assess the level of her suicidality without knowing the meanings of suicide to Chinese-Americans? Lacking such culturally informed understandings, was it possible for me to accurately evaluate Tina's state?

Zoran

A 20-year-old immigrant from Sarajevo in the former Yugoslavia sought psychological treatment for help in managing his steadily worsening anxieties. Zoran complained that he was increasingly preoccupied by fantasies of personal catastrophe. Afraid of what might befall him in the world outside, he had taken to spending whole days in his room. Zoran told me that he was frequently unable to sleep, and that when he slept he was awakened by frightening nightmares.

Zoran and his mother had immigrated to the United States nearly seven years ago to escape the war in Yugoslavia. At the time of their arrival, Zoran was almost 14 years old. The child of a mixed marriage between a Serb and a Muslim, his Serbian father had remained behind with no intention of moving to America. Neither Zoran nor his mother had had contact with him since, and his whereabouts, as well as his safety, were unknown.

In the initial consultation, Zoran recounted a brief narrative of uprootings, separations, and violence. His sense of personal fragmentation was obvious. Indeed, he said that as a result of having spent his life in two different countries, and of having spoken two different languages, he had come to experience himself as two separate people. Zoran clearly wished to distance himself from his past. When I asked about his early years in Yugoslavia, his memory often failed him. Although Zoran seemed to feel trapped by his history, he took pains to separate previous events from the anxiety that currently overwhelmed him.

Listening to Zoran's story, I was once again confronted by complex clinical questions. Could a conventional clinical treatment adequately address the traumas of cultural dislocation and loss that Zoran had suffered? Might his anxieties be culturally patterned in ways unfamiliar to me? How was I to treat someone who described himself as having two separate cultural selves, one of which he had disavowed?

SHIFTING PARADIGMS

More and more frequently, psychotherapists are called upon to treat patients like Jennifer, Tina, and Zoran. Some patients, like Jennifer, may have been born in the United States to immigrant parents who resisted the press of assimilation to American society, and who attempted to ground their children in their native language and culture. Other patients, like Tina, may have grown up in well-established ethnic communities in the United States, communities in which strong ethnic identities flourish and languages other than English predominate. Still other patients, like Zoran, may be immigrants to the United States. They may have immigrated to the United States permanently, they may be refugees who seek political asylum, or they may be temporary residents who plan to return home once they have completed a job or a course of study.

Patients like Jennifer, Tina, and Zoran present psychotherapists with significant challenges. By and large, therapists have tended to work with patients whose cultural backgrounds are similar to theirs—patients with whom they share fundamental, culturally determined conceptions as to "what is automatic, habitual, assumptive, and unwitting in conduct and thought" (Wohl 1989, p. 81). As a rule, they have found it unnecessary to generate culturally informed understandings of human behavior and mind, or to consider the ways in which cultures shape individual psychologies. Under conditions of cultural similarity between patient and therapist, culture has generally been viewed as irrelevant to the personal beliefs and behaviors under therapeutic investigation. Indeed, under such clinical conditions culture often seemed nonexistent, fostering the ethnocentric belief that "others have culture, while we have human nature" (Schwartz 1992, p. 329). This is not to suggest that any patient and therapist ever completely share cultural worlds. Individual differences in class, ethnicity, religion, and gender, as well as in interpretations and enactments of cultural ideals and norms, ensure that no two persons are culturally identical (Goodenough 1976, Schwartz 1978). Every therapeutic dyad therefore contains some degree of cultural variation, and every psychotherapy is, to some extent, intercultural.

I maintain, however, that the cultural variation that exists between patients and therapists who are of different nationalities, and between patients and therapists of different ethnicities who are native speakers of different languages, is of another order. When their cultural and linguistic backgrounds diverge in these ways, patient and therapist cannot be expected to share culturally shaped worldviews, assumptions, habits, or patterns of thought. As a result of their varying histories and conceptual frameworks, patient and therapist are likely to experience difficulties in creating the shared, culturally organized meanings on which successful psychotherapeutic treatments depend.

Psychotherapists are not alone in confronting this newly reconfigured world. The current press to render professions more culturally relevant and responsive cuts across a variety of disciplines. Lawyers have created the "cultural defense" to protect foreign-born clients who have engaged in activities that are legal in their native societies, but that violate American laws (Magnarella 1991). Teachers struggle to educate students of varying nationalities and ethnicities whose culturally shaped patterns of thinking, learning, and interacting differ from theirs (Erickson 1997). Medical specialists confront variations in the ways in which patients from diverse cultures experience and exhibit the diseases that the specialists have conventionally constructed as universal (Good 1994, Kleinman 1980).

Many practicing psychotherapists recognize that these changing historical circumstances pose new challenges to clinical theory and practice. Some who have treated patients from other cultures have observed firsthand that their foreign and ethnic patients' experiences of psychological difficulty are powerfully shaped by non-Western and other alternative cultural meanings. They have noted that the static (Saleebey 1994) of received psychological theory prevents them from listening to their foreign and ethnic patients' narratives in an unbiased way, and that preconceived Western diagnostic categories cannot comfortably contain such patients' accounts of psychic imbalance and distress. These psychotherapists recognize that the increasingly multicultural and international nature of their practice demands that they move beyond conventional, universalizing models of treatment. And yet calls to create new cultural models of psychotherapy, to adapt existing treatment models so that they incorporate cultural perspectives, and to train culturally competent clinicians (Sue 1998) have produced few concrete results.

Moreover, even as appeals for culturally informed psychotherapies multiply, universalizing conceptions of mental life draw fresh support from neurobiological research. Perhaps Freud would have welcomed such developments. As a consequence of his professional training in neurology, he believed that medical science would someday discover the exact physiological correlates of the mental processes and disorders that his metapsychological formulations imperfectly described. Today, Freud's vision is increasingly realized. Newly elaborated universalizing conceptions of the mind—conceptions that are based not on metapsychological formulations but on the underlying structure and chemistry of the brain—increasingly inform psychiatric accounts of mental disability and distress. By virtue of this recent paradigm shift in the field of psychiatry, neurochemical explanations of behavior now strongly compete with psychological ones; in many cases, they have supplanted them. To create a catalogue of mental diseases whose etiologies reside in biochemical rather than in psychological phenomena, there has been a concerted effort to dissociate discrete psychiatric symptoms from their intervening precipitants (Good 1992). By doing so, however, psychiatrists have divorced mental disorders not only from their personal meanings and histories, but from their cultural contexts and significations as well. The clinical ramifications of such practices are clear. Psychotherapists who privilege biochemically based psychiatric perspectives on the mind need not spend clinical time exploring the cultural dimensions of their foreign and ethnic patients' experiences of psychological distress. Nor need they think twice before diagnosing foreign and ethnic patients in terms of the ostensibly universal psychiatric categories that are legitimized by their links to the biological workings of the human brain. Clearly, such reductionistic perspectives on human functioning fail to provide clinicians who practice in a world of increasing cultural variety with the necessary means of conceptualizing the particular cultural psychologies of their foreign and ethnic patients. At the same time, they fail to generate more effective strategies for serving the growing numbers of international and multicultural individuals who seek psychological help.

INTERDISCIPLINARY PARADIGMS

It is not that there has been a complete absence of efforts to bring culturally informed approaches to the study of human behavior and mind. Indeed, current thinking on the interconstitution of culture and mind belongs to a long tradition in the history of Western ideas that asserts their inseparability (Jahoda 1993). In recent times, a number of anthropologists and psychologists have attempted to join cultural and psychological perspectives. The middle decades of the twentieth century, for example, saw interdisciplinary ventures such as the Culture and Personality School, which sought to understand the interrelationships between cultural patterns and personality types by identifying the basic or modal personalities of particular societies. Other interdisciplinary ventures examined cross-cultural variation in such conventionally psychological topics as child development, perception, and memory, eventually culminating in the subfields of cross-cultural psychology, psychological anthropology, and cultural psychology (Bock 1980, Shweder 1990, Spindler 1978).

The middle decades of the twentieth century also saw the emergence of the Cultural School of psychoanalysis (Thompson 1950). Breaking with Freud, this small group of psychoanalysts argued that normal and abnormal development were rooted not in innate and universal instinctual drives, but in environmental pressures that varied across historical periods and cultural contexts. In their view, individuals were not autonomous, decontextualized, biological entities. Rather, persons were inextricably embedded in social interactions and in societies, and their psychologies took shape in response to cultural norms and ideals (Fromm 1941, Horney 1937, Sullivan 1953).

Although the members of the Cultural School contested many of the universalizing orientations and premises of psychoanalysis, their clinical examinations of the cultural dimensions of human behavior and consciousness were quite limited. Sullivan's orientation was more ecological and interpersonal than cultural, while Fromm's generalizations about national character, as well as his broadly existential considerations of the effects of cultural pressures on the development of the self, lacked direct clinical application. And while Horney explored the cultural and historical origins of particular neurotic types, like the other psychoanalysts of the Cultural School she failed to develop cultural models of clinical practice. The Cultural School had little impact on the majority of practitioners, and it failed to reconfigure psychoanalysis in either theory or practice.

As the currents of postmodernism have challenged disciplinary boundaries in recent years, interdisciplinary endeavors have intensified. Among cultural anthropologists, there has been a resurgence of interest in psychological anthropology, with research proliferating on the self, the body, gender, and emotion (Abu-Lughod 1986, Daniel 1984, Lutz 1988, Ortner 1996, Shostak 1981). At the same time, the newly constituted field of cultural psychology, by inviting general psychologists to adopt cultural perspectives on human functioning and to work toward a "credible theory of psychological pluralism" (Shweder 1993, p. 498), has spurred psychological research on the cultural patterning of cognition, motivation, and human development.

Like their interdisciplinary predecessors, however, both psychological anthropology and cultural psychology speak primarily to researchers in the field and in the laboratory. Neither field directly addresses practicing psychotherapists who treat patients from other cultures. Further, despite the obvious importance of research in psychological anthropology and in cultural psychology to the development of cultural approaches to psychotherapy, their findings have yet to be synthesized and adapted for a clinical audience. As a result, their usefulness to psychotherapists—whose experiences with the interconstitution of mind and culture take the form of clinical encounters with persons from other cultures—has been slight. Although therapists may recognize that the presenting complaints and personal histories that foreign and ethnic patients bring to psychotherapy take non-Western cultural forms and enfold non-Western cultural meanings, they lack the conceptual frameworks that would assimilate such cultural content into clinical theory and practice.

FOLIES À DEUX

Because cultural perspectives generally remain outside the parameters of psychotherapy, clinicians who conduct intercultural treatments encounter difficulties of many varieties. Lengthy lists of the problems that are common to such treatments have been compiled, yet few effective solutions have been produced. As a result, many intercultural treatments resemble folies à deux. Some are plagued by premature terminations, with many foreign and ethnic patients abandoning psychotherapy after a single session. Those that continue often contain therapeutic missteps, collisions, and accidents; frequently, they are played out in the clinical consulting room between mutually uncomprehending, and sometimes mutually incomprehensible, clinical parties.

Anthropologists have warned that when the stories non-Westerners tell are interpreted through Western theoretical frames, misunderstandings inevitably ensue (Rosaldo 1989). The same holds true for intercultural psychotherapies. Misunderstandings commonly occur in such treatments when psychotherapists view their non-Western patients through the lenses of Western psychological theories: when therapists evaluate their foreign and ethnic patients by Western norms and standards; when they interpret patients' culturally normative behaviors as impediments to achieving Western ideals of selfhood, or as resistances to treatment (Chin 1993); and when they reduce culturally specific patterns of emotional disturbance to variations on "universal" psychological disorders (Koss-Chioino and Vargas 1992, Littlewood 1990, Saleebey 1994).

Additional difficulties in intercultural treatments stem from the conventions of psychotherapeutic practice, which frequently violate the norms of other cultures. Simply by asking their patients to reveal intimate personal material, to recount family histories, to express emotional reactions, and to air interpersonal disputes, psychotherapists may demand types of disclosures and interactions that their foreign and ethnic patients' indigenous cultures prohibit (Draguns 1985, Varma 1988). Moreover, psychotherapy's interest in fostering highly separated, individuated, and autonomous selves is contrary to indigenous cultural values that emphasize collective welfare, interrelatedness, and interdependence (Ewalt and Mokuau 1995, Landrine 1992). The working relationship between patient and therapist is another problematic element of many intercultural treatments. Egalitarian and nondirective psychotherapists can unsettle patients who are more comfortable with hierarchical and directive professional interactions (Koss-Chioino and Vargas 1992), while distant, unresponsive, and impersonal psychotherapists can upset patients who wish to establish warm, reassuring, and familial treatment relationships (Varma 1988).

More serious problems can result from the misdiagnoses that occur in intercultural treatments. As Benedict (1934) observed, ideas of psychological normality and of psychopathology are culturally defined, varying from one society to the next. Just as Western cultures foster "gratifications of the ego which according to any absolute category would be regarded as abnormal" (p. 75), behaviors that Western clinicians consider deviant may be highly valued elsewhere. Indeed, psychotherapists who work with patients from other cultures often find it difficult to interpret their symptoms and behavioral cues, and to correctly distinguish practices that are culturally syntonic to the patient from those that signal psychopathology (Kakar 1985, Roland 1988). Psychotherapists can err by overpathologizing behaviors that are normative in the patient's native culture, but that seem aberrant when taken out of context, and by underdiagnosing particular syndromes that are common to the patient's native culture but with which they are unfamiliar (Abel et al. 1987). Another type of misdiagnosis that has been found to occur in intercultural psychological treatments involves classifying depressed patients as psychotic. In some such cases—especially those involving the use of interpreters—clinicians have failed to detect depressed patients' suicidality, with tragic results (Sabin 1975).

When therapists lack cultural perspectives, they are less able to engage their foreign and ethnic patients in creating the shared conceptions of experience that are essential to psychotherapy. Premature terminations, as well as misdiagnoses, culturally inappropriate interventions, and fragile treatment alliances, frequently ensue. Intercultural treatments that are ineffective—and in some cases, countertherapeutic— are likely to persist as long as cultural perspectives remain outside the parameters of psychotherapy.

THE CONSTRUCTION OF CLINICAL KNOWLEDGE

Therapists who conduct intercultural treatments regularly confront such daunting clinical challenges. Yet little clinical research specifically examines the role of culture in psychotherapy. Moreover, the scant research that exists on culture and psychotherapy, and on intercultural treatments, rarely has been informed by the views of foreign and ethnic psychotherapy patients; instead, most of this research has been based almost entirely on therapists' points of view. The result is that foreign and ethnic patients' assessments of their clinical treatments have entered consideration as the constructions of their psychotherapists.

Why has research on culture and psychotherapy so consistently failed to examine patients' reactions to their treatments? It could be that studying psychotherapy patients presents daunting challenges to methodology and confidentiality. But a more plausible explanation for the conspicuous exclusion of patients' voices from clinical research is that despite newly influential relational and egalitarian treatment approaches —and despite recent clinical commitments to learning from the patient (Casement 1985)—clinical knowledge, including the capacity to evaluate the courses and outcomes of psychological treatments, continues to be located in the hands of its practitioners.

If the clinical literature constructs therapists as more knowledgeable sources than patients, then it also constructs them as more credible ones. Many psychotherapists appear to believe that patients make unreliable informants. This point was driven home to me when I presented a group of clinicians with material drawn from my interviews with an Indian man who had been treated by an American psychotherapist (for further discussion, see Chapter 3). I chose to present this material, which detailed the Indian man's largely unfavorable reactions to his treatment and to his therapist, in the hopes of sparking a critical discussion on intercultural treatments. But because the Indian man had been a psychotherapy patient, the clinicians in attendance seemed unwilling to seriously consider his comments. Instead, they discredited the man's capacity to report on his own psychotherapy by quickly and neatly pathologizing him. In their view, the material that I presented did not contain data that might inform intercultural treatments; rather, it contained pathologies that required interpretation and diagnosis. By the end of my presentation, these clinicians had concluded that the Indian man was severely depressed and character disordered, and that his negative reactions to his treatment were motivated primarily by unresolved transferential angers toward his therapist.

Whatever rationales have been formulated to justify the systematic exclusion of patients' voices from studies of psychotherapy, such practices weaken the discipline. There is simply no legitimate basis for the conclusion that psychotherapy patients—even those who have been diagnosed with psychological disorders—have nothing of importance to convey to clinicians about psychological treatments. Were representations of psychological treatments restricted to those guaranteed to be in perfect mental health, the clinical literature would be very thin indeed. Yet such practices persist, with unfortunate results. The reflections, speculations, and conclusions concerning intercultural treatments that are disseminated to clinical audiences continue to be dramatically one-sided, while the primary sources that might inform and enrich intercultural psychotherapies are shut out of the discussion.

Moreover, when therapists are called upon to speak about, to write about, and to theorize about patients' psychotherapy experiences, their opinions and expertise are further legitimized. The underrepresentation of patients' views in clinical research thus reinscribes analytic authority.

THE CONSTRUCTION OF PSYCHOTHERAPY PATIENTS

The suggestion that clinical researchers interview foreign and ethnic patients about their psychotherapies with American therapists not only runs counter to the conventions of clinical research but it contradicts psychotherapeutic theory and practice by foregrounding the cultural dimensions of clinical treatments. For especially in the preliminary evaluation of patients, psychotherapeutic conventions customarily erase non-Western and other alternative cultural issues from the emerging clinical picture.

The medical practice of constructing its objects by transforming the individuals it treats into persons with medical problems (Good 1994) has a clear analogy in the field of mental health. In psychological clinics, those who seek psychotherapy come to be represented as persons suffering from Western psychological disorders. The first step in transforming individuals into Western clinical entities is often accomplished by means of the standardized forms that many mental health settings require patients to complete before commencing treatment. These forms commonly solicit a variety of personal data in such categories as family composition, medical history, educational level, and occupational background. Commonly, they require prospective patients to complete checklists of the psychological symptoms and syndromes that they have experienced—every item of which is rooted in Western psychiatric categories.

Although the forms solicit a wealth of material on the patient's background, the information they request about the patient's culture of origin is virtually nil. Frequently, the patient's cultural identity disappears from the forms completely. In other cases it emerges haphazardly, as a by-product of some other piece of information requested by the forms. For example, foreign patients are often only identifiable when some bit of data, such as the address of a relative or of a family physician, reveals ties to another land. The forms are even less reliable in identifying patients with mixed cultural backgrounds and patients from ethnic subcultures whose family names have been anglicized.

Because the forms are generally completed prior to the first treatment session, therapists frequently read them before setting eyes on the patient. In these circumstances, the forms provide psychotherapists with a preliminary map of the patient's psychological landscape. Because the forms are usually available only in English, they also require patients to use the categories of what is to them a foreign language in describing themselves and their difficulties. The net effect of the forms, therefore, is to replace the patient's culturally organized account of emotional disequilibrium—containing, for example, indigenous worldviews, values, emotions, systems of meanings, and conceptions of mental health—with a set of predetermined psychological problems that the discipline recognizes, and for which it prescribes specific and culturally sanctioned courses of treatment. Indeed, it is conceivable that the very exercise of filling out clinical forms trains prospective patients to translate their culture-bound syndromes and difficulties into conventional psychological categories, and to present themselves to their therapists in these terms, rather than in the terms of their indigenous cultures.

A second step in the creation of the psychological patient is accomplished by the means of case conferences, the weekly staff meetings common to many mental health facilities where therapists present their patients to other clinicians on staff. These meetings are usually attended by a variety of mental health professionals—social workers, counseling and clinical psychologists, psychoanalysts, and psychiatrists. In mental health settings that function as training institutions, case conferences provide invaluable educational experiences for students and other trainees, who find their understanding of psychotherapeutic practice enriched by the array of clinical viewpoints presented there.

From the perspective of a cultural psychotherapy, however, perhaps the most striking feature of the many case conferences that I have attended is the way in which patients' ethnic and cultural identities are almost immediately erased from the clinical picture. As patients are presented, their native cultures are commonly reduced to exotic backdrops against which the usual psychological stories are claimed to unfold. At other times, the patients' native cultures are represented as purely descriptive features of their lives, ones with no deeper hold on their psyches than, for example, their make of car. Once the presenter has stated that a particular patient was born in a certain country, or has a parent of a specified nationality, cultural considerations are deemed satisfied. Frequently, they are not discussed at all. Psychiatric symptomatology, developmental history, family dynamics, and other presenting information are then presented and evaluated without an exploration of their potential non-Western or other cultural meanings, reflecting the prevailing conviction that cultural differences are superficial, and can be comfortably subsumed by universalizing psychological formulations.

The conventions of the clinic thus effectively construct foreign and ethnic psychotherapy patients as psychologically indistinguishable from Western patients. The conversion of such patients' indigenous understandings of their distress into conventional psychiatric categories works to silence their native cultural voices and material, and to remove them from the therapeutic arena. At the same time, such conversions diminish the possibility that therapeutic interventions that consider and respond to patients' indigenous cultures will be offered in intercultural psychotherapies.

THE CONSTRUCTION OF PSYCHOTHERAPISTS

If procedures such as the forms and case conferences construct the patients of psychotherapy, then they also, if indirectly, construct its practitioners. Such clinical conventions permit psychotherapists who are unfamiliar with the psychological workings of culture, and with the means for its clinical investigation, to restrict their attention to the predetermined psychiatric categories that are listed on the forms. These are categories with which psychotherapists have considerable familiarity and experience, especially in comparison with their foreign and ethnic patients. Their prior knowledge of the specific causes and treatment requirements of Western psychiatric disorders then structures therapeutic encounters.

The conventions of the clinic commonly operate in tandem with the universalizing models of psychotherapy that dominate clinical practice. These models disregard foreign and ethnic patients' indigenous conceptions of the mind and of the self. Instead, they direct psychotherapists to sift through the culturally shaped material that their foreign and ethnic patients present in search of recognizable symptoms, syndromes, and behavioral patterns. They then encourage psychotherapists to focus their attention on this preselected set of psychological problems. Such universalizing models spare psychotherapists the challenges of confronting psychic constellations that are unfamiliar, unfathomable, and strange. Authorized to dismiss their foreign and ethnic patients' culturally shaped perceptions of their experiences, clinicians are free to reframe them within the boundaries of conventional theoretical constructs.

Together with the conventions of the clinic, the standard models of psychological treatment construct psychotherapists as expert and empowered in relation to their patients from other cultures. Through their applications of Western psychological knowledge to their foreign and ethnic patients' mental operations—knowledge that they alone possess—psychotherapists attain a degree of authority and power akin to those of the "omniscient" practitioners of classical psychoanalysis. Intercultural treatments thus can be seen as dialogic engagements in which patients who are culturally deracinated, and who have been stripped of their native psychological understandings, are treated by experts in universalizing models of the mind.

In intercultural psychotherapies, factors that go beyond clinicians' authoritative constructions of human behavior and mind add to analytic authority and power. Anthropologists remind us that all intercultural encounters occur between individuals who have particular personal and cultural histories, and who occupy specific social, economic, and political positions (Abu-Lughod 1991, Ortner 1996). Such issues of positionality affect intercultural treatments, undermining notions of equality between patients and therapists. For example, many international patients who seek psychological treatment in the United States are foreigners in their therapist's home country. In addition to being positioned as outsiders, their immigration status and their sense of security in America may be tenuous. Some ethnic patients belong to minority groups with long histories of political oppression and disempowerment; many receive psychological treatment from members of the majority culture. Speaking a nonnative language in psychotherapy can further exacerbate foreign and ethnic patients' sense of disadvantage in the treatment relationship.

Foucault (1963, 1980) is among those who have argued that psychoanalytic encounters are asymmetrical in power, and that they are skewed inexorably in the clinician's direction. Foucault, of course, wrote with a different clinical era in mind, one that predated the spread of relational and intersubjective models of treatment. He therefore could not have considered contemporary clinical approaches which seek to balance the power within the clinical consulting room by defining therapeutic knowledge as mutually created by patient and psychotherapist. Although such new approaches explicitly reject the notion of analytic authority, from a Foucauldian perspective the privileging of therapists' knowledge is an inevitable consequence of the institutional linkages between psychotherapy and established structures of Western power. According to this view, psychotherapy is formally connected to psychology and to the academy. As such, it belongs to the discourse of science, which represents knowledge and truth in the West. It is these institutional connections that authorize and empower psychotherapy's discourses as well as its practitioners, while simultaneously discrediting the unscientific, indigenous discourses of foreign and ethnic psychotherapy patients.

THE CULTURE OF THE CLINIC

Conventional clinical procedures not only construct the participants in psychotherapeutic encounters in ways that disempower patients and empower clinicians, but they also help create the culture of the psychological clinic. As discussed above, these procedures endorse standard psychotherapeutic discourses, discourses that both impose Western metapsychologies and subjugate alternative cultural conceptions of mental health and healing. The many foreign and ethnic patients who enter psychotherapy with alternative cultural metapsychologies—that is, with specific, culturally shaped ideologies of emotional imbalance and psychic healing—are likely to find that these indigenous metapsychologies are silenced and invalidated in their sessions. Despite the fact that when patients and therapists are from different cultures the clinical consulting room is, in effect, a multicultural space—and a space that frequently contains non-Western as well as Western cultures—the hegemonic discourses of psychotherapy, which the forms and case conferences reinforce, screen out patients' indigenous cultures. Thus, as they begin their psychological treatments, foreign and ethnic patients confront the built-in Western culture of the psychological clinic.

1

The Culture of Theory

THE PRESENCE OF THE FOUNDER

Despite competing explanations of human behavior and mind, Freudian psychoanalysis continues to exert an extraordinary hold over contemporary clinicians. Even those who actively seek to revise Freudian
theory and technique acknowledge that the founder of psychoanalysis
is a perpetual presence, and that classical psychoanalytic concepts are
very much alive (Mitchell 1997). Certainly Freudian psychoanalysis is
very much alive for the many practicing clinicians who embrace its
universalizing precepts, who consider the cultural backgrounds of their
foreign and ethnic patients to be of minor psychic significance, and who
practice psychotherapy as if people who inhabit different cultural worlds
remain essentially the same. Freudian psychoanalysis is equally alive for
practicing clinicians who, rather than modifying received classical theory
and technique to accommodate patients from other cultures, dismiss
potential non-Western or ethnic patients as unanalyzable or untreatable
(Foster 1996b, Moskowitz 1996). Practicing in the perpetual presence
of the founder of psychological treatment, psychoanalysts and psycho-

therapists alike have failed to develop the theories and methods that would more effectively deliver psychotherapy to patients from other cultures.

THE CULTURE OF PSYCHOTHERAPEUTIC THEORIES

The standard models of psychoanalysis, which provide the theoretical moorings for the contemporary practice of psychotherapy, are a case in point. What Pine (1990) has called "the four psychologies," in reference to Freudian psychoanalysis, ego psychology, object relations theory, and self psychology, generally assume that the underlying causes, dynamics, and treatment requirements of psychological disturbances—as well as the psychological disturbances themselves—are invariant across cultures. As a result, these models neglect to consider the cultural dimensions of psychological problems and the cultural requisites of psychological treatments. Proponents of newly prominent "two-person" or relational models of treatment similarly fail to address the particular features and problematics of intercultural clinical encounters. Through their deliberate exclusion of cultural considerations from the therapeutic frame, these dominant theories of psychological treatment position themselves as transculturally valid.

Such universal claims, however, run counter to contemporary views of theory. According to these views, to which I subscribe, all theories, even those that are rooted in the supposedly objective sphere of science, are the products of particular cultural and historical contexts (Proctor 1991). Like all other theories, psychotherapeutic theories, which include ideologies of the self, of mental health and illness, and of psychological repair, are culture specific and historically contingent. Indeed, these theories represent contemporary Western conceptions of the mind and of the self rather than a transhistorical and transcultural human nature.

Contemporary psychoanalysts and psychotherapists might agree that selected aspects of classical psychoanalysis are culturally and historically contingent. Many clinicians recognize that Freud was a creature of his time (Mitchell 1993) and that his preoccupation with sexual repression was a consequence of the particular time and place he inhabited

—Victorian-era Viennese society. These clinicians do not anticipate that issues of sexual repression will be central to their contemporary Western clientele, and they shift their attention to other matters (Bettelheim 1990, Cushman 1990, Pine 1990). Yet some of the same psychoanalysts and psychotherapists who have come to the conclusion that many Freudian notions fail to resonate for their late twentieth-century American patients less readily accept the proposition that the psychological maladies and maladjustments that preoccupy them are equally culturally contingent and historically specific. Nor do they believe that the models of treatment that they employ to treat such problems might be restricted in application.

Yet evidence of the cultural and historical specificity of clinical theory and practice abounds. Both clinical theory and clinical practice embed taken-for-granted "meanings, interpretations of reality, values, standards of right and wrong, health and illness, and norms of conduct" (Wohl 1989, p. 81), which are particular to limited segments of Western societies at the turn of the twenty-first century. Moreover, despite its claims that it is scientifically objective and value-free, psychotherapeutic practice works to produce a relatively narrow set of treatment outcomes, all of which embody contemporary Western ideals of selfhood and behavior. Both psychoanalysis and psychodynamic psychotherapy promote, for example, the Western developmental objectives of separation and individuation; Western forms of relationship, which are founded on the principles of independence and egalitarianism; and Western modes of cognitive and affective functioning, which privilege logical thinking and emotional expressiveness. At the same time, such psychological treatments discourage forms of behavior, consciousness, and relationship that are highly valued by other populations, but that do not resonate positively in the West.

The cultural and historical specificity of clinical theory and practice is further evidenced by their emphasis on the individual. Psychology emerged in an era in which a new ideal type of personhood, that of the individual possessed of free will and unencumbered by social relations and obligations, came to be viewed as the basic social unit in many parts of the industrializing West. Psychotherapies generally retain this focus on the individual, taking the socially decontextualized person both as the principal object of their theories and as the primary locus of their interventions. Because clinical theories privilege clients' intrapsychic and interpersonal realities, they direct practitioners to locate problems inside and between individuals and to disregard the broader sociocultural factors that affect psychological formation and adaptation. As a rule, such theories reduce struggles around issues of cultural identity, migration, and sociopolitical discrimination to matters of personal psychology (Chin et al. 1993, Koss-Chioino and Vargas 1992).

THE CULTURAL SPECIFICITY OF THE FOUR PSYCHOLOGIES

Although the four psychologies are properly four theories of psychoanalysis, they also constitute the standard models of psychodynamic psychotherapy. Many psychotherapists who are currently in practice were trained in these psychoanalytic models, and remain attached both to their understandings of human behavior and to their conceptions of clinical technique. The four psychologies thus supply many of the fundamental theoretical assumptions and frames that guide practitioners as they conceptualize the psychic lives of their patients, as they interpret their patients' disclosures, and as they make clinical interventions.

Despite their pervasive influence on clinical theory and practice, because the four psychologies are based on Western conceptions of the self and of the mind, they can be ill-suited to clinical work with persons from other cultures. Assuming a universality of human mind, and assuming there to be a cultural fit between the patient and the clinician and the patient and the outside world, these clinical models steer practitioners toward conventional Western meanings and interpretations. In consequence, they fail to cultivate a receptivity to alternative—and especially non-Western—cultural content.

Freud's (1912) instruction to the psychoanalyst to listen to patients' verbalizations with "evenly hovering attention" is an ideal that is impossible in practice. Rather, clinical listening is theory driven, as psychoanalysts or psychotherapists selectively attend to particular aspects of patients' disclosures that most closely correspond to preexisting theoretical constructions of human mind and behavior (Hartmann 1958).

By guiding practitioners' attention and response, psychoanalytic models not only "order the data of lives," but deeply affect "the entire conduct and presumably the outcome" of treatment (Pine 1990, p. 44). The tendency of psychoanalytic theory to "order the data" into predetermined patterns becomes especially problematic in intercultural psychological treatments. In such treatments, Western clinicians commonly employ Western models of psychotherapy to treat foreign and ethnic patients. Focusing their attention on specific portions of patient material that conform to these models, they overlook important, culturally shaped psychological content, content that such models neither encompass nor explain. The data are then ordered into configurations that reflect Western ideologies of psychological instability and imbalance, but that fail to mirror the internal worlds and lived experiences of their patients. Significant discrepancies between the ways in which Western psychotherapists and their foreign and ethnic patients construct psychological meaning and experience compromise intercultural treatments. Yet clinicians have found no alternative, culturally informed means of ordering the data of foreign and ethnic patients' lives.

In the following sections I briefly describe the basic features of the four psychologies. I also consider two-person models of treatment. I then identify a number of their central concepts that remain influential in contemporary clinical treatments, but that are specific to Western cultures. Finally, I show how cultural perspectives might be incorporated into these treatment models to better serve patients from other cultures.

Drive Theory

Freudian psychoanalytic theory, which is also known as classical psychoanalysis, views the human psyche as biologically based and hence as universal. At the same time, it views the person as instinct driven, conflict ridden, and unconsciously motivated. Classical psychoanalysis directs analytic attention to the patient's psychic reality, or interior world, and to its conflicts, to the near exclusion of the patient's external world. While it is impossible to offer a comprehensive review of Freudian theory here (for a more complete discussion, see Brenner

1974), I discuss two of its central concepts in terms of their relevance to intercultural treatments.

The Universality of Transference

The classical transference concept as elaborated by Freud refers to feelings that emanate from early relationships or from another source rather than from the therapeutic relationship, that the patient has nonetheless transferred onto the therapist (Freud 1924). Like many other Freudian constructs, the concept of transference has been revised in recent decades and now assumes divergent forms and functions in various psychoanalytic models. Although the concept of transference has undergone extensive revision, however, and although some practicing clinicians now focus their transference investigations on transferences that exist in the here and now, genetic transferences that resemble those described by Freud remain an important component of many contemporary psychotherapies.

While there is a vast literature on transference, discussions of its cultural properties are relatively rare. Most such discussions have concentrated on the transferential complications of intercultural treatments (Abbasi 1996, 1997, Ticho 1971, Varghese 1983). Therapists' inabilities to grasp transference constellations patterned on forms of relationship that are common in the patient's culture but not in theirs, have been noted (Taketomo 1989). Patients' negative transference reactions, including feelings of estrangement, mistrust, and hostility, have also been observed (Basch-Kahre 1984), as have patients' confusion and alienation when their therapists focus on the transference rather than on the real patient–therapist relationship (Roland 1988). Transferences that take the form of ethnocultural stereotypes present additional difficulties in intercultural treatments (Comas-Diaz and Jacobsen 1991). Accordingly, it has been argued that when therapist and patient have different cultural backgrounds, various cultural facets of transference can compromise both the therapist's technical and diagnostic skills and the therapeutic alliance.

Such discussions provide some sense of the transference reactions that are common in intercultural psychotherapies. Yet they fail to grasp a principal feature of the concept of transference—that transference is a construction of human relations that realizes its conventional meanings only in cultures in which a particular version of self-reliant individualism is the primary means by which personhood is understood and experienced, and only for cultures in which social relations are organized around highly separated and individuated persons. These in themselves are relatively restricted phenomena, the rise of this kind of individualism having occurred relatively recently in the context of human history, and primarily in the industrialized West (Kirschner 1996, Sampson 1989).

The commonsense view of emotions prevalent in the West constructs feelings as entities that well up from within (Heelas 1986), that are felt for others, and that properly belong solely to the specific events and interlocutors that elicit them. The transference concept itself rests on a corollary to this view, one that holds that patients' feelings for their therapists do not properly belong to their therapists, but are rather visited on them as mere repetitions of emotions that the patients have previously experienced toward other, more primary, objects. As such, transferences are thought to be composed of feelings that patients experience inappropriately, and that their psychotherapy must resolve.

Indeed, the concept of transference is based on a Western view of the person. While cultural variation in the construction of the self is discussed in the following chapter, the anthropologist Clifford Geertz (1983) raises a point that is relevant here:

> The Western conception of the person as a bounded, unique, more or less integrated motivational and cognitive universe, a dynamic center of awareness, emotion, judgment, and action organized into a distinctive whole and set contrastively both against other such wholes and against its social and natural background, is, however incorrigible it may seem to us, a rather peculiar idea within the context of the world's cultures. [p. 59]

This "peculiar idea" is the foundation upon which the concept of transference rests. Yet as Geertz suggests, the fierce individualism that is the hallmark of Western civilization is resolutely devalued and eschewed in many cultures. Geertz's (1973, 1983) descriptions of the Balinese, for example, detail their efforts to de-emphasize individual characteristics and to behave in ways prescribed by their social statuses and roles. What is of importance to the Balinese is not the individual per se, but rather the part that the individual plays and the category that the individual occupies in the social order. In Bali, Geertz maintains, persons are esteemed not because they possess idiosyncratic histories, sensibilities, and qualities, but because they embody social types.

This de-emphasis on the individual is illustrated by the Balinese system of naming. In Bali, children are not referred to by their personal names but by their place in the birth order, which begins with first-born, continues through fourth-born, and then repeats. The result is that both the first and fifth-born children of a family are called first-born, and that multitudes of children across Bali share the same name. Similarly, a single kinship term refers to one's parents, aunts, and uncles, and another refers to one's sons, daughters, nieces, and nephews; such terms fail to distinguish the particular persons within them. Even this degree of generational differentiation—which is minimal by Western standards—is not maintained throughout the network of kin, however, as all members of both one's great-grandparents' generation and one's great-grandchildren's generation are called by the same name.

Clearly, for the Balinese, the ideal is *not* to respond to others as individuals, either in thought or in feeling. Many social relationships take place not between persons who have distinct individual features and identities, but between the interchangeable occupants of culturally constituted roles. As a result, emotions are properly thought to belong to, and to be directed toward, not particular individuals, but rather classes or categories of people to whom one owes culturally defined constellations of obligation and feeling. As the Balinese case demonstrates, the Western habit of differentially responding to others based on their personal characteristics and quirks is not necessarily practiced elsewhere. Transference, therefore, while having particular meanings in the West by virtue of the general cultural agreement as to the impropriety of displacing the feelings originally felt for one person onto another, cannot be assumed to have the same significance in other cultures. In fact, it is imaginable that the concept of transference might be meaningless to patients from societies in which feelings are supposed to be transferable from one person to another, and in which responding emotionally to one person as one has previously responded to others defines normal and expectable behavior.

To make such a statement is not to suggest that therapists totally abandon explorations of transference in intercultural treatments. It is, however, to recommend that therapists who work with patients from other cultures ground their transference analyses in the context of such patients' culturally specific senses of self, of others, and of relationship. It is also to recommend that therapists who conduct intercultural treatments seriously consider how their foreign and ethnic patients might react to transference interpretations, and to recommend that they conceive of intercultural treatments as opportunities to explore the divergent forms transference takes for patients from other cultures.

Culture and the Unconscious

In Freud's early formulations of psychoanalysis, he identified both the primary objective and the source of cure in psychoanalysis as "the translation of what is unconscious into what is conscious" (1920, p. 541). Although Freud later revised the role the unconscious plays in psychoanalytic treatments, he continued to grant the unconscious a pivotal role in psychoanalytic theory and technique. The unconscious as conceptualized by Freud referred both to a set of mental contents and to a system of mental activities. Freud's "unconscious proper" (1940, p. 17) contained fantasies, ideas, impulses, and wishes, and was governed by the laws of primary process. Although forcefully kept out of awareness by mental procedures that he likened to censorship, Freud contended that unconscious psychic products and processes were powerful determinants of behavior. To those who questioned the existence of the unconscious, Freud (1915) offered the proofs of dreams, hypnotic states, parapraxes, neurotic symptoms, obsessions, and sudden, unexplained thoughts and ideas.

It was Freud's (1915) contention that the nucleus of the unconscious was composed of inherent mental functions, so that the contents of the unconscious and its laws of operation, like all psychic structure, were intrinsic and culturally invariant. From this assumption of psychic uniformity, the concept of analytic authority—and the fact of analytic power—naturally flowed. For if psychoanalysts were, in essence, scientists expert in unearthing and decoding the hidden and disguised but eternal truths of the psyche, then only through analytic intervention could patients become aware of their innermost thoughts, actions, and desires.

Freud (1915) conceptualized the unconscious as a stratum of the multilayered mental topography which made psychoanalysis a depth psychology. This metaphor of depth illustrates the critical distinction psychoanalytic theory made between individuals' conscious awareness, which Freud dismissed as disguised, distorted, and epiphenomenal, and the mind's true contents, which inhabited its depths. In light of this fundamental distinction, Freud declared that an essential psychoanalytic goal was to penetrate beyond the surface phenomena that composed patients' limited field of awareness to reveal the real meanings and motives that lay hidden beneath them.

Freud not only elaborated the contents and laws of the unconscious, enumerated the proofs of its existence, and explained its refusal to enter awareness, he also claimed to have developed the necessary techniques for uncovering it. In Freud's view, a number of mental functions and products provided a window on otherwise unavailable unconscious meanings and motives. Freud (1900a) believed that dreams revealed mental processes and contents that were excluded from consciousness. And he contended that certain categories of errors in cognitive functioning, or parapraxes, offered the analyst clues to the unconscious wishes that caused them (Freud 1900b).

How was the unconscious to be made conscious? The analyst's task, as Freud saw it, was to investigate the patient's dreams, parapraxes, and neurotic symptoms. From such derivatives of the unconscious, the analyst was to "construct a sequence of conscious events," filling in the gaps between what was conscious and what was not. Analytic intervention therefore entailed "making plausible inferences and translating it [sic] into conscious material." According to Freud (1940), psychoanalysis depended on the "binding force of these inferences" (p. 16).

Despite Freud's claim that the unconscious was inherent and universal, some practicing psychotherapists accept Bettelheim's (1990) argument that Freud's sociohistorical surround, with its sexual repression, imperial decline, and fascination with death, colored his constructions of the unconscious. The precise contents of the unconscious have consequently been reconfigured to reflect contemporary Western family dynamics, residence patterns, and social realities rather than those of Freud's Vienna. Yet although some psychotherapists concede Freud's sociohistorical specificity, they neglect to acknowledge their own. Many therapists resist the suggestion that their view of the unconscious is as shaded by the particular circumstances of their history and culture as was Freud's. Assuming that the local and modal family structures and customs with which they are familiar are globally widespread, they imagine the newly reconfigured unconscious to be universal. Regardless of their patients' cultural backgrounds, many practicing psychotherapists continue to interpret their patients' unconscious motivations, fantasies, and conflicts in light of "middle-class Westernized psychodynamics" (Herron 1995, p. 523).

Increasingly, there are grounds for refuting the existence of a singular, universal unconscious and for proposing the existence of multiple unconsciouses—unconsciouses that are influenced by culture—in its stead. Conceptualizations of the "ethnic unconscious" (Herron 1995, Javier and Rendon 1995) and of the "cultural unconscious" (Adams 1996) rest on two propositions. The first proposition is that mental processes and products are neither inherited nor universal but are acquired through culturally mediated experiences, and are therefore cross-culturally variant. The second proposition is that the contents of the unconscious extend beyond instinctual wishes and their derivatives to embrace the sociocultural surround, cultural mythologies and cosmologies, cultural idealogies of selfhood and relationship, ethnic identifications, and the historical past that members of a cultural group share.

Some cultural conceptions of the unconscious seek to link particular unconscious wishes, motivations, and fantasies to the diverse forms of family structure and parent–child relationship that exist across cultures. Kakar (1985), for example, has argued that Indian children who sleep with their mothers until adolescence, or who share sleeping quarters with their parents and frequently witness their sexual activity, develop fantasies of sexuality that differ markedly from those of American children who lack such intimate contact. Cohler (1992) has written that the fantasies of children raised in polymatric societies may involve a number of women rather than the singular mother of monomatric societies. Given the extensive cross-cultural variation in early childhood experience and the effects of early experience on the development of the mind, there is bound to be a wealth of such "distinctive culturally colored fantasies" (Javier and Rendon 1995, p. 516).

Cultural conceptions of the unconscious raise important questions concerning analytic authority. For if the unconscious contains not only culturally colored fantasies but also, as suggested above, culturally specific experiences, ecologies, and ideologies, then how is the analyst to understand the culturally different patient's unconscious? Moreover, if analytic authority depends on "making plausible inferences" and on "construct[ing] a sequence of conscious events" (Freud 1940, p. 16) to fill in the gaps between the conscious and the unconscious, then how is the psychoanalyst who is unfamiliar with the patient's culturally mediated intrapsychic and extrapsychic realities to accomplish this?

Cultural conceptions of the unconscious also raise questions concerning analytic access to the unconscious. Dreams, according to Freud (1900a), were the "royal road" to the unconscious, with typical formats and contents that held the same meaning for everyone. Dreams, however, contain culturally particular symbols, narratives, and meanings, so that they cannot be accurately interpreted without some knowledge of their larger cultural context (Kakar 1990, Tedlock 1987). The parapraxes, which Freud considered to be an alternative route to understanding unconscious psychic material, must be similarly reconceptualized in light of cultural conceptions of the unconscious. Many parapraxes concern errors in language use. Yet languages contain idiomatic expressions and metaphors whose connotations escape those who are not their native speakers. Further, when psychoanalysis is conducted in the patient's second language, slips of the tongue, plays on words, and other verbal bridges often vanish at the moment of their translation into the language of analysis. As a result, in intercultural treatments many of the customary routes of access to unconscious motives and meanings are closed.

A more thorough cultural critique of the concept of the unconscious, and one that renders its use problematic in psychotherapies both with non-Western patients and with patients from ethnic groups within Western societies, also warrants mention. As noted above, Freud constructed psychoanalysis as a depth psychology. Yet to subscribe to this metaphor of depth is to invoke culturally and historically particular views of the self. Adherents of psychoanalysis are heirs to conceptions of selfhood that developed in late eleventh-century Europe. Novel in their time, these conceptions of selfhood strictly separated observable behaviors from inner states, such as thoughts, morals, emotions, and intentions. Accordingly, individuals were no longer defined by their actions, but by their interior states. The practice of self-investigation acquired value, and a "vocabulary of inner intent" flourished (Rosen 1985, p. 67).

Freud's psychoanalytic theory reinforced this separation between internal life and external acts. It privileged the inner self, or intrapsychic reality, and prescribed the acquisition of self-awareness. But in addition, Freud gave this inner landscape a distinct topography. Freud's (1915) model of the mind had a depth dimension, so that its inner self was buried in the depths of the mind. Distinguishing the manifest from the latent and the epiphenomenal from the profound, Freud (1940) designed an unconscious that could not be directly observed, but that could only be "inferred, recognized, translated into conscious form" (p. 17).

This notion of the inner self, which is central to the theory and practice of psychoanalysis, is unfamiliar to many cultures. Rosen (1985) writes that in Morocco, internal states are constructed as neither inaccessible nor secret; instead, they are viewed as directly corresponding to overt behaviors. According to Rosen, the internal and external worlds of Moroccans do not lie at different depths, but occupy the same plane. Acts and intentions become comprehensible not through the professional decoding of hidden significances, but through culturally contextualized knowledge of the actor's personal character and interpersonal ties.

Those who object to Freud's universalizing conceptions of the unconscious have reconceptualized many of its central features. Critics of the universal unconscious suggest that the unconscious is plural and cross-culturally variable rather than singular and universal; that it is acquired through experience rather than innate; that it includes the cultural environment rather than instincts exclusively; and that it is contingent upon culturally particular views of the self. Applying the ideas of culturally relativized and socioculturally informed unconsciouses to intercultural treatments suggests that when therapists treat patients from other cultures, they will hear not only the patients' culturally colored unconscious fantasies; they will hear a wide spectrum of culturally colored unconscious impulses, motivations, wishes, identifications, and histories as well.

When confronted with such material, the concept of analytic omniscience crumbles. For unless psychotherapists completely deny the existence of cultural differences, they can no longer presume to have absolute access to the deeper reaches of their patients' minds or to the deeper significances of their therapeutic disclosures. Instead, they must recognize that when they treat patients from other cultures, the unconscious motives that they may conventionally ascribe to Western patients do not necessarily apply.

Ego Psychology

Ego psychology developed out of Heinz Hartmann's wish to both broaden Freudian theory and alter its tenor. At odds with the classical psychoanalytic view of human behavior as instinct driven, conflict ridden, and pathological, he imagined a healthier, ego-centered psyche that was capable of rational and conflict-free activity. Dissatisfied with psychoanalysis's neglect of such psychological processes as perception, learning, and language, he returned them to the therapeutic domain. And rejecting psychoanalysis's singular preoccupation with the patient's intrapsychic reality, he emphasized the human need to adjust to the demands of the external world.

By enlarging the domain of psychoanalysis to embrace extrapsychic realities as well as internal ones, Hartmann introduced the sociocultural environment into psychoanalytic theory. Claiming that different behaviors were adaptive in different social structures, and that behavior and development were shaped by "collective thinking," "worldviews," and "handed-down principles, self-evident propositions rooted in traditions, and the like" (p. 68), Hartmann suggested that all human behavior was culturally situated, and that a complete understanding of human functioning was impossible without a grasp of its cultural surround. Although ego psychology's basic premises provided a promising foundation for cultural approaches to clinical practice, Hartmann failed to extend the theory of ego psychology in this direction. Instead of investigating the ways in which differences in worldviews and social structures across cultures produced variations in human adaptation and behavior, he turned his attention to similarities in human functioning. As a result of Hartmann's retreat from a culturally informed view of human mind and behavior, ego psychology's basic assumptions and concepts retain an ethnocentric cast that makes them problematic for clinical work with foreign and ethnic patients.

The Average Expectable Environment

Hartmann (1958) regarded the individual's ability to navigate the "average expectable environment" (p. 55) to be a prerequisite of mental health. Yet he neither explained what he meant by "average" and "expectable" nor discussed the psychological ramifications for patients whose environments he viewed as neither. While Pine (1990) has argued that "it is the precise individual environment, and not the average expectable one, that matters in development" (p. 62), Hartmann generally assumed that his patients inhabited "normal" environments; he therefore found it unnecessary to explore their precise, individual surrounds in treatment. This stance discouraged the investigation not only of patients' atypical environments, but of their culturally distinctive ones as well. The project of cultural analysis was thus excluded from ego psychology.

Although it is inadequate as it stands, the concept of the average expectable environment can be adapted to accommodate cultural perspectives. Therapists might begin by recognizing that what constitutes an average expectable environment varies from culture to culture (LeVine 1990). They might proceed by assuming that the home environments of their foreign and ethnic patients will differ in significant ways from the environments with which they are familiar. Such patients' sleeping arrangements, household composition, patterns of residence of kin, and ecologies, to name but a few factors, are likely to diverge from those of their therapists. Not only are the home environments of foreign and ethnic patients likely to be variously inhabited, defined, and organized, but they frequently will fail to support the Westernized versions of individuation and personal autonomy that ego psychologists consider essential to healthy psychological development.

Just as foreign and ethnic patients' native environments are likely to be unfamiliar to their therapists, the therapist's environment, which is the new home of foreign and ethnic patients, is apt to seem odd and unpredictable to them. Therapists should therefore expect that their foreign and ethnic patients will experience a lack of fit between themselves and their new environments, which often results in the impairment of their habitual means of mediating between internal and external realities and of negotiating the outer world. Such impairments can then be understood not as cognitive deficits or psychopathologies, but as the natural consequences of cultural displacements. In addition, once therapists conceptualize their foreign and ethnic patients' native cultural environments as other than average and expectable, they will be better positioned to closely investigate these environments and to assess their impact on psychic functioning.

Ego Functions

Hartmann identified a set of particular psychological processes whose smooth operation, in his view, provided incontrovertible evidence of mental health. He referred to these processes as ego functions. Although Hartmann (1958) sounded like a cultural relativist when he proclaimed, "Knowledge is bound to existence and place" (Hartmann 1958, p. 67), he represented the ego functions as mechanical operations of the psychic apparatus and considered them to be universal.

Contrary to Hartmann's view, ego functions are not simply physiological operations that are devoid of cultural content. Instead, they represent Western ideals of thought, feeling, and relationship. For example, the ego functions of reality testing, judgment, and logical thinking privilege particular cognitive processes that are valued in the West, but not necessarily valued in other cultures. Ego functions that designate optimal relations between the world and the self are based on Western, individualistic constructions of the self as completely distinct and apart from others and from the world. Yet such relational boundaries vary extensively across cultures, as exemplified by Hindu views of transpersonal selves, selves that continually exchange substances with their local environments and with the cosmos (Kakar 1985). The ego function concerned with the regulation of drives, affects, and impulses similarly fails to reflect the fact that patterns of emotional expression are culturally prescribed.

Despite Hartmann's failure to consider cross-cultural variations in ego functioning, a cultural approach to ego functions can be added to ego psychology. Hartmann's suggestion that ego functions adapt to external expectations can be extended, so that ego functions are reconceptualized as developing differentially in response to divergent cultural demands. This reformulation allows psychotherapists to anticipate that the ego functions of their foreign and ethnic patients may differ from those that ego psychology considers standard. It also encourages therapists to investigate the culturally specific features of external demands, and the ego functions' particular developments in response to them, as part of the treatment of foreign and ethnic patients. A culturally informed view of ego functions thus seeks cultural information and explores the precise relationships among culture, culture change, and human functioning. At the same time, it cautions therapists against the expectation that they will find Western versions of ego functions in their patients from other cultures.

Ego Assessment

Ego psychologists evaluate their patients' mental functioning by assessing the ego's strength. Ego strength is principally determined by judging the proper operation of the various ego functions, as well as by assessing the personality's stability and consistency across situations. Problems in determining the psychological functioning of foreign and ethnic patients according to these criteria arise on two fronts. First, evaluations of ego operations are confounded by the Western cultural specificity of the ego functions Hartmann identified, as discussed above. Therapists who encounter unfamiliar patterns of thought, emotion, and attachment in foreign and ethnic patients without understanding their non-Western or other alternative cultural features are likely to misjudge such patients' ego functions, resulting in misdiagnosis.

Second, the goal of personal integration central to ego psychology belongs to the Western ideal of personhood and is particular to segments of Western cultures. The ideal of the integrated personality is foreign to cultures that value selves that can adapt to, and that are constituted by, situational and social requirements, rather than selves that display a consistent identity across situational contexts and interpersonal interactions (Shweder and Bourne 1984). What might seem to the therapist to be evidence of personal disintegration or instability might represent to the patient culturally sanctioned and context-appropriate shifts in the presentation and experience of the self.

Therapists who work with foreign and ethnic patients should be aware of the ways cultural variations in selfhood can complicate ego psychological assessments. More accurate assessments depend on evaluations of patient functioning that consider cultural constructions of the self, cultural norms of social interaction and behavior, and their interface with prior and current environmental demands.

Developmental Theory

Ego psychology's view of child development is closely linked to Mahler's (Mahler et al. 1975) separation-individuation paradigm. This developmental model proposes that the intense mother–infant relationship in the early months of life, or "symbiosis," gradually, through a predetermined series of specific subphases, gives way to the dyad's physical and psychic separation. This process both allows the infant to realize its separateness from its mother and compels the infant to develop into a distinct, independent, self-contained individual.

The separation-individuation paradigm depends in large part on its characterization of the infant as possessing an innate desire for autonomy. According to this paradigm, development is a process that is driven by the child's internal push for independence and differentiation. Development proceeds as a series of progressive movements away from dependence on and enmeshment with the mother, and toward self-sufficiency and distinct self-other boundaries. Although this paradigm clearly promotes the Western cultural values of autonomy and individuation, and although it offers a Western construction of the child as an inherent seeker of independence and self-reliance, its cultural specificity is largely unacknowledged. Instead, the separation-individuation paradigm is generally portrayed as a universal developmental sequence, one, moreover, that is the cornerstone of normal development.

The developmental objectives of this model, however, are not pancultural developmental goals; rather, they reflect the ideals and demands of highly individuated Western cultures. Such cultures, given their lack of community, extended family, and nuclear family supports, require their members to function as separate and self-reliant persons. It is therefore not surprising that contrasting patterns of infant development have been observed elsewhere. Among certain cultural groups in East and West Africa, for example, the physical inseparability of mother and child during the first few years of life gives infants few opportunities to develop the autonomy-seeking behaviors that Mahler considered to be universal in infancy. Accordingly, instead of being seen as the inevitable product of biological maturation, the process of separation-individuation may be better understood as the product of particular, culturally determined child-rearing practices common to a limited number of Western cultural groups (Muensterberger 1969).

In addition, although theorists from Klein (1935) and Bowlby (1958) to Winnicott (1960b) and Mahler (Mahler et al. 1975) have conceived of the infant as situated in a matrix composed solely of itself and its biological mother, the mother–child dyad that is the focus of separation-individuation theory is not the main socializing unit across cultures. Rather, it is a phenomenon that is restricted to the nuclear family common to the industrialized West, and that is in decline even there due to women's increased employment outside of the home. In many societies, infants are cared for by more than one mother figure or by an extended social group, making their attachment to multiple caregivers the norm (Kurtz 1992, Tronick et al. 1987).

Because the theory of separation-individuation is based on ideals of autonomy and individualism, conceptions of the child, patterns of child care, and family structures that are culturally specific, it does not accurately describe the developmental trajectories of all cultural groups. Foreign and ethnic patients are unlikely to conform to Western expectations regarding matters of autonomy, differentiation, and attachment. Their culturally distinctive patterns of separation and individuation merit therapeutic investigation.

Object Relations Theory

Object relations theory grew out of the preliminary observations made by early psychoanalysts regarding the role of objects, or other people, in psychic functioning. Object relations theorists rejected several basic postulates of Freudian psychoanalysis. Most importantly, they refuted Freud's claim that human behavior was primarily designed to satisfy instinctual drives, and that human relationships acquired significance secondarily, as a by-product of their association with drive reduction. Object relations theorists proposed alternative views of human functioning. Claiming that people were inherently predisposed to seek human contact, they argued that object relations were not only essential to human development and survival, but were significant ends in themselves.

It is true that various object relations theorists posited different and sometimes contradictory conceptions of objects, and of the psychological laws that governed them, and that they split into competing factions or schools (cf. Greenberg and Mitchell 1983). Despite their theoretical divergences, however, object relations theorists shared several fundamental assumptions, and it is to these core assumptions that I refer when I describe object relations theory. Above all, object relations theorists embraced the shift from a drive model to a relational model of human behavior. They also supported the view that early object relationships, which were internalized, mediated ongoing external realities, coloring—and frequently distorting—new interpersonal experiences. By analyzing the internalized objects that inhabited their patients' intrapsychic worlds, object relations therapists sought to understand the precise ways in which individuals unconsciously repeated these early relationships, remaking subsequent attachments in their image (Fairbairn 1941, 1943, Klein 1935). Perhaps because they offer illuminating perspectives on interpersonal relationships, which invariably become the focus of many psychotherapies, object relations approaches are widely used in contemporary psychological treatments.

Object relations approaches have also been found to be useful in intercultural treatments. Kakar (1985) contends that object relations theory is more suited than classical psychoanalysis to the clinical treatment of non-Westerners because it lacks universalizing assumptions and detailed metapsychologies, and because it emphasizes interpersonal connections. A close examination of object relations theory, however, demonstrates that like classical psychoanalysis, it contains Western and universalizing conceptions of objects, of the self, and of relationships. Indeed, object relations theory's inattention to the cultural properties of objects complicates its application in the treatment of foreign and ethnic patients.

The Cultural Nature of Objects

Object relations theory's representation of objects is incomplete by virtue of its omission of culture. For although object relations theory conceives of internalized objects as embedded in a relational matrix, it fails to situate objects in their cultural worlds. By considering objects who are culturally decontextualized, object relations theory implies that objects are the same across cultures. Yet persons and systems of relationship do not have universal meanings and properties, but are instead culturally constructed.

Flegenheimer (1989) remarked, "If a patient tells me about a farmhouse connected with his childhood, I am reminded of a farmhouse which I know, which may be different from the farmhouse the patient has in his mind" (p. 381). The same can be said for objects. Although words such as *mother, father, wife,* and *friend* might seem to refer to universal human relationships, they actually represent cultural categories, the contents of which vary extensively across cultural settings. Most Indian languages, for example, distinguish between relatives on the maternal and paternal sides of the family. Unlike English, which has single terms for aunt and uncle, these languages have separate terms for mother's sisters and brothers and for father's sisters and brothers. Such terms both designate specific biological relationships and evoke particular constellations of obligation and interaction. The cross-cultural variability of the categorization of objects is an important issue for intercultural clinical work, because the objects which Western therapists have in mind when terms of kinship arise in treatment are likely to differ from those of their foreign and ethnic patients. The complete exploration of objects' specific cultural roles and meanings thus becomes a crucial piece of intercultural treatments.

Objects are also culturally shaped in that they are containers of cultural values, norms, and assumptions about reality. The objects with whom children interact are always cultural objects, because they perform culturally defined psychic functions, enact culturally specific behaviors, and embody cultural ideals. Children's internalization of objects, therefore, necessarily entails their internalization of culture.

Moreover, objects function not only as containers of culture, but as transmitters of culture. As culture carriers (Gehrie 1979) they reproduce, albeit with some degree of individual variation, cultural meanings and practices. Parents, for example, enact cultural practices by deciding when and with whom their infants sleep, how to interpret and respond to their cries, and when and what to feed them (Small 1998). Through their caregiving activities, they mediate their children's physiological and emotional needs and structure their children's environments according to cultural values and norms. Objects thus transmit and recreate culture through their habitual, everyday activities.

Another cultural aspect of objects overlooked by object relations theory concerns the variation which exists across cultures in what constitutes and composes objects. Restricted by Western conceptions of the person, object relations theory narrowly defines objects as "external and internal (real and imagined) other people" (Greenberg and Mitchell 1983, p. 14). In contrast with this limited view, in many non-Western cultures the category of objects is more diverse, more complex, and more inclusive. In other societies, the range of objects with whom one interacts can include ancestral spirits, objects that lack fixed identities, cosmic forces, and supernatural beings (Landrine 1992). Instead of conforming to the Western view of objects as fundamentally separated from the external environment and from others, other societies conceive of objects as containing aspects of the physical world and unindividuated dyads. Objects that fall into these categories can be internalized, mediating self- and object-representations and interpersonal relationships in ways that may be unpredictable to Western psychotherapists.

As long as therapists and patients are from similar cultural backgrounds, they are likely to share culturally influenced assumptions about objects and object relationships. When therapists and patients are significantly culturally different, however, patients' internalized objects and patterns of relationship are likely to differ from those that their therapists consider familiar and natural. Because such differences can cause therapists to misunderstand crucial features of their foreign and ethnic patients' culturally colored object worlds, with deleterious effects on their psychotherapeutic treatments, it is important for therapists to routinely investigate the cultural nature of their patients' internalized objects.

The False Self

In the view of many therapists, the codified diagnostic categories of psychiatry as well as the less formalized conceptions of psychological difficulty that inform their clinical practice define universal standards of psychopathology. As a result, they overlook the fact that these diagnostic categories and conceptions embody ideals of self and of mental health that refer only to segments of Western cultures. A further potential hazard of practicing psychotherapy without regard for the patients' cultural backgrounds concerns the misapplication of Western diagnostic concepts and categories to foreign and ethnic patients.

The object relations construct of the false self provides one such example. Although never explicitly acknowledged as such, this construct contains conceptions of psychological health that are specific to Western cultures. Winnicott (1960a) described the false self as a psychological disturbance in which an artificial self develops in order to shield the authentic or true self from exposure to an environment that would destroy it. Winnicott gave the psychopathology of the false self a distinct etiology and symptomatology. In his view, the false self was the product of an early object relationship in which the mother habitually subverted her infant's efforts toward self-expression and spontaneity. As evidence of the false self's existence, Winnicott pointed to overly compliant demeanors, to profound feelings of personal inauthenticity, and to self-effacing self-presentations and modes of interpersonal attachment.

What Winnicott failed to note is that the false self construct is rooted in Western ideologies of the self. First, this construct presumes a Western view of the infant as a distinct, separate, self-motivated individual who is involved in a dyadic relationship with the mother. Second, it reflects the Western belief that psychological dangers await those whose self-expression is thwarted; in contrast, in many other cultures, self-expression is discouraged in order to preserve group harmony. Third, the false self construct presumes the existence of a true self—an authentic personality that is fixed, stable, and essential. This Western presumption regarding the self conflicts with conceptions of the self that are common in many other cultures, and that construct the self as context-dependent and shifting (Shweder and Bourne 1984). Finally, the compliant demeanor and primary attunement to the needs of others that provide Western psychotherapists with evidence of false self psychopathology represent behaviors that are normative in other societies; indeed, their absence in those contexts would be deemed unacceptable. Consider, for example, the case of the Indian patient whose family identified his primary symptom as an excess of "unnatural autonomy" (Kakar 1985, p. 446). In the eyes of this patient's family, nothing would be more welcome than for him to exhibit what object relations therapists call a false self.

Because the idea of the false self rests on Western ideals of development, selfhood, and behavior, its usefulness to psychotherapists in understanding patients of other cultures is restricted. Indeed, the cultural analysis above shows the false self construct to be a Western, culture-bound syndrome rather than a pancultural psychic disorder. It therefore suggests that other Western diagnostic categories and concepts be similarly analyzed, so that their relevance to the clinical treatment of foreign and ethnic patients might be determined.

Self Psychology

Like object relations theory and ego psychology, self psychology was brought into being because its founder, Heinz Kohut, considered classical psychoanalysis's representations of human psychological functioning inaccurate and inadequate. Kohut focused self psychology on the entity of the self and its disorders rather than on isolated psychic structures and processes. He explained psychopathology as the result of the self's insufficiently nourishing early experiences with others—whom he called *selfobjects*—rather than as the result of intrapsychic conflict. Kohut's self psychology thus subordinated Freudian drive theory to what it proposed was a more comprehensive view of human functioning (Kohut 1977, 1984).

Self psychology supported object relations theory in its contention that fundamental human needs and motivations were gratified through the matrix of interpersonal relationships rather than through the mechanics of drive discharge. Self psychology went beyond object relations theory, however, in constructing selfobjects not merely as ends in themselves, but as essential to the psychological existence of the self. Indeed, Kohut (1977) maintained that children's need for "an empathic, responsive human milieu" (p. 85) of selfobjects was equal to their need for oxygen. Kohut thus created a psychology of the self in which individuals' needs for particular types of human responsiveness, or for particular self-selfobject relationships, were granted an absolute primacy in the formation of an intact self.

Kohut (1984) claimed that the human need for selfobjects was a lifelong one, so that infants experienced early or "archaic" selfobjects as a part of the self, and older individuals drew ongoing emotional sustenance from selfobjects. In Kohut's view, optimal psychological development was dependent on parents providing their children with the necessary emotional infusions of empathy and responsiveness. While he argued that occasional parental lapses provided children with opportunities to internalize mature coping behaviors, Kohut blamed chronic early parenting failures for later psychic disintegration. According to Kohut, the child who consistently lacked attentive and supportive parenting would accrue enduring defects in his or her sense of self.

In the course of developing his theory of psychoanalytic practice, Freud had concluded that narcissistic patients were untreatable by psychoanalytic methods. One of Kohut's original objectives in formulating self psychology was to develop a psychoanalytic cure tailored to the needs of such patients. Kohut understood that the narcissistic personality was not a universal, biologically based phenomenon, but that it was produced by particular sociocultural conditions. In his view, the fragmentation of the family and the rapid pace of social change were responsible for the spread of the narcissistic personality disorder in the industrialized West. By describing the social and historical origins of narcissism, Kohut implied that self psychology would be of restricted utility in treating patients who had grown up in other parts of the world because their sense of self, having developed under different conditions, would be unlikely to exhibit the narcissistic features that self psychology had been designed to treat.

Kohut's concerns regarding the application of self psychology to patients for whom it was not intended would appear to have been put to rest by recent revisions in self psychological theory that broaden its scope (Lichtenberg et al. 1992). Because self psychology no longer focuses exclusively on narcissistic patients but now addresses a widened range of human psychological difficulty, it would seem to have become more applicable to patients from other cultures, patients who have been less affected by the Western sociocultural transformations that Kohut identified as causative of psychopathology. But for self psychology to become more applicable to foreign and ethnic patients, more than its focus on narcissistic personalities needs to be revised. For in its understandings of parenting, of selfobjects, and of the therapist's role as well, self psychology remains bound to Western cultures.

The Functions of Parenting

Kohut maintained that parents' activities as primary caregivers were critical to the psychological development of their children. Asserting that parents shaped their infants' innate potentials by mediating environmental conditions and by selectively reinforcing their behaviors, Kohut (1971) argued that parents wielded a virtually exclusive influence over their children's developing sense of self. Kohut's discussion of parenting, however, was not informed by cultural perspectives. Despite Kohut's identification of particular parenting functions that he claimed were essential to psychological health, there are no absolute or universal standards of parenting. Instead, parenting objectives and activities are culturally shaped and vary extensively cross-culturally. When parents and other primary caregivers selectively respond to children, and when they mediate their environments, they do so not simply as expressions of their individual personalities and preferences. Rather, parenting behaviors are determined by the norms and standards of their culture, and by the specific types of selves that particular cultures seek to reproduce.

In Kohut's elaborations of the functions of parenting, he failed to recognize that in many societies child caregiving is the work of persons other than, or in addition to, the biological mother and father. There are extensive differences across cultures in which particular individuals contribute to the child's developing self and in the precise nature of their contributions. Among the Efe of Zaire, for example, infants are cared for by several members of the community in addition to their biological parents. What is more striking to many Westerners is that Efe infants are nursed by a number of lactating women in addition to their biological mothers (Tronick et al. 1987).

Further, the parenting functions that self psychology takes to be natural, normal, and necessary are not found across all cultural groups; in fact, parents in many societies deplore Western caregiving practices. Recent work on parent–infant interactions in other cultures supports this point. Infant researchers in parts of Kenya and Mexico have found that Kenyan and Mexican mothers refrain from the active engagement with their infants that self psychology considers essential to infants' affective and social development. According to these researchers, these mothers are interested in training their babies to be quiet and undemanding rather than active and vocal, so that they might be better adapted to their cultural surrounds (Brazelton 1977, LeVine 1990).

For self psychology to become more useful to the clinical treatment of patients from other cultures, its conceptions of parenting need to be broadened so that they include cultural perspectives. For psychotherapists who treat patients from other cultures, this might require investigating the culturally specific features of the parenting their foreign and ethnic patients received, rather than assuming the existence of transcultural parenting practices. The concept of the *developmental niche* proposed by Super and Harkness (1986) offers assistance in this regard. This concept, which was originally formulated to guide research on cross-cultural child development, focuses attention on three dimensions of the cultural context of childhood: the physical settings of childhood; its customary child-care practices; and its ideologies of human nature, human needs, and human behavior. When adapted for clinical practice, the concept of the developmental niche offers psychotherapists a framework for exploring their foreign and ethnic patients' parenting histories in a culturally contextualized way, and for understanding the parental failures their patients experienced in the terms of their native cultures rather than through the lenses of Western expectations and norms.

Cultural Selfobjects

Closely linked to self psychology's conception of parental functions and central to its theory are its representations of selfobjects. As noted above, self psychology originally concentrated on psychopathology's interpersonal rather than intrapsychic origins, tracing the psychopathology of the self almost entirely to the quality of parental attention children received. It was Kohut's (1977) contention that parents, as their children's primary selfobjects, had to fully satisfy their children's basic psychological needs to ensure healthy development. Kohut identified these basic psychological needs as mirroring, which he defined as gratifying children's needs for admiration and for expressing ambition; idealization, which he defined as creating opportunities for children to idealize their parents; and twinship, which he defined as children's need for an alter ego.

The concept of selfobjects is problematic for intercultural treatments because Kohut represented selfobject functions as universal. Self psychology assumes that all children everywhere have identical needs for mirroring, idealization, and twinship. Yet these selfobject needs are specific to segments of Western cultures. They are due, in part, to the "radical individualism" (Roland 1996, p. 102) that prevails in the West, compromising interpersonal ties and demanding independent functioning. Because selfobject functions are as culturally variant as the parental functions described above, a view of selfobjects as grounded in culturally specific patterns of relationship is required.

In his later writings, Kohut (1984) advanced the concept of cultural selfobjects, and identified two of their primary functions. First, according to Kohut, cultural selfobjects embody cultural ideals, frequently in heroic proportions. In this way, he maintained, cultural selfobjects provide other cultural members with a sense of moral uplift. Second, in Kohut's view, cultural selfobjects constitute the collectivity of alter egos that populate the social environment. Through their very presence, they reinforce individuals' values, morals, and activities, and sustain their sense of self.

But Kohut overlooked the more fundamental point about selfobjects. Because all selfobjects enact particular, culturally valued interpersonal roles and functions, and because they correspond to culturally specific ideals of the self, all selfobjects are cultural. This more broadly conceived, cultural view encourages psychotherapists to explore the precise and multiple ways in which culture permeates and shapes all of their foreign and ethnic patients' selfobjects. Further, by suggesting that the self develops through its interactions with culturally suffused selfobjects, this view anticipates the extensive variation that actually characterizes patterns of human connectedness, psychological need, and interpersonal expectation across cultures.

The Japanese concept of *amae* provides an example of culturally specific patterns of psychological need and interpersonal attachment, and of the particular selfobject relationships that satisfy them. As explained by the Japanese psychiatrist Takeo Doi (1981), *amae* refers to interpersonal dynamics of intense interrelatedness and interdependence. Although its symbiotic nature makes *amae* the antithesis of Western ideals of autonomous adult functioning and firm self–other boundaries, Doi describes *amae* as psychologically foundational to the Japanese sense of self. For *amae* to emerge so that the self can develop in accordance with Japanese ideals of personhood clearly requires a set of cultural selfobject functions that are far removed from the middle-class American selfobject functions of mirroring, twinship, and idealization.

A second cultural dimension of selfobject functions concerns their role in children's psychological development. When Kohut discussed selfobjects, he focused on their contributions to the development of a stable individual identity. Gehrie (1979), however, has emphasized that optimal selfobject experiences play an important role in developing positive cultural identities as well. Because they enact culturally approved behaviors and ideals, selfobjects show children how to become competent members of their cultures.

The above discussion of cultural selfobjects undoubtedly provides but a partial listing of the cultural dimensions of selfobjects. Through close attention to the cultural patterning of their foreign and ethnic patients' psychological needs, and through close attention to the interpersonal expectations and requirements of such patients as they arise in therapeutic relationships, psychotherapists will surely discover additional cultural properties of selfobjects.

The Therapist's Role

Self psychology's novel conceptions of psychopathology produced new understandings of how psychotherapy cured. They also led to reformulations of the therapist's function and role. Kohut (1984) discouraged self psychological practitioners from emulating the emotional neutrality and detachment of classical psychoanalysts. Instead, he recommended that they treat their patients with responsiveness, warmth, and empathy. Kohut did not believe that the analyst's task was to make the patient's unconscious conscious by interpreting concealed motives and meanings. In his view, analysts were to repair patients' early deficits and fragmented selves by supplying them with the emotionally supportive developmental experiences that they had missed. Subsequent theorists of self psychology have refigured the therapist's role. Instead of emphasizing the therapeutic function of psychic repair, which they contend is necessary only in the treatment of severely disturbed narcissistic patients, they seek to provide all varieties of patients with an empathic and attuned therapeutic presence (Lichtenberg et al. 1992).

Despite these revisions in clinical technique, self psychology's constructions of psychological treatment remain problematic for intercultural psychotherapies. First, in the cases of severe self pathology for which self psychology holds extreme lapses in parental empathy responsible, the prototypical self psychological cure involves repairing self structures by providing patients with the missing selfobject experiences of mirroring, twinship, and idealization. Yet self deficits are not culturally invariant. Instead, they reflect culturally particular ideals of selfhood, psychological needs, and relationships, and are differently configured across cultures. Self psychologists who treat patients from other cultures must ascertain the culturally specific nature of their patients' relational needs before they can provide them with the necessary selfobject experiences.

Second, newly revised self psychological theories hold that most patients have selfobject needs that are unrelated to deficits in the self. Such patients are thought to require responsive treatments rather than reparative ones, and self psychologists are encouraged to offer them empathic attunements. Because psychological needs for attunement are strong among those foreign and ethnic patients who are accustomed to highly interdependent interpersonal relationships, it would seem that self psychological treatments are tailor-made for them. Yet cross-cultural differences in the precise nature of selfobject needs, in ideologies of relationship, and in modes of interpersonal communication raise questions as to whether American psychotherapists can offer foreign and ethnic patients the precise types of attuned selfobject experiences that they require. For example, many Indian and Japanese patients are used to nonverbal modes of communication and means of attunement. These include numerous varieties of silences, each of which conveys particular feelings and meanings (Roland 1996). Few Western psychotherapists are equipped to supply such patients with these specific types of therapeutic interactions. Such patients may feel embarrassed and insulted by their Western therapists' verbalizations, and experience their therapists as uncaring as a result of them. In intercultural self psychological therapies, then, it is quite likely that the treatments therapists offer will be out of tune with foreign and ethnic patients' selfobject needs.

For self psychology to become a more useful approach to cross-cultural treatments, its conceptions of parenting, of selfobjects, and of the therapist's roles and functions must be reconfigured to include cultural perspectives. As discussed above, even then its effectiveness may be restricted in some cases due to therapists' inabilities to perform culturally specific selfobject functions. Yet only when self psychology expands its frameworks, so that they include the exploration of patients' cultural beliefs and expectations regarding what is necessary and nourishing in interpersonal relationships, will it acquire the possibilities of offering better methods for evaluating, and for meeting, the emotional needs of foreign and ethnic patients.

THE CULTURAL SPECIFICITY OF OTHER PSYCHOLOGIES

Perhaps the most significant shift in clinical theory and practice in recent years concerns the increasing numbers of practitioners who have abandoned the practice of one-person psychotherapies in favor of two-person models of treatment. Variously referred to as interpersonal, relational, and interactional psychotherapies, such models generally stress the reciprocal, collaborative, dialogical, and egalitarian features of therapeutic encounters. For the purposes of this discussion, such varying clinical approaches are grouped together and categorized as two-person models of treatment.

Sullivan's Interpersonal Theory

Contemporary two-person models of psychological treatment show an affinity with Harry Stack Sullivan's theory of interpersonal psychiatry. While Sullivan's clinical theory is too elaborate to be fully presented here (for comprehensive statements of his interpersonal theory, see Sullivan 1953, 1954, 1956), selected theoretical and technical elements that have captured the analytic imagination in recent years are summarized.

Sullivan (1953) went against the tide of mid-century psychoanalytic conservatism. Rejecting Freud's conception of individuals as isolated organisms, Sullivan viewed human beings as embedded in social worlds and as predisposed toward social interaction. Refuting Freud's biologically based explanations of psychological conflict, Sullivan located the origins of psychological problems within the matrix of human relationships. His conception of personality was similarly socially rooted. Sullivan argued that personality was constituted by interpersonal relationships, and that personality development was a process of acculturation by which individuals' sense of self assimilated the reactions of an ever-expanding social environment. Individuals struggled to accommodate themselves, first to the dynamics of their families, and then to the requirements of their larger communities. The anxiety that individuals suffered when their actions met with disapproval interfered with their cognitive functioning and distorted their perceptions of others. Such problems were incorporated into the evolving personality and surfaced in subsequent interactions.

Sullivan extended his theoretical emphasis on social interaction into the clinical domain, reconfiguring psychological treatment as an interpersonal encounter. For Sullivan, the therapeutic relationship was a real and mutual social exchange. Further, by insisting that the analyst's personality entered the analytic frame, Sullivan repositioned the clinician from a place of detached investigation to one of participation. Sullivan's reconception of psychological treatment as an interpersonal process—one in which both patient and clinician influence the production of clinical material rather than as one in which an uninvolved psychoanalyst observes the patient's intrapsychic world unfold—is the hallmark of contemporary two-person treatment approaches.

Two-Person Models of Treatment

As noted above, in recent years two-person models of psychological treatment have undergone a revitalization in clinical practice. Some contemporary two-person treatment models stem directly from Sullivanian interpersonal theory; others claim alternative genealogies in philosophy, in object relations theories, or in self psychology (A. Roland, personal communication). This section focuses on the features that many two-person clinical models share.

Contemporary two-person treatment models endorse Sullivan's modifications in the clinician's position and role. Indeed, by doing away with all of the "pillars of classical technique" (Mitchell 1997, p. 12), they go beyond Sullivan's reconceptualizations of analytic comportment. But two-person models do more than banish analytic abstinence, anonymity, and neutrality; they also dismiss notions of analytic objectivity and omniscience. Rejecting the classical claim that practitioners have scientific and privileged knowledge of their patients' intrapsychic realities, such models construct the clinical encounter as a joint and egalitarian enterprise in which interpretations of reality and attributions of meaning are collaboratively determined by patient and clinician. Contemporary two-person models thus contradict Sullivanian theory, which maintained that despite their involvement in therapeutic encounters, clinicians retained their objectivity and therefore were the authoritative interpreters of clinical interactions.

Another feature common to many current two-person models is their concentration on patients' present circumstances and concerns rather than on their past experiences. In this respect as well they break with Sullivanian theory, which viewed historical reconstructions of patients' early years as having at least an equal therapeutic importance. More closely in tune with Sullivanian theory, by constructing psychological treatment as an interaction between patient and clinician, such models reconceptualize the patient's mind. No longer is the psyche seen as a bounded and separate internal space. Rather, according to two-person models, it is embedded in the relational field of the therapeutic encounter.

The Culture of Interpersonal Relationships

Sullivan was viewed as part of the Cultural School of psychoanalysis (Thompson 1950). Indeed, Sullivan (1953) identified cultural anthropology as a tributary that contributed to his theory of psychiatry. As a result, it is often imagined that interpersonal approaches, along with other two-person models of treatment, are more hospitable than conventional one-person models to intercultural psychotherapies. Yet Sullivan's concept of culture was actually quite restricted. Typically, he invoked the idea of culture to signal that his theory differed from Freud's, in that it conceptualized psychic processes as socially rather than endogenously determined. For Sullivan, the idea of culture signified no more than the social rules and prescriptions that, in his view, shaped individual personality.

Sullivan's limited interest in culture is further demonstrated by the fact that he concerned himself neither with psychological development in cultures other than his own, nor with cross-cultural variations in psychological functioning. Clearly expressing his preference for universalizing psychological perspectives, Sullivan (1953) stated that he was not interested in human differences across cultures, but in human similarities. Moreover, despite his focus on interpersonal interaction in clinical encounters, Sullivan failed to consider either the cultural contexts in which therapeutic relationships unfold or the particular ways in which cultural differences between patients and clinicians affect therapeutic interactions.

Current relational theorists similarly neglect to address the cultural dimensions of two-person treatments. While it is true that two-person models generally eschew Western universalizing metapsychologies and closely ground themselves in actual clinical interactions (Friedman 1988), this does not render them culturally neutral. Nor does this extricate two-person models from the Western assumptions that pervade psychotherapeutic theory and practice. Moreover, as I argued in the Introduction to Part I, the clinical consulting room is not a culturally neutral space in which patient and therapist freely negotiate shared understandings of ongoing therapeutic interactions; rather, it is a Western cultural environment that constructs patients, therapists, and therapeutic knowledge in particular ways. Thus, although two-person models contend that therapeutic relationships and understandings are reciprocally and newly created within each clinical dyad, both are strongly determined by the Western cultural frames in which they are set.

If the built-in Western culture of the clinical consulting room compels foreign and ethnic patients to accept their psychotherapists' Western cultural frame, then it also compels them to adapt themselves to it. Upon entering psychological treatment, many foreign and ethnic patients adopt a Western manner of presenting themselves and a Western manner of interacting with their therapists, thereby silencing indigenous cultural voices in their treatments. Further, by privileging patients' current situations, two-person models distance foreign and ethnic patients from the primary cultural identifications that are moored in early experiences, memories, and relationships. Two-person models are thus likely to induce and to reinforce Westernized cultural selves in foreign and ethnic patients, selves that may be detached from more profound and enduring difficulties and concerns.

A final consideration regarding the use of two-person approaches in the psychological treatment of foreign and ethnic patients concerns their ethos of egalitarianism. It is perhaps ironic that this ethos, which is reflected in two-person models' emphases on patients' and therapists' mutual contributions to the therapeutic relationship and to therapeutic knowledge, might render these approaches inappropriate for some foreign and ethnic patients. Egalitarian relationships are themselves Western ideals. As such, they offer no clinical advantage to the many foreign and ethnic patients who are more comfortable with hierarchical relationships, and who expect their healers to be powerful and authoritarian—patients, in other words, who would prefer that their therapists more closely resembled the traditional practitioners of classical psychoanalysis.

Intersubjective Approaches

Intersubjective approaches are another influential current in contemporary clinical theory and practice. Incorporating postmodern ideologies, they represent truth and knowledge as situational, multiple, shifting, and constructed, rather than as knowable, objective, and absolute. Encompassing relational theories, they conceive of human psychology as bound up in interpersonal experience. And rejecting classical psychoanalysis's view of the mind as a collection of isolated psychic processes, they locate psychopathology in the intersubjective contexts in which, they claim, it originated (Stolorow et al. 1994).

Like two-person models of psychological treatment, intersubjective approaches are free of many of classical psychoanalysis's rigidities in theory and technique. They possess little metapsychology and do not presume the existence of core intrapsychic conflicts. Intersubjective approaches thus liberate clinicians from preconceived theoretical positions and allow them to respond more directly to their patients' clinical material. Compared to classical psychoanalysis, they permit greater technical flexibility, allowing both a broader range of interventions and a more compassionate understanding of patients' resistances to treatment and change (Rabin 1995).

Practitioners who advocate intersubjective approaches embrace even more radical reformulations of the analyst's role than those that two-person models of treatment contain. Intersubjective practitioners, like clinicians who endorse two-person models of treatment, contend that the psychoanalytic ideal of the detached and neutral scientist who dispassionately analyzes the data of patients' lives is impossible to achieve. They argue that clinicians are active participants in psychological treatments, and that every instance of clinical intervention, response, and restraint is colored by their personal characteristics, values, and beliefs. Going beyond some two-person models, intersubjective approaches conceptualize the clinician's subjectivity as a source of important countertransference information, one which enriches and deepens psychological treatments (Renik 1993).

Cultural Subjectivities

In endorsing analytic subjectivity, intersubjective approaches acknowledge that clinicians' personal characteristics inevitably influence psychotherapeutic treatments. Yet such approaches fail to consider that the personalities, moralities, and ideologies that compose practitioners' subjectivities are not simply individual psychological products, but rather are culturally shaped. Intersubjective approaches thus neglect to examine the ways in which therapists' cultural subjectivities affect intercultural treatments.

It has been argued that "only a *part* of concrete reality is interesting and *significant* to us, because only it is related to the *cultural* values with which we approach reality" (Weber 1963, pp. 384–385, emphasis in the original). This Weberian proposition, which asserts that cultural values differentially ascribe significance to experience, has clear implications for intercultural psychological treatments. Indeed, the cultural values that inform practitioners' subjectivities powerfully influence both how they approach their foreign and ethnic patients' realities and which particular aspects of these realities they find interesting and significant. When clinicians and patients have differing cultural values, they may hold varying opinions as to which aspects of patients' worlds require therapeutic attention and intervention. Psychotherapists whose cultural values privilege individuals' self-determination, for example, are likely to focus on issues of individuation and to encourage autonomy, even when their patients' cultures value interdependence and self-sacrifice (Ewalt and Mokuau 1995). Moreover, psychotherapists' cultural subjectivities configure the therapeutic relationship in particular ways. Commonly, clinical interaction is shaped to conform to Western notions of relationship, even when such relationships contradict the needs and expectations of foreign and ethnic patients (Tsui and Schultz 1985). By failing to reflect on the cultural subjectivities at play in intercultural therapeutic encounters, intersubjective approaches neglect to examine such concerns.

Dialectics and Dialogues

Intersubjective approaches conceptualize psychotherapeutic encounters as dialectical. By this, they mean that clinicians and patients participate in mutually influencing interactions, interactions in which they continually generate multiple and shifting constructions of each other (Ogden 1994). But intersubjective discussions of patients' and psychotherapists' reciprocal constructions have been restricted to their constructions of each others' personal characteristics. The cultural factors that contribute in essential ways to their reciprocal constructions therefore have been overlooked.

Evidence from cross-cultural treatments, however, strongly suggests that patients and clinicians imbue each other not only with particular individual characteristics, but with cultural ones as well. Abbasi's (1996, 1997) discussions of intercultural treatments demonstrate that white American patients culturally construct their non-Western clinicians, that they attribute specific ethnic identifications and socioeconomic positions to them, and that these identifications profoundly affect their psychotherapies. Hollingshead and Redlich's (1958) well-known study showed that clinicians culturally construct their patients as well, ascribing an excessive degree of pathology to patients whom they perceive as non-white. These examples show that within therapeutic encounters, therapists and patients create each other not only as distinct individuals but also as cultural objects, and that their reciprocal attributions of cultural identity can alter the tone and the course of treatment. Clearly, intersubjective perspectives need to be broadened to consider the ways in which cultural subjectivities affect intercultural clinical treatments.

CONCLUSION

The conservative legacy of Freudian psychoanalysis deeply affects the theoretical assumptions and technical methods of contemporary psychotherapies. Classical psychoanalysis's universalizing views have established Western ideals of the mind and of the self as pancultural psychological norms. By doing so, they have diverted therapeutic attention from the cultural dimensions of foreign and ethnic patients' psychologies. At the same time, the Freudian claim that psychoanalytic theory and methods are culture free has discouraged practitioners from developing clinical models that are better suited to intercultural treatments. The enduring influences of classical psychoanalysis have thus worked against the creation of a cultural psychotherapy.

A cultural psychotherapy depends not only on reconceptualizing clinical models of treatment, but on generating culturally informed understandings of the topics that are the usual subjects of clinical encounters, including the mind, the self, emotion, and development. In Chapter 2, I argue that cultural anthropology's approaches to these topics can be useful to clinical theory and practice, and I discuss their potential applications to intercultural psychotherapies.

2

Psychotherapy and Anthropology

BOUNDARY CROSSINGS

In this chapter, I suggest that cultural anthropology and related subfields, including psychological anthropology, ethnopsychology, comparative human development, and linguistic anthropology, offer culturally informed understandings of human behavior and mind that are integral to intercultural treatments. I then identify the categories of anthropological research that are most important to the clinicians who conduct such treatments. In particular, I discuss the potential contributions of anthropological research on culture, selfhood, emotion, child development, and language to clinical practice. This chapter is not meant to be an exhaustive catalogue of the anthropological knowledge that would inform clinical practice. Rather, it constitutes a starting place for interdisciplinary efforts.

To transmit cultural anthropology's understandings of human behavior and mind to clinical psychology, however, requires more than identifying the specific anthropological findings that are most relevant to psychotherapists. Such boundary crossings also depend on undoing the resistances that clinicians have traditionally displayed toward integrating cultural material, and especially anthropological renderings of human behavior, into their theory and practice. Addressing the possibility that psychotherapists have resisted anthropological material because they have found it impenetrable or abstruse, in this chapter I have converted this material into forms that are suitable for clinicians. Perhaps, after having reviewed more accessible cross-cultural findings, psychotherapists will be encouraged to assess potential anthropological contributions to the study of human mind and behavior and to employ such approaches in their intercultural clinical work.

ANTHROPOLOGICAL CONTRIBUTIONS TO PSYCHOTHERAPY

The Nature of Culture

The tendency among psychotherapists to disregard the cultural dimensions of human psychology can be explained in various ways. Certainly, as I have maintained earlier, therapists' inattention to the cultural backgrounds of their foreign and ethnic patients is a logical consequence of psychology's universalistic models of mind. In addition, because psychotherapists and their patients have customarily shared Western cultural backgrounds, the universalistic features of the standard models of treatment have not been strongly challenged. Further, as suggested above, the anthropological data that would inform intercultural psychotherapies have yet to be introduced directly into the clinical domain. Yet psychotherapists' traditional dismissals of the cultural dimensions of their patients' psychologies might also be understood as a result of their unfamiliarity with new directions in anthropological theory and research.

Formerly known as a field that studied social heritage to the exclusion of the individual human organism and the interpersonal situation (Sullivan 1953), some might argue that cultural anthropology has taken a psychological turn in the past two decades. Much recent anthropological research focuses on individuals rather than on large-scale social groups (Abu-Lughod 1997, Behar 1993), and on topics that have conventionally been contained within the disciplinary boundaries of psychology. Among such topics are the self, human development, cognition, intentionality, gender, and emotion (Abu-Lughod 1986, Astuti 1998, Daniel 1984, Lutz 1988, Ortner 1996, Rosen 1985, White and Kirkpatrick 1985). Within this new body of findings, both the general nature of cross-cultural psychological variation and its precise characteristics in particular cultural settings are clearly detailed. This chapter describes the vast and rapidly growing store of anthropological data on cross-cultural variation in the topics that most concern psychotherapists.

Just as psychotherapists might have been unaware of the new anthropological interest in psychological subjects, they might also be unfamiliar with more recent anthropological conceptions of culture. When psychotherapists have written about culture, they have tended to represent it in ways that many current anthropologists consider outmoded. They have reduced culture to specific behaviors or practices (Applegate 1990), and they have generally relegated it to the extrapsychic world of human experience that is external to their concerns (Winnicott 1971). Many psychotherapists continue to conceive of culture as a unitary entity that belongs to the social group, rather than to the individual, that is located in the external world of materials and products rather than within the internal world of thoughts, emotions, and ideas, and that is embodied in group ritual and custom rather than in individual action. Given these understandings of culture as exterior, concrete, and collective, it is not surprising that psychotherapists continue to regard it as irrelevant to the individual psychological experience that is their usual domain, and to effectively banish cultural analysis from therapeutic encounters.

Among clinicians who recognize culture as an aspect of their patients' identity that merits psychotherapeutic investigation, essentializing views of culture predominate. In their writings about culture, they tend to represent all members of a given cultural group as possessing a fixed and homogeneous set of values, behavioral habits, and beliefs. Typically providing psychotherapy to persons of particular ethnicities, these clinicians prescribe the acquisition of cultural knowledge and the adoption of culturally specific therapeutic techniques as solutions to the problems of intercultural clinical work (Morones and Mikawa 1992, Rogler et al. 1987, Tsui and Schultz 1985).

While acquiring knowledge about specific cultural groups might be of help to therapists who deliver a limited number of intercultural treatments, it is inadequate as an overall strategy for conducting psychotherapy with foreign and ethnic patients. Such essentializing conceptions of culture overlook significant intracultural variation and encourage the cultural stereotyping of patients. They also fail to provide psychotherapists with the necessary methods for discovering, understanding, and treating the multiple cultural identifications and internalized cultural conflicts that are common among multicultural patients. For the many contemporary psychotherapists who practice in clinical settings that have a culturally diverse clientele, learning about the culture of every foreign and ethnic patient is an impossible task. More importantly, research has shown that therapists' knowledge about their patients' cultural backgrounds has no bearing on patients' therapeutic progress (Sue and Zane 1987). Rather than learning about the stereotypical characteristics of particular cultures, psychotherapists need to become familiar with the general characteristics, categories, and functions of culture per se (Devereux 1958).

To propose that contemporary cultural anthropologists would support this view is not to suggest that there exists a singular, definitive conception of culture that all anthropologists embrace. On the contrary, on the subject of culture, anthropologists have consistently, and famously, failed to reach a consensus. In their writings about culture per se, anthropologists debate its character, its location, its functions, and its distribution within and across populations. Some anthropologists debate its existence, asserting that the concept of culture no longer describes today's complex, ethnically heterogeneous, and geographically mobile societies (Abu-Lughod 1997, Gupta and Ferguson 1992). Conceptions of culture that continue to influence anthropologists and are relevant to clinicians who conduct intercultural psychotherapies are summarized below.

Perhaps the most important culture statement for contemporary psychotherapists is found in the work of Clifford Geertz. Geertz (1973) reinvented American cultural anthropology in the 1970s, conceptualizing the field "not as an experimental science in search of law but an interpretive one in search of meaning" (p. 5). Indeed, Geertz supported

Weber's (1963) assertion that cultures order otherwise chaotic environments by suffusing them with meaning. In Geertz's view, cultural meanings, values, and worldviews are shared by the members of cultural groups and are contained within thematically consistent and organized systems of social symbols, which it is the anthropologist's task to decode.

Of central interest to psychotherapists are Geertz's (1973, 1984) arguments against universalizing conceptions of human nature and human mind. A cultural relativist, Geertz contended that culturally specific meanings inhabit and shape individuals' thoughts, emotions, and motivations, and that every culture provides its members with particular and distinct ways of perceiving, evaluating, and experiencing the world. According to Geertz, the psychological processes that psychotherapists construct as internal and individual actually embody collective, culturally created meanings. In other words, because thoughts, emotions, beliefs, and ideas are culturally determined, they are public and shared.

Post-Geertzian anthropologists reject many of Geertz's central claims. Rather than locating culture within the public domain, some contemporary anthropologists place it within the individual, and examine the varying motivations of individual cultural actors (Obeysekere 1990). Other anthropologists, instead of distributing culture homogeneously and evenly across all members of a given group, construct culture as differentially interpreted and reproduced according to individuals' varying subjectivities and social positions. These anthropologists describe the distinctive ways in which members of the same culture differently understand the same cultural realities (Abu-Lughod 1997, Schwartz 1978). Still other contemporary anthropologists, rather than ascribing distinct cultures to persons within finite, geographically bounded spaces, conceive of culture as dispersed across national boundaries due to transnational migrations and diasporas and to globalized media and economies (Gupta and Ferguson 1992, Rouse 1991). Also relevant to the theory and practice of psychotherapy are conceptions of culture inspired by Bakhtin's (1981) claim that cultural voices and meanings reside within individual speech and action. Bakhtin's ideas have spurred dialogic approaches to culture, which propose that cultures are "continuously produced, reproduced, and revised in dialogues among their members" (Mannheim and Tedlock 1995, p. 2). This view of culture as emergent and as reciprocally created through conversations allows psychotherapists to understand treatment sessions as cultural events that are multivoiced, reciprocally constructed, and mutually interpretable by patients and therapists. It also provides patients and therapists with a means of recovering the cultural voices that are routinely overlooked and devalued by Western therapeutic discourses.

Contemporary cultural anthropologists thus offer psychotherapists various new ways of thinking about culture. They suggest that culture exists in the individual mind, shaping perception and experience, thought and emotion, and values and worldviews, as well as in the public sphere. They propose that cultural meanings are individually interpreted and enacted in addition to being, to varying degrees, shared by the members of a society. They claim that culture is expressed in both individual and collective action, and that it resides in private conversations as well as in social symbols. By focusing on individuals, on their psychological processes and characteristics, and on their social worlds, these new conceptions of culture directly address clinical interests. At the same time, they provide psychotherapists with the necessary tools for generating more accurate understandings of the subjectivities and experiences of foreign and ethnic patients. To more explicitly extend such cultural inquiry into the clinical domain, in the sections below I consider anthropological inquiries into topics of psychotherapeutic interest.

The Cultural Construction of the Self

If the formation of a cultural psychotherapy is contingent upon therapists familiarizing themselves with contemporary notions of culture, then it also requires them to acquire an appreciation of the self as a cultural product. Cultural anthropologists refute the universalistic conceptions of the self and of human nature that underlie the standard theories of psychotherapy (Geertz 1973, 1984, White and Kirkpatrick 1985). They also reject psychological views of selfhood that restrict culture's influence on the self to superficial overt behaviors, as distinct from individuals' basic feelings and conflicts (Ticho 1971).

Cultural anthropologists claim not only that culture fully penetrates the self, but that the self assumes a virtually unlimited variety of forms in diverse cultural environments. In their view, Western versions of the self as located inside an individual body, as consistent across contexts, introspective, and capable of change, and as a "bounded, unique, more or less integrated motivational and cognitive universe, a dynamic center of awareness, emotion, judgment, and action" that is "organized into a distinctive whole" (Geertz 1983, p. 59), have little in common with the particular ways in which selves are constructed and experienced across cultures.

Cultural conceptions of the self hold that the self is neither a biological given nor a genetic imperative, but that it is instead a sociocultural construction. By suggesting that every culture and every historical era produce specific and distinctive configurations of the self, cultural conceptions of the self provide perspectives on selfhood that are absent from clinical theory. Although they are sometimes flawed by an inattention to intragroup differences, anthropological accounts of cross-cultural variation in the self are helpful to psychotherapists who work with patients from other cultures because they portray the vast range of possible human selves. The examples below illustrate some of the ways in which selves diverge across cultures.

One important aspect of cross-cultural variation in selfhood concerns the extent and nature of individuation in the self. Some societies doubt the very existence of separate, individual selves. The people of Sabarl island in Papua New Guinea, for example, lack native terms for individual persons, perhaps because their identities are realized almost entirely through social interactions (Battaglia 1990). The selves of the Lohoring of East Nepal are similarly communal in nature, although they are very differently configured. For the Lohoring, selves are not experienced as having fixed locations within individual bodies, but as migrating from one person to another (Hardman 1981). A more individuated sense of self exists among the Tamil of south India. There, the essences of selves are believed to be constituted, in part, through the mixing of individuals' bodily substances with the substances of the soil of their native villages (Daniel 1984). The highly individuated selves of the Kaqchikel Maya of highland Guatemala are further distinguished by their capacities to assume animal forms and animal natures at night (Warren 1995).

Another aspect of the self that is constructed in markedly different ways across cultures is gender (cf. Ortner 1996). Cross-cultural variation in the construction of gender includes the degree to which male and female are perceived as separate, nonoverlapping categories. The sharply defined boundary between the sexes in Taroudannt, Morocco, is reflected in the near total segregation of men and women in public life. Constructions of women as deficient in intelligence and as possessing uncontrollable sexual desires contribute to the seclusion of Taroudannt females (Dwyer 1978). Among the Sambia of Papua New Guinea, contact with women is believed to endanger the masculine war-making capacities of the male population because it allows female pollutants to invade men's bodies. Sambia males repeatedly subject themselves to painful episodes of bloodletting to purge themselves of the feminine contaminants that weaken their masculine systems (Herdt 1990). However, among the Vezo of Madagascar, strict divisions between male and female are absent and the similarities between the sexes are emphasized. The result is a society of comparatively ungendered persons (Astuti 1998). A further dimension of cultural difference in gendering occurs in India. There, man and woman are joined together not only in Hindu deities that contain both male and female genders, but in human selves that are alternatively gendered as *hijras*. This third gender category defies conventional Western notions of male and female in its construction of *hijras* as neither man nor woman, but as man *plus* woman (Nanda 1994).

Other anthropological accounts of selfhood demonstrate that patterns of behavior, modes of thought, constellations of affect, states of consciousness, constructions of identity, ideologies of agency, and modes of relationship—both with other persons and with the natural and supernatural worlds—vary greatly from culture to culture. These accounts illustrate the ways in which the self's experience of time, space, relationship, and identity, as well as its ways of constructing meaning, are highly variable cross-culturally. Because anthropological accounts of the self also demonstrate that the self's experience of health and illness, including the locus and meaning of pathology, is culturally specific, ethnographic studies of the self have an obvious relevance to the psychological treatment of patients from other cultures.

Recognizing the flaws inherent in universalistic conceptions of the self, some psychologists have developed alternative models of selfhood. Variously referred to as the individualist and the collectivist self (Triandis 1995), the egocentric and the sociocentric self (Sampson 1988), and the independent and the interdependent self (Markus and Kitayama 1991), psychologists have filled in the outlines of these basic self orientations by correlating them with a number of emotional dispositions, cognitive styles, and interpersonal behaviors. While these models of the self take the important step of introducing mainstream psychologists to the concept of cultural variation in selfhood, their limitations are substantial. First, their binary and mutually exclusive categories tend to produce, and to support, cultural generalizations and stereotypes. More importantly, because these models assume there to be a series of distinct oppositions between Western and non-Western versions of selfhood, they fail to examine the culturally specific categories of the person that are required in intercultural psychotherapies.

The deficiencies of psychology's binary models of the self reinforce the importance of assimilating anthropological understandings of selfhood into clinical theory and practice. In intercultural psychotherapies, the culturally specific constructions of the self that are particular to each patient cannot be assumed, but must be discovered anew in every case. This approach has been put into practice by Kakar (1997) and by Roland (1988, 1996), psychoanalysts who, in the course of intercultural treatments, have tried to understand the specific ways in which individualities and collectivities are differently configured in particular non-Western cultures. Therapists who follow their example, recognizing cross-cultural variation in selfhood and exploring the precise cultural characteristics of the self in clinical encounters with foreign and ethnic patients, not only will be able to conduct culturally informed psychotherapies, but also will be in a position to contribute to interdisciplinary conversations about selfhood across cultures.

Emotion Across Cultures

The therapeutic enterprise revolves around the patient's experience of emotion. Many patients who enter psychotherapy seek insight into emotional reactions that trouble them, and wish to establish more adaptive patterns of affective experience and response. Therapists who are unable to understand their patients' emotional states often find it difficult to grasp their interior and exterior worlds. Moreover, the empathic therapeutic stance that some psychotherapies advocate cannot be achieved unless psychotherapists can connect with their patients' subjective emotional realities. Therapists' difficulties in accurately assessing and responding to their patients' emotional states intensify when they treat patients from other cultures, because such patients' emotional reactions and expressions differ in significant ways from those that are considered to be natural and normal in the West. Thus another way in which anthropological knowledge can inform intercultural psychotherapy treatments involves applying anthropology's cultural perspectives on emotion to foreign and ethnic patients' affective histories and experiences.

Psychologists have been deeply influenced by naturalist conceptions of emotion. Accordingly, they tend to conceive of emotions as inherent and fixed biologically based essences, as instinctive endogenous entities that well up from within (Heelas 1986) and contain meanings that are exclusively psychological. Informed by these views, psychologists generally have assumed there to be transcultural uniformity in the human experience of emotion. But as Lutz (1988) argues, many of mainstream psychology's ostensibly scientific conceptualizations of affect are actually rooted in North American constructions of emotionality as irrational, as potentially uncontrollable and dangerous, and as essentially female.

Recent anthropological work portrays the vast diversity in affect that exists across cultures. Persons who inhabit different cultural settings acquire dramatically divergent emotional repertoires. And because these varying emotional repertoires are fundamentally related to "different ways of being a person in radically different worlds" (Kleinman and Good 1985, p. 3), translating emotion words across cultures is not simply a matter of identifying equivalent terms in another language. Rather, it requires an understanding of the radically different cultural worlds in which emotions are situated.

One dimension of cross-cultural variation in emotional repertoires concerns the differences from one cultural setting to the next in the particular emotions that are culturally significant. The emotion known as *amae*, for example, which refers to profound feelings of interpersonal interdependence and interconnection, is highly valued among the Japanese and yet is unmarked in the American emotional repertoire (Doi 1981). Even emotions that seem to exist in the same form across cultures are variously experienced in different cultural settings and serve varying social ends. Thus the shame experienced by the Ilongot headhunters of the Philippines diverges from the American sense of shame, serving not to discourage inappropriate personal behaviors but to repair the situations of social inequality that the Ilongot find intolerable (Rosaldo 1983).

But cross-cultural variation in emotion extends beyond the specific contents of emotional repertoires. There is also extensive cross-cultural variation in where emotions are situated and in what causes them. Some cultures locate emotions internally, and experience them as either psychological or bodily processes. Other cultures locate emotions in the external world, and attribute them to the actions of other human beings or of supernatural entities. The Maori of New Zealand, for example, do not experience emotions as originating inside of the mind or the body, but as caused by impersonal forces that inhabit the external world (Smith 1981). The Tahitians, on the other hand, have been reported to locate emotions internally, experiencing them as emanating from their stomachs (Levy 1973). The tendency to transform emotional upsets into physical symptoms, or to somaticize, has been found to be especially common in Chinese societies (Kleinman and Kleinman 1985).

Further cross-cultural variation in emotion concerns the ways emotions are managed. Contrary to Western psychotherapeutic perspectives, which recommend that emotions be acknowledged and released, particular types of emotional expression are eschewed in many cultural settings. Living among the Utku Eskimos, Briggs (1970) discovered that they strictly prohibited expressions of irritation and anger. Observers of the Balinese have described the ideal presentation of self in Bali as one that entails the elimination of all traces of individual emotional re-action (Geertz 1973).

Claiming that emotions are cultural constructions rather than psy-chobiological essences, contemporary anthropologists situate emotions within larger cultural systems of values, norms, and morals (Abu-Lughod 1986, Lutz 1988). Arguing that emotions are socially rather than indi-vidually owned and produced, current anthropological work suffuses them with sociocultural meanings. Recent research on the Islamic Re-public of Iran described the government's demand that its citizens pub-licly display grief to prove their loyalty to the dominant regime. This study underscored the role emotions play in communicating political messages and in achieving political ends (Good and Good 1988).

Anthropological accounts of the varieties of emotional experience and expression across cultures illuminate several aspects of emotion that are of importance to psychotherapists who treat foreign and ethnic pa-tients. First, such patients are likely to have emotional repertoires that differ from those with which their therapists are familiar. Second, when foreign and ethnic patients whose native language is other than English use English words to describe their emotions in therapy, they are likely to be translating into English indigenous conceptions of emotion that the English words imperfectly convey. As a result, important informa-tion about their emotional states is lost. Third, such patients are likely to have different ideas concerning the proper means of managing emo-tions. American therapists who urge their foreign and ethnic patients to outwardly express their emotions might unsettle those for whom cer-tain types of emotional expression are culturally unacceptable. Adopt-ing anthropological perspectives on emotion can not only increase psy-chotherapists' sensitivities to cross- cultural differences in emotion, but also encourage therapeutic explorations of the precise nature of foreign and ethnic patients' emotional worlds.

Comparative Human Development

When Freud introduced his theory of the psychosexual stages of devel-opment, he provided what was perhaps the original example of a devel-

opmental theory embedded in a more comprehensive human psychology. Many contemporary therapists reject this universalizing psychosexual developmental scheme, however, regarding with skepticism the
Freudian (1905) pronouncement that every child on earth must master
the Oedipus complex.

Yet even as they reject particular features of Freud's psychosexual
theory, many practicing psychotherapists continue to endorse universalizing conceptions of development. They also accept a central premise
of Freud's developmental scheme, agreeing that the experiences of early
childhood contribute in important ways to the development of the adult
personality. Consequently, in many psychological treatments, psychotherapists encourage their patients to describe the course and temper of
their early development. Even therapists who focus on the treatment
relationship and on current psychological functioning pay special attention as their patients recall childhood patterns of attachment, frustra-
tions and conflicts, and areas of mastery, listening for indications of
divergence from developmental norms. What some psychotherapists fail
to recognize, however, is that the norms in question are Western ones,
and that such universalizing constructions of normal development pervade clinical theory and practice.

The tendency among psychotherapists to accept universalizing
constructions of human development begins with the assumption that
the infant is situated in a matrix composed primarily of itself and its
biological mother. The infant is then expected to exhibit the particular
patterns of attachment (Bowlby 1958), modes of interpersonal responsiveness (Stern 1985), processes of separation and individuation (Mahler
et al. 1975), and senses of self (Winnicott 1960b) that psychologically
trained observers of infancy have identified as normal. These particular
developmental outcomes do not appear universally, however. Rather,
they represent culturally structured, Western developmental goals and
ideals, and are restricted to certain populations even in the industrialized West.

Psychology, by and large, has constructed human development as
the biological maturation of innate potentials. Yet it is clear that human
development is more complex and various than the predetermined unfolding of physiological capacities, as the prolonged period of infantile

dependence on others for its survival inevitably marries biological maturation to the acquisition of culture. Psychology's assumption that all children follow the same developmental path regardless of their sociocultural surround is uninformed by observations of children in other cultural settings (LeVine 1990); recently, it has begun to be questioned by culturally oriented developmental psychologists. But because the standard models of psychotherapy have incorporated psychology's universalizing views of development, many psychotherapists continue either to disregard significant variations in the early experiences of their foreign and ethnic patients or to evaluate these variations in light of Western developmental standards and norms.

Just as the establishment of a cultural psychotherapy requires that therapists investigate their foreign and ethnic patients' culturally constructed selves and emotions, it also requires that they explore such patients' culturally specific developmental histories. Here again, anthropological findings are available to inform clinical perspectives. Anthropological studies of comparative development counter psychology's conception of a unitary developmental path with detailed examples of extensive variation across cultures in the sequence, timing, and character of development. Such studies also provide specific examples of deviations across cultures from what psychological theory claims to be universal, stage-specific milestones and tasks. As anthropological accounts of cultural diversity in human development demonstrate, Western developmental norms are sociocultural products rather than biological imperatives (Harkness 1992).

Much of the research on comparative human development has focused on infancy. This research is guided by the supposition that because infants have had limited exposure to culture, universal biological processes should predominate and cross-cultural differences should be minimal. Yet research on infants in other cultural settings fails to replicate the patterns of development observed among American infants. The robust and intellectually responsive babies Stern (1985) described bear little resemblance to the sickly, listless babies of northeastern Brazil, who are constructed as innately predisposed not to activity and relationship, but to weakness, illness, and death (Scheper-Hughes 1990). Nor do Stern's highly stimulated and socially engaged American infants resemble the more placid infants of the Gusii of West Africa, whose parents refrain from placing them in the center of social attention (LeVine 1990).

Ethnographic studies of human development illustrate that development during other parts of the life span also shows a considerable plasticity across cultures. In her pioneering study of female adolescent development in Samoa, Margaret Mead (1928) demonstrated that contrary to popular belief, the emotional storms of adolescence are culturally contingent rather than inevitable biological consequences of puberty. Along similar lines, recent anthropological studies of adulthood indicate that middle-class North American conceptions of middle age, which emphasize physical and cognitive decline, are based on culturally distinctive assumptions regarding aging, the body, and the self rather than on biological considerations alone (Kakar 1997, Lock 1998, Shweder 1998).

Many psychotherapists agree that early childhood experiences significantly shape adult psychologies. To extend this assumption to cultural experiences would be to suggest that the cultural aspects of early childhood experience also contribute to later psychological makeup. Indeed, children whose early experiences occur in, and are shaped by, cultural worlds that differ from those of the Western middle-class children upon whom most developmental theories and norms are based might be expected to acquire divergent psychologies. Further research is necessary to determine how the cross-cultural variations in early developmental tasks and goals that cultural anthropologists have reported are related to adult psychological capacities.

Assumptions of uniformity in human development work against foreign and ethnic patients whose early histories and experiences cannot be contained or explained by Western developmental schemes. When these patients are evaluated in terms of Western developmental frameworks and goals, their psychological functioning—including their divergent patterns of attachment, of interpersonal relationship, of cognition, and of emotion—is likely to appear deficient or deviant. Bringing anthropological perspectives on the cultural shaping of human development into a dialogue with clinical theory can counter psychology's universalizing developmental narratives. By suggesting that therapists intensively explore their foreign and ethnic patients' culturally specific developmental pathways, such perspectives offer ways to enrich intercultural clinical understandings.

Anthropology and Language

Like classical psychoanalysis, psychotherapy is primarily a talking cure. Indeed, psychotherapy depends in large measure on verbal interactions between patients and therapists. But despite the obvious importance of fluid and mutually comprehensible conversations to the therapeutic enterprise, the ramifications for psychological treatment in cases where psychotherapist and patient do not share a native tongue, and especially in cases where the patient undergoes therapy in a non-native language, have been insufficiently examined. Several aspects of language use that complicate intercultural therapeutic encounters are discussed below.

The lack of a common native language between psychotherapist and patient frustrates psychotherapeutic progress on various fronts. Patients who speak a foreign language in treatment are continually translating from their native tongue into a foreign one. Such constant translation requires considerable intellectual effort, distracting patients from the emotional work of treatment. But in addition, culturally specific concepts defy easy translation. When central conceptual terms from the patient's native culture lack semantic equivalents in the language of their psychotherapy, patients must construct lengthy and laborious explanations of them. Words that refer to subjective perceptions, interpersonal connections, psychological states, and emotional reactions—in other words, the primary topics of psychotherapy—are notoriously resistant to translations that capture their cultural shadings and social implications.

As a result, many patients who speak a second language in treatment find it difficult to provide their therapists with clear and precise portraits of their psychological distress (Basch-Kahre 1984). When patients' translations are less than fluid, and when therapists and patients experience difficulties in communication, the therapeutic alliance frequently suffers. Under such clinical conditions, therapists are inclined to overpathologize their patients (Russell 1988), and patients are likely to experience the feelings of being inarticulate, incompetent, and unimportant that are common to foreign language speakers (Morley 1991). Moreover, in cross-linguistic encounters, the linguistic nuances, relational cues, idiomatic expressions, and changes in intonation that inform verbal communication are frequently lost (Flegenheimer 1989).

The patient's use of a nonnative language in psychotherapy has still further implications for intercultural treatments because native languages are fundamentally bound up with early emotional experience. The mother tongue, which is acquired in infancy and in early childhood, acquires an association with primitive affects, fantasies, and conflicts, and with primary sensory experiences and relationships (Greenson 1949). Second languages, on the other hand, typically are acquired later in life, and frequently are learned in impersonal institutional settings. In consequence, they are often detached from the intense early feelings and formative events that were experienced in the native tongue. When patients speak a second language in treatment, rich personal associations as well as primary feelings and experiences are often unavailable to them, and therefore to their psychotherapists (Amati-Mehler et al. 1993).

Languages are also fundamentally bound up with the organization of memory. Specific emotions and experiences become encoded in particular languages, and are then remembered primarily in those languages. Bilingual patients may not have access to significant portions of their memories when their therapy is in a second language, and their monolingual therapists may be unable to trigger important emotional associations (Javier 1995). Some patients may choose to undergo treatment in a second language in order to keep difficult feelings and events, which are remembered exclusively in the native tongue, out of awareness. Other patients may embark on psychotherapy in a second language in order to conceal aspects of their inner life from therapeutic scrutiny, or to support a new self that has taken shape in a second language (Kaplan 1993).

Perspectives drawn from the areas of sociolinguistics and linguistic anthropology further illuminate the problematics of cross-linguistic and intercultural therapeutic encounters. These perspectives suggest that in addition to having inadequate access to primary psychological experiences and inadequate command of the language of their treatment, patients who speak a non-native language in psychotherapy are likely to be unaware of the culturally organized communicative demands that govern the use of the second language in culturally defined situations (Gumperz 1972). Specifically, many such patients will be unfamiliar with the discourse patterns that characterize the psychotherapeutic encounter. They may be unsure of how to speak and how to listen in psychotherapy sessions, and of how to address their therapists. They may be bound by indigenous linguistic conventions that prohibit the highly personal and emotional verbal disclosures that therapists generally expect from their patients. Some foreign and ethnic patients may consider language to be a less effective means of communication than silences or other nonverbal behaviors.

Maintaining that all language use is rule governed, linguistic anthropologists and sociolinguists seek to identify both the general parameters of language use that are specified by cultural rules and the particular sociolinguistic rules that operate in given cultural settings. One parameter of language use that is rule governed concerns who is allowed to speak in various culturally defined circumstances. Women who seek medical advice in parts of Bangladesh, for example, do not have the right to discuss their own problems with their healers. Rather, females are accompanied by family members who are authorized to tell their stories and to convey their complaints for them (Wilce 1995). A second parameter of language use that is rule governed defines the types of speech that are required in given social situations. In the villages of highland Yemen, tribesmen must produce specific formulas of greeting in order to imbue social interactions with the culturally required components of mutual honor and respect (Caton 1986). A third parameter of language use that is rule governed concerns the particular ways in which ideas are phrased. Thus the Chinese avoid explicit statements in their speech, instead tending to use indirect references and circumlocutions (Young 1994).

When conversational partners do not share a native language, they are likely to use language very differently. At the same time, they are unlikely to be aware of the ways in which their varying patterns of language use affect their reactions to each other. Mismatches in language use commonly produce uncomfortable patterns of interaction, mutual misperceptions, and misunderstandings (Erickson and Shultz 1981, Young 1994). When such mismatches exist between patients and therapists, they complicate psychological treatments. Chinese patients who are accustomed to indirection in language, for example, are likely to experience their American therapists' direct questions as aggressive and intrusive. To their American therapists, who expect explicit answers, the circumlocutions with which their Chinese patients respond to their questions are likely to signify evasiveness and disengagement.

Although the dissonant patterns of interaction and the misperceptions of the other that commonly result from divergent usages of language undermine clinical judgment and disturb therapeutic alliances, they remain undertheorized aspects of psychotherapy. Bringing the perspectives of sociolinguistics and linguistic anthropology to bear on intercultural encounters better equips clinicians to understand the ways in which psychological treatments are affected when patients undergo psychotherapy in a non-native language.

CONCLUSION

Some contemporary anthropologists have come to mistrust the concept of culture. They argue that it inclines them to deny similarities and exaggerate differences between themselves and their informants, and to construct ethnographic subjects as distanced and exoticized "others" (Abu-Lughod 1991). While this is a serious matter for cultural anthropologists, a different set of issues confronts psychotherapists. For if the field of cultural anthropology has been compromised by its emphasis on the profound variation among persons from different cultures, then the discipline of psychotherapy has been compromised by its insistence on their profound sameness.

Contemporary psychotherapists need not be wary of conceptualizing their foreign and ethnic patients as radically and unrecognizably "other," but of conceptualizing them as indistinguishable from mainstream American patients. Anthropological perspectives, such as those that are described in this chapter, can help psychotherapists recognize and explore the varying psychologies of their foreign and ethnic patients.

By providing theoretical models that explain the ways in which culture infuses every aspect of human experience, and by providing specific examples of differences in human behavior and consciousness across cultures, they offer psychotherapists the possibilities of understanding such patients in their own terms, rather than in the universalizing terms of Western categories and concepts. Anthropological perspectives thus make essential contributions to a cultural psychotherapy.

Part II
_____

From the Patient's
Point of View

Introduction: The Patient and the Clinical Encounter

As discussed in the previous chapters, psychotherapists have paid little attention to the role of culture in psychotherapy, and even less attention to the ways in which their foreign and ethnic patients experience psychological treatment. Because patients' perspectives are underrepresented in the psychotherapy literature, psychotherapists who wish to learn about intercultural treatments have had to rely on the reports of other clinicians. In Part II, I attempt to redress this imbalance. In contrast with clinical research that exclusively investigates the views of psychotherapists, for this research I studied psychotherapy patients. To learn about intercultural psychotherapies from the patient's point of view, I conducted extensive and in-depth interviews with six subjects who had undergone psychological treatment with therapists whose cultural backgrounds and native languages differed from theirs. Part II examines these subjects' evaluations of their psychotherapies.

Before I analyze these interviews, several of their features need clarification. By design, I chose to study individuals who had been treated by other psychotherapists rather than by me. In my view, the literature on psychotherapy is deeply flawed by its consistent privileging of the therapist's voice, and I wanted to refrain from interpreting the data I collected from therapeutic perspectives. Interviewing subjects who had been treated by other psychotherapists allowed me to listen to narratives of treatment without my prior and intimate knowledge of their personal, family, and psychiatric histories intruding on the material. Presumably, it also allowed the subjects of this research to speak about their treatments more freely and to evaluate them more critically. If in the course of investigating these subjects' reactions to their treatments, I have at times challenged the clinical care they received, I have done so in the interest of developing culturally informed approaches to psychotherapy that may enhance intercultural clinical treatments.

Although each research subject's cultural background was distinctive, the following interviews share a specific configuration of cultural difference between psychotherapist and patient. Chapters 3 through 8 analyze psychotherapies in which the therapist was North American and the patient was either of another nationality or from an ethnic subculture within the United States. While many of the issues raised in the following chapters may be relevant to intercultural treatments regardless of the precise cultural composition of the therapeutic dyad, examining this particular therapist–patient configuration undoubtedly poses issues that are specific to this type of intercultural therapeutic relation. Alternative therapist–patient combinations—for example, psychotherapies set in the United States in which the therapist is from another country and the patient is North American—are likely to raise additional issues that are specific to them. Each cultural combination of psychotherapist and patient requires separate consideration.

This research is a qualitative rather than an experimental study. I did not control for the subjects' clinical diagnosis, for their therapists' theoretical orientations, or, in a systemic sense, for any other variables. Further, I do not claim that the six subjects constitute a representative sample. Because this study was set in a university town, most of its subjects were students. Certainly, foreign and ethnic students, like other immigrants and ethnic group members, frequently seek psychological help because of the enormous cultural gulfs they must navigate and because of the intense social pressures they face. Yet I do not claim that these six subjects represent all foreign and ethnic patients, nor do I claim that any of these subjects speaks for his or her entire cultural group.

I used a consistent format in conducting the interviews on which Part II is based. I began the interviews by informing the subjects of my interest in intercultural psychotherapies and by asking them to narrate the courses of their treatments. I then raised precise and exploratory questions about the cultural dimensions of their treatments and the cultural dynamics of their interactions with their psychotherapists. My interviewing style incorporated some of the methods I use in my clinical work with patients. For example, I first asked the subjects of this research to tell me their thoughts and feelings about their treatments. I then explored the replies I received, considered the possibilities of alternative interpretations and views, confronted defensive responses, and attempted to uncover the multiple subjective meanings of the material they disclosed. But my interdisciplinary orientation to these interviews caused me to combine the techniques of a psychotherapist with an anthropologist's sensitivity to non-Western and other cultural forms and to linguistic usages. As a result, I also listened for and explored non-Western and other cultural categories and concepts, and I investigated relevant images and terminologies in the subjects' native languages. Further, I tried to link the individual psychodynamics and relational patterns that are the conventional topics of the clinical consulting room to manifested sociocultural systems of meaning other than the Western ones that the standard theories of psychotherapy automatically or implicitly impose.

Some might contend that because I was a white, American psychotherapist asking foreign and ethnic patients about their psychological treatments with other white, American psychotherapists, these interviews reproduced the problematics and resistances of the subjects' therapeutic relationships. The subjects, however, maintained that these interviews afforded them welcome opportunities to openly reflect on their treatments, to assess their successes and failures, to express lingering gratitudes and resentments, and, above all, to think through the Western and non-Western cultural issues that their psychotherapies had raised but, in every case, had failed to adequately address. Indeed, many of the subjects experienced this research as a sort of "metatherapy" that both identified and clarified the cultural impediments to their treatments.

The act of interviewing foreign and ethnic patients about their psychotherapies with American psychotherapists is itself contrary to the conventions of psychotherapeutic practice in that it foregrounds the cultural aspects of treatment that standard clinical procedures customarily dismiss. Such standard clinical procedures effectively erase non-Western and other alternative cultural constructions of the self and of psychological health and replace them with Western ones. As a result, when foreign and ethnic patients begin psychotherapy, they inevitably confront the built-in Western culture of the psychological clinic.

Chapters 3 through 8 examine the varying ways in which six foreign and ethnic psychotherapy patients experienced this confrontation and the strategies they employed to manage it. As these chapters illustrate, in different ways throughout the course of their psychotherapies, these subjects were preoccupied by the cultural inflections of their treatments. None of the subjects I interviewed conceived of psychotherapy as a culture-free activity that took place on culturally neutral terrain. Rather, each viewed psychotherapy as a foreign and essentially North American endeavor that unfolded in a distinctive, culturally suffused landscape. Nor did the subjects of this research regard their therapeutic encounters as having occurred between culture-free individuals. Instead, they constructed both their therapists and themselves in cultural terms. Each subject invoked a multiplicity of cultural voices in treatment, selectively choosing among them to achieve desired therapeutic ends and to reproduce socioculturally patterned relationships with his or her therapist.

For these subjects, the Western culture of the clinical consulting room was reinforced by the language in which their psychotherapies were conducted. All of the subjects of this research underwent treatment in the—to them—non-native language of English. In consequence, in every psychotherapy session, each subject had to manage the complex tasks of speaking and acting as a patient in a foreign tongue. The subjects of this research were required to translate both culture-specific concepts and highly charged personal material into English. A further level of translation required them to convert their cultural metapsychologies— their specific, culturally determined, non-Western notions of emotional imbalance and psychic healing, which frequently contradicted those of their psychotherapists—into the concepts and categories of conventional psychotherapies.

These subjects experienced intense ambivalences about their psychological treatments, ambivalences that often arose as they identified psychotherapy with the larger Western cultural world. The subjects expressed these ambivalences by distancing themselves from their therapists, by silencing affectively salient non-Western and other cultural voices, by withholding personal information, and by missing sessions entirely. In the next six chapters, I examine the terms of these foreign and ethnic subjects' engagements with, and disengagements from, their psychotherapies, and I explore the various ways in which their continuing negotiations of the built-in Western culture of the clinical consulting room affected the progress of their treatments. Finally, in concluding reflections on each case, I begin to consider the ways in which a cultural psychotherapy might have enriched each subject's psychological treatment.

3

Negation: Prakesh

Born and raised in India, Prakesh began psychotherapy when he was a graduate student in physics at an American university. Although he appeared to participate in his treatment fully, in his own mind he systematically negated every aspect of it. Prakesh rejected psychotherapy's theoretical assumptions, mistrusted its methods, and failed to conceive of himself or of his difficulties in the terms of Western psychology. Psychotherapists might interpret Prakesh's total negation of therapy as a psychological resistance to treatment, yet perhaps it is better understood as the result of a dramatic collision of cultures. Certainly, in Prakesh's eyes, there were such profound cultural gaps between himself and his American psychotherapist that his therapist was incapable of understanding him. Nor was Prakesh willing to accept his psychotherapist's Westernized constructions of his problems. Indeed, what could it possibly have meant for Prakesh to be diagnosed and treated for depression when he claimed that his native language had no term for depression as a clinical entity?

Prakesh's negation of psychological treatment was further grounded in his identification of psychotherapy with North American society. He was highly critical of the United States and of American foreign policy; he castigated the United States for its bullying of less powerful nations, including his native India. In this chapter, I examine the ways in which Prakesh's psychotherapy was affected when he brought the adversarial political relationship between America and India into the clinical consulting room, first by constructing his American therapist as the representative of a country that oppressed and dominated his, and then by using his psychotherapy sessions to overturn this power relationship.

"POTSHOTS IN THE DARK"

Prakesh is a 30-year-old man from Calcutta. The only child of a pair of scientists, Prakesh, a Brahmin by birth who had previously disavowed his caste, grew up in a middle-class household. His native language is Bengali. He began to learn English in school when he was 6 years old, and although this language assumed ever greater prominence in his life as his education advanced, prior to coming to the United States his English use was restricted to academic settings. Perhaps it is for this reason that the English he speaks today, although fluent, has a somewhat formal quality.

Prakesh arrived in the United States for the first time in the early 1990s, and began a doctoral program in physics at an American university. His work progressed at a normal pace, but after two years in school, as he was completing his courses, he began to experience difficulties in his hearing. Prakesh tried to ignore this problem, and it was only in the course of a routine physical examination that he learned that he had an auditory disorder. He immediately underwent surgery, but it was too late. Because he had delayed in seeking medical attention, his ear had suffered permanent damage. Prakesh spent the entire summer recuperating from his ear operation. He described this as an extremely difficult time; he was in pain, unable to work, short of funds, and completely demoralized.

Prakesh intended to resume his graduate studies the following fall. But when he attempted to focus on his studies, residual abnormalities in his hearing disturbed his concentration. Blaming himself for his problems, and worrying that his academic career was finished, Prakesh considered quitting his program and returning to India. He also considered committing suicide. This he imagined in great detail. He conducted a great deal of research on the subject, and went so far as to "experiment" with the method of suicide that he found the "most practical"—tying a plastic bag around his head with a string. He became discouraged, however, when he realized that even this most practical method was "extremely uncomfortable, because, you know, it gets hot, and terrible. So I realized that I wouldn't even be able to do that if I needed to. So that made me even more upset, because I realized that I wouldn't even be able to kill myself."

At the urging of a professor who knew of his difficulties, Prakesh took a year's medical leave. That winter, he returned to India and moved back into his parents' house. Prakesh recounted his anguish during that time at the uncertainty surrounding his future. For several months, he said,

> I would just lie in bed for most of the day and sleep. I was thinking about death a lot at that time. I kind of felt that I had already died; that was the feeling that was operant in me, that I wasn't alive anymore. I felt that my life was basically over, because I wasn't doing the things that I would have wanted to do, which I would have been doing if the ear problem and all of this mess hadn't happened.

Prakesh's mother was deeply alarmed by her son's condition. She sought the advice of a cousin who studied psychiatry, and the cousin referred Prakesh to a local psychiatrist. Prakesh did not appreciate the referral. For one thing, he did not conceive of his difficulties as psychological in nature. On the contrary, "I felt that this was a physiological problem, not a psychological one, because it had to do with the ear." Further, although Prakesh was aware that mental health professionals practiced in his city, he considered them to be of no use to him. In his view, Indians who sought psychiatric help were unlike him; either they were addicted to various substances, or they had behaved unusually for no apparent reason, or they simply had excessive wealth and wished to spend their money. Despite his admittedly desperate state, Prakesh did not think that he was experiencing psychological problems; therefore, he saw no reason to seek psychological treatment.

Moreover, from what he had read in Indian newspapers, Prakesh had formed strong opinions about mental health treatment, all of which disinclined him to seek it:

> They make you lie on a couch, and they suggest things to you, and that seemed very medieval, like medieval doctors. They didn't know how things worked within the body, and so they would try out all these solutions and chemicals without quite knowing what would work and what wouldn't. And a lot of it was based on faith, rather than science.

The practitioners of this "medieval" treatment, according to Prakesh, were

> basically charlatans. . . . In the case of the human mind, no one knows how any of it works. . . . So if you don't really know what's going on inside, all you can do is trial and error and taking potshots in the dark, hoping that something will work. So that seemed to me not very different from quackery.

When considered in light of the history of psychoanalysis in India, Prakesh's disdain for psychological treatment acquires significant sociocultural dimensions. The Indian Psychoanalytic Society was founded in 1922 during the period of British colonial rule, and never broke free of its taint. For many Indians, psychoanalysis did not represent a new and universal science of the mind; rather, it represented a further manifestation of European imperialism, one that sought to subjugate indigenous conceptions of consciousness to Western systems of knowledge. The fact that some British psychoanalysts wrote disparagingly of Indian culture and character reinforced the Indian construction of psychoanalysis as a British colonial enterprise (Nandy 1995).

Despite Prakesh's obvious cynicism about mental health treatment, he agreed to see the psychiatrist, Dr. T., because "it will make my mother happy." Dr. T. prescribed an antidepressant and arranged subsequent visits to monitor Prakesh's medication; according to Prakesh, he was not offered psychotherapy. Noting the psychiatrist's prescription of an antidepressant as well as Prakesh's account of his state of mind at that time—the suicidality, hopelessness, inability to concentrate, social withdrawal, and inactivity that he described are the classic symptoms of depression—I asked Prakesh whether he remembered having felt depressed at that time. He answered:

> The word *depression* is something that I only learned after all this happened. I never knew that depression—I mean, I knew the English word *depression*, but I didn't know depression as a clinical term. I only learned that after I went to the psychiatrist and he told me "You are suffering from depression." . . . I wasn't aware of the fact that there is something called depression, which is a clinical term. And the word *depression* in its clinical connotation doesn't exist in Bengali or, I believe, in any Indian languages. There isn't any term for depression as a psychological state of mind.

Given such claims, how are we to understand the fact that it was Prakesh's Indian cousin who urged him to see a psychiatrist, and that it was an Indian psychiatrist who first diagnosed him with depression? Lacking information about Prakesh's family, we cannot determine their familiarity with Western systems of medicine. Lacking information about his psychiatrist, we cannot ascertain his therapeutic orientation. From Prakesh's descriptions of his psychiatric treatment, however, we might infer that, like many Indian psychiatrists, Dr. T. followed the medical model, and that English was the language of Prakesh's psychiatric treatment. We might therefore conclude that although Prakesh's initial psychological treatment occurred in India, it was Western in orientation.

Borrowing a technique from linguistic anthropology, I asked Prakesh to tell me the Bengali term that described how he had felt at that time, and he offered the word *mushkil*. He translated *mushkil* as "I'm in trouble," or "I'm in a terrible mess." I then asked Prakesh to tell me about other situations to which *mushkil* might refer, and he provided the examples of boarding a bus without money for the fare or of being in debt. The differences between *mushkil*, as Prakesh defined it, and the

English *depression* are striking; *mushkil* refers to an external rather than an internal state of affairs, is devoid of psychological and emotional content, and lacks connotations of illness and incapacity. Yet Prakesh maintained that this word accurately portrayed his suicidality and despair.

Over the next few months Prakesh's state slowly improved, and he returned to the United States to resume his studies after the new year. Upon his return, he followed Dr. T.'s recommendation that he continue his treatment. Having confirmed that his insurance would cover its cost, he entered psychotherapy with Dr. Lane, an American psychologist. But soon after treatment began, Prakesh realized that Dr. Lane knew very little about his cultural background.

> For example, he asked me about whether I have any significant other, or whether I have any girlfriend. And so at the time when I was seeing him, I had just asked someone, a friend of mine, to marry me, and she had at that point said that she was thinking about it. So he asked me more about that, he asked me how long I had been courting her. And she's from Calcutta as well, and I found that somewhat difficult to answer, because the concept of courting someone in a formal way, that concept doesn't exist in my culture. . . . So I asked him to explain what he meant by the word *courting* because I wasn't sure what he meant. So he asked me, you know, whether we would go to movies together or hold hands, and things like that. But that's not done in the culture that I come from; I mean, it would be considered very impolite to the other person as well if you suddenly grab her hand, and you know, start maybe, you know, kissing in public or maybe holding hands in public. It's considered very rude and offensive, not only to people around you, but to the other person as well.

As Prakesh described the details of his family life in India to Dr. Lane, he grew increasingly concerned that his therapist not only might be unfamiliar with his culture, but also might incorrectly consider his family circumstances bizarre and his socioeconomic background deprived.

Dr. Lane asked me when I was growing up how many rooms were there in the house, and how many people were living there. And there was just like two rooms. And one room was like my parents and me, and the other room was my grandmother, who was very old. So to an American, that sounds very bizarre—especially, like, middle-class Americans who are used to like, you know, living in these houses that are palatial compared to Third World standards, and I come from the Third World myself. But you know, to Dr. Lane it seemed very unnatural. But in a Third World middle-class situation, that's very common, you know. The kind of social origins that I come from, it's very usual. And in fact, by the standards of my country, that would be quite a privileged life. But someone sitting here might feel that this person had a very deprived childhood.

As these statements indicate, Prakesh was concerned that his therapist neither comprehended the most basic features of his life nor shared his basic ideas of what was natural and normal. He commented, "There were a few things that I felt wouldn't be worth saying to him, because he probably wouldn't be likely to understand them." In fact, Prakesh soon recognized that he could never be sure "whether he [Dr. Lane] was getting what I was saying or not." When I asked Prakesh how he had felt about this he replied,

I felt a little amused, in the sense that he might be drawing completely wrong conclusions about me, maybe because of the fact of his ignorance of the culture. So I felt kind of like, you know, when you watch a show on TV and you see some kind of a person talking about something, and the person is thinking about something completely else. And what does that induce? That induces laughter, amusement. So that's the kind of feeling that I had.

But Prakesh was not merely amused when he realized that his psychotherapist might be drawing completely wrong conclusions about him due to the cultural breach between them. His account of his first impressions of his psychotherapist's office illustrates that he also harbored more negative feelings toward Dr. Lane.

I thought to myself, "This is an incredibly large room. Why is this
room so large?" . . . What I had felt at that time was a feeling that I
get a lot of times in this country, is that people here waste a lot of
things, I mean, waste a lot of resources. And I thought that there was
absolutely no reason why a room in which you're just a doctor talking to a patient is so incredibly large. And I thought that this is just
like an American thing, you know, that they have all this money and
they build this incredibly large room, and they're wasting a lot of
space, and not making good, optimum use of it.

Prakesh then linked his condemnation of the clinical consulting
room as an "American thing" to more broadly held criticisms of the
United States, reinvoking the theme of American waste. "My views were
quite negative—that it was a very highly consumeristic society where
people consume much more resources than they need, and there's a lot
of waste." Some might conclude that Prakesh was suggesting that his
therapy, too, was a waste. What he made more explicit was his profound
resentment of the United States government's policies toward India.

My impressions of America were mostly from what I read in the newspapers and things like that, which basically meant that my impressions
of America were impressions about American foreign policy. I thought
it was atrocious because basically it's a very powerful country, and it
basically tries to impose its will on a lot of different weaker nations
around the world, and I didn't like it. I mean America, I perceived it to
be somewhat anti-India in its policies because whenever India has had
a war, America has usually supported the other party. . . . So I didn't
think that America had a very favorable policy toward India.

Although Prakesh clearly viewed the relations between his native
country and the country of his psychotherapist as adversarial, he insisted
that this had no bearing on his feelings toward Dr. Lane. "That wasn't
anything against Dr. Lane personally, but it's more like, my views on
American society coming to the fore, rather than my views of American
people as individuals."

Yet despite Prakesh's assertions to the contrary, it was clear that the political antagonisms between India and the United States influenced his constructions of his American psychotherapist. For Prakesh, Dr. Lane was not merely an individual who practiced mental health, but rather an American cultural object. In the transference, Prakesh experienced his therapist both as an example of American greed and excess—as evidenced by his denigration of Dr. Lane's "incredibly large" consulting room—and as a representative of the powerful society that had "imposed its will" on his nation. In fact, Prakesh went on to state that he viewed his psychotherapy as more than an encounter between a therapist and a patient; to him, it was a "First World–Third World issue." Once Prakesh had constructed his psychotherapy as a confrontation between a powerful First World therapist and a weak Third World patient, he struggled to take control of it. Having imposed this particular power differential on the treatment, he labored to reverse it. Having constructed his therapist as an oppressor, he worked to throw him off.

Whether Prakesh's fears of being dominated are in part characterological cannot be determined from the data provided here. Any such assessments must be informed by understandings of culturally normative relational patterns. What is clear, however, is that this particular construction of his psychotherapy induced struggles around issues of domination in Prakesh, and gave him a sense of moral advantage. When I asked him whether he thought the "First World–Third World issue" had affected his feelings about his therapist, Prakesh replied,

> I think the way it affected it was that it made me feel very kind of morally superior to the person. . . . Basically, if someone has a lot of privilege or affluence and if someone else doesn't have that, then— I'm not saying that this is rational or anything, but this is just the way I felt, this might not be a good way of feeling or it might not even be rationally explainable—you feel that this person hasn't done as much to deserve this. It's just that he happened to be born into a society at a particular point of time. So another person who hasn't kind of had the same good luck is morally superior.

Clearly, Prakesh transformed his therapist, whom he had originally experienced as the dominant partner in their relationship, into his moral inferior in order to gain a measure of power in his treatment. More strikingly, he empowered himself by subverting his treatment's very nature. In his own mind, and unknown to Dr. Lane, Prakesh turned his treatment into something entirely different. Here is how Prakesh viewed his psychotherapy:

> It was very good English conversation practice. You know, I had to pay a co-pay of ten dollars, and I would get, you know, a captive listener to listen to my bad English for one hour every two weeks. And that was a very good opportunity for me to practice my English.

In this passage, Prakesh's wishes to reject his psychotherapy and to invert the terms of the therapeutic relationship are clearly expressed. Refashioning his psychological treatment as English conversation practice allowed Prakesh to defend himself against a therapeutic encounter in which he felt disempowered, misunderstood, and misjudged. It also allowed him to evade his therapist's perceived authority, which for Prakesh carried the added weight of the First World's authority over the Third World. If Prakesh had once seen himself as the weaker party in the thrall of a powerful therapist, by making his therapist into a captive on whom he could inflict his bad English, he successfully turned the tables. And by denaturing his treatment in this way, Prakesh provided himself with another source of amusement of which Dr. Lane was unaware. In my last interview with Prakesh, I asked him for a final assessment of his mental health treatment. He reflected on its impact on him, and then he further negated it:

> Actually, in a way I think it was bad, because you know, talking about these things kind of brings back a lot of memories, and it makes you feel disturbed when you, you know, think about these things, because you forget most of them. Then you see him [Dr. Lane] in the morning, and you talk about all these things, and you feel disturbed for the rest of the day.

When I asked him if he had found anything helpful about his treatment, Prakesh replied,

> Basically, talking coherently to someone on a topic for one hour helps to organize your thoughts. And like, when you're doing a Ph.D., or when you're going into academics, you basically live by talking; I mean, you have to give presentations about your research, and give talks and so on. So talking on a particular topic is a very good exercise . . . especially in English.

I then asked him whether he had learned anything from his psychotherapy, and he answered, "It helped Dr. Lane learn a lot about me, but it didn't help me learn a lot about myself, or learn a lot new about myself."

Continuing this line of inquiry, I asked Prakesh if he was worried that his depression would recur. He responded that if he was, it was only to the same extent that

> you were worried that when you walk out of your home in the morning, you were going to be run over by a car—that possibility is always there. You're afraid that when you walk to school, like when it's like today, you can slip and fall and break your leg. So there are a lot of things that are always worries at the back of your mind, and this wasn't any extra special worry.

As my insistent questioning of Prakesh demonstrates, I was initially skeptical of his accounts of his treatment. I refused to believe that his treatment had been of no benefit to him. Further, despite my determination not to analyze Prakesh from psychotherapeutic perspectives, I viewed him as defensively denying his depression, and I wondered why he persisted in doing so. I found myself trying to convince him that he had, in fact, been depressed. The more I pressed him for confirmation, however, the more he resisted. For example, when I asked Prakesh what Dr. Lane's recommendation that he continue to take antidepressants had meant to him, he answered, "It didn't mean anything to me." He added,

I know that people in this country tend to prescribe things a lot. You know, a huge number of people here are on these psychological drugs anyway. And I would have been surprised if he didn't, because prescribing is very common here.

Setting aside the fact that it was his Indian psychiatrist who had first prescribed "psychological drugs" for him, I asked Prakesh why he had continued to take the medication when, in his view, it had had no effect on him. He replied, "The co-pay was very small, like five dollars for buying the drug. It wasn't costing me any money, so I just continued taking the drug." I then asked him why he had sought psychological help once he had returned to the United States, given that he viewed psychotherapy as quackery. He answered, "Dr. T., whom I had been seeing in Calcutta, had told me that once I come back here, I should continue the treatment. And I was merely following the instructions."

Clearly, Prakesh had negated every aspect of his psychotherapy. But how might such extreme negative reactions to intercultural clinical treatments best be understood? Were we to regard this case from conventional psychotherapeutic perspectives, we might construct Prakesh as resistant to psychological treatment. We might suggest that his intrapsychic conflicts, characterological style, strategies of defense, and interpersonal relations warranted closer examination. Further, we might view Prakesh's reactions to Dr. Lane as a negative transference in which Prakesh felt overpowered and abused, and in which he displayed sadomasochistic tendencies.

Can such standard psychological formulations accurately characterize a patient who was born and raised in India? To construct Prakesh in such conventional terms is to impose Western frames of analysis—including Western metapsychologies, Western ideals of relationship, and Western constructions of individual psychodynamics—on a non-Western patient, and to dismiss both Prakesh's cultural formation and the cultural meanings that suffuse his reactions to treatment.

Alternatively, a culturally informed analysis would take Prakesh's Indian background into account in examining his rejection of his psychotherapy. Rather than assuming that relationships have the same features and meanings across cultures, a cultural analysis might investigate Prakesh's construction of his relationship with Dr. Lane in terms of Indian interpersonal norms. Therapists might explore how the caste-based, hierarchically ordered Indian society in which Prakesh spent the first three decades of his life had influenced his conceptions of relationships; they might seek to understand whether Prakesh's construction of his relationship with Dr. Lane along hierarchical lines reproduced relational patterns that, although in conflict with American ideals of egalitarianism, are normative in his native society.

This type of analysis might also include inquiries into the sociopolitical aspects of the antagonisms that characterized Prakesh's engagement with his psychotherapist. Instead of reducing such antagonisms to individual psychopathology, a culturally informed analysis provides access to other important dimensions of Prakesh's experience. Clearly, Prakesh was upset by America's domination of India, and was concerned that his relationship with Dr. Lane mirrored this power differential. Perhaps in his therapeutic relationship with Dr. Lane, Prakesh heard the echoes of British colonialism as well. To consider such significations in analyzing Prakesh's antagonism toward his psychotherapist is to restore him to the cultural and historical contexts in which his subjectivities developed. It is also to understand that by negating his psychotherapy, Prakesh symbolically enacted his greater wish to reject the whole of Western hegemony. That this wish evidently remained unexpressed in his psychotherapy with Dr. Lane might have further pressured Prakesh. Privately rejecting his psychological treatment, but obliged by Indian rules of relationship to treat doctors with deference and respect and to follow their orders (Roland 1988), Prakesh complied with the therapeutic regimen his doctors prescribed, regularly attending his psychotherapy sessions and obediently ingesting his medication. Perhaps the contradictions that Prakesh experienced in this regard contributed toward his disdain of Dr. Lane.

A cultural analysis of Prakesh's intercultural psychotherapy might further demonstrate that Prakesh's rejection of his treatment was the result of conflicting cultural metapsychologies. After psychoanalysis arrived in India in the early 1920s, a few Indian psychoanalysts devoted themselves to the project of spreading Freud's teachings throughout the Indian subcontinent. But psychoanalytic theory failed to capture the imagination of the Indian populace. Some blamed this failure on psychoanalysis's fundamental incompatibilities with India's indigenous ideologies of the mind (Nandy 1995).

Certainly, the clash of cultural metapsychologies was an impediment to Prakesh's psychological treatment. Socialized into Indian ideologies of psychic disability and repair, Prakesh rejected Western psychotherapy's most basic assumptions. By insisting that he had not attended psychotherapy out of a need for professional treatment, but rather because "I wanted to keep my conscience clear," because "I wanted to make my mother happy," because "it didn't cost much," and because he was "merely following the instructions" of his psychiatrist, Prakesh severed the connections between the experience of psychological distress and the desire for psychological help. Nor did Prakesh conceptualize his inability to function in psychological terms. Despite his paralyzing hopelessness and despair, Prakesh did not consider himself depressed; he was merely "in a terrible mess." Although his condition improved following treatment, Prakesh credited neither his Indian psychiatrist nor his American psychologist for the relief he experienced. Instead, he claimed that his medications had not perceptibly brightened his mood, and that his psychotherapy, while providing a "very good exercise" for his English, had left him feeling "disturbed."

What makes this clash of metapsychologies especially troubling for Western clinicians is that Prakesh did not view his suicidality as a symptom of a psychological disorder. Instead, he detached his suicidality from its conventional Western etiologies and frames of reference. Although I repeatedly asked Prakesh what had brought him to the brink of suicide, his explanations made no sense to me; I understood only that he viewed his suicidality as a rational response to his hearing problems. Because, as the particular features of Prakesh's case demonstrate, the precipitants and meanings of suicidality differ cross-culturally, this case raises important questions regarding the identification and treatment of suicidality in foreign and ethnic patients.

If it is clear that Prakesh consistently dismissed the causal relationships and systems of meaning on which the culture of psychotherapy depends, then it is equally clear that at the heart of his psychotherapy were webs of incompatibilities. Some of these webs were spun from culturally discrepant ideologies of the mind, including culturally specific notions of mental dysfunction and healing. Others were made of the enduring historical antagonisms of colonialism and of contemporary political tensions. As a result of these incompatibilities, when Prakesh received the diagnosis of depression it lacked its customary resonance. Rather than signifying a familiar psychological syndrome and indicating an accepted course of treatment, this diagnosis signified a foreign affliction—one that belonged to a culture that Prakesh experienced as immoral, dominant, and hostile—and one that he therefore needed to reject.

4

Seduction: Jun

Jun is a 31-year-old woman who was born in South Korea. As a consequence of having spent several years of her childhood in the United States, however, Jun considers herself bicultural. In Jun's view, her bicultural self is split between contradictory Korean and American ideals of selfhood, systems of morality, patterns of relationship, and cognitive and affective styles. Jun continually experiences tensions between these conflicting cultural voices, and attempts to calm them by maintaining positions of disengagement and marginality in both her Korean and American worlds.

This chapter examines the encounter between Jun's Western psychological treatment and her bicultural self. As we will see, Jun's sense of being torn between the freedoms and opportunities available to her in the United States and her native culture's demands for self-sacrifice and political involvement extended to her psychoanalysis. In Jun's treatment, her desire to realize a highly individuated, autonomous, sexually expressive, Westernized sense of self conflicted with her need to contain such wishes, which by Korean standards were forbidden. This chapter examines the failure of Jun's treatment to repair these splits, itself becoming the subject of intense cultural loyalty conflicts. It then considers the ways in which Jun's need to resist the American "seduction," with which she associated her psychoanalysis, significantly compromised her participation in her treatment.

"FORBIDDEN WISHES"

Jun came to the United States seven years ago from her native Seoul, the capital of South Korea. This was not her first sojourn in North America. When Jun was a young girl, her father had brought the family to the United States, moving them from city to city over a period of years while he pursued a corporate career. The 8-year-old Jun, who upon arriving in the States had spoken no English, suddenly found herself a pupil in an American elementary school. She picked up English quickly, and the fluid, unaccented English that she speaks today suggests her mastery of the foreign tongue at an early age.

Having rapidly achieved English fluency, Jun made friends with her American classmates. And yet, she recalled that her most nourishing relationships during her early years in the United States were with the characters of the "vast network of fantasy" that she created during that time. Hers was a secret, private, and richly detailed fantasy world, and it was populated almost exclusively by Americans.

One of Jun's favorite fantasies involved her imagined encounter with a boy she called Daniel. Daniel, she said, was "a blond, blue-eyed person."

> The fantasy was always the same. I'd run into this guy in the park, like I'd be a little kid, he'd also be a little kid—or actually he'd be kind of adultish, I'd be a little kid. And I'd run into him in the park, and this is so funny—I would bang my head against something, like against him, and then this catastrophe would bring us together. And then we'd sit on the park bench and talk—like this was my idea of romance at the time—and I would have this intense crush on him, and he would have this intense crush on me, and you know, sort of like, what little girls talk about. I enjoyed that fantasy so much.

Jun's repeated imaginings of her love affair with the American boy were a frequent source of pleasure to her. Yet at the same time, while living in the United States thousands of miles away from her relatives, she yearned for her Korean kin. And so, every day after school when she and her mother drank tea together, Jun asked her mother to tell her stories about their ancestors. Her mother complied, "telling me about everybody in my family, going back generations."

> She used to tell me about her grandmother in very specific detail; about her mannerisms, what kind of person she was—and she was really sort of a *grande dame* in all of the senses of the word—and I just grew up having a sense of longing, intense love, and a very strong sense of connection to all these women—it was actually like stories of women—all these women who came before me, who went through such difficult times with such courage. . . . My sense of being a Korean, my Korean identity, is really centered around these people, who were very much in my mother's mind, who are now very much in my mind.

Thus, even as Jun was growing up in American society and dreaming of union with a blond, blue-eyed American boy, her identity as a Korean deepened. It was as though a dual sense of self were being forged in her, one part of which wished to be permanently tied to the land in which she temporarily resided, and the other part of which had her Korean ancestors "very much in my mind."

The dual identifications and contradictions of cultural affiliation that emerged during her time in America, however, soon appeared to be put to rest. When Jun was 12, her father found a new job in Korea. Just as abruptly as Jun had been thrust into the American mainstream four years before, suddenly she was required to reestablish herself in Korean society. Jun felt obliged to renounce her fascination with America. Even the fantasy of her romance with Daniel, which had brought her so much joy, had to be abandoned.

> When I went back to Korea, I think I really relinquished this idea of
> . . . I don't think I ever had the idea that I would actually really marry

an American person. I think I always knew that I'd have to marry a
Korean person. But this is the thing—I think for a long time I needed
to sort of tamp down on any possible attraction I could have felt for
American guys, or anything like that.

Like many other Korean adolescents, Jun became fully occupied
with the pressures of preparing for the highly competitive college en-
trance examinations. Although she had a passion for the theater, her
father would not permit her to live the unstable life of an artist in Korea,
and steered her toward an academic career. Suppressing her ambivalence—and bound by convention to obey her father—Jun followed her
father's directives. At the age of 26 she went to the United States for the
second time, and began graduate study in history at an American university. Two years later, she entered psychoanalysis. Jun explained her
reasons for seeking treatment:

> I didn't really have anywhere to go with my feelings about things, and
> I had this vague sense that I had a lot of issues that I hadn't really thought
> about in any great depth. . . . There really wasn't a place in my life where
> I had a space to just sit and think about what my life was about.

Jun's decision to enter clinical treatment was an unusual one for a
Korean. Although there has been some change in recent years, in Korea
the "seeds" of mental disorders generally have been seen as both conta-
gious and contaminating. The result has been a stigmatization of psychological illness so complete that Koreans with mentally disordered
relatives can be condemned to lives as unmarriageable outcasts. With
the predominance of such metapsychological notions in Korea, mental
health treatments have been available only to the most severely disturbed.
Those with less serious emotional problems usually would not be offered psychological help. Instead, they would provided for by family,
by friends, and by the church, which were obliged to care for them and
to return them to the fold.

Indeed, Jun portrayed her desire for a "space to just sit and think what
my life was about" as rare in Korean culture. Like many Koreans, she recognized fundamental contradictions between the Confucianism that deeply

shaped Korean worldviews, ethics, relationships, family structures, and senses of self, and American values and mores (Slote 1996). In Jun's view, the Confucian ethic had focused the activity of introspection in Korea on questions other than those that one would tend to contemplate in the West. The questions that Koreans were likely to ask, she said, did not focus on issues of individual identity; they did not concern "who you were, what you were doing, where you wanted to go."

> The introspection has mostly not been about what am I . . . but more sort of like, what should I *do*? . . . The way they thought about the problems was, How should I deal with this? What is the best way to deal with this? Versus, Why am I feeling like this?

Jun suggested that emotions, too, were conceptualized and treated differently in Korea than they were in the United States. She credited the Confucian ethic with defusing the impact of emotion, so that, "for example, instead of thinking about how angry I am, or what am I feeling right now, the question is, how should I *deal* with this feeling?" Koreans were expected to "deal with" particular feelings, Jun said, in accordance with the cultural codes that governed social and family relationships.

> See with the Confucian thing, there is this very strong idea of hierarchy, such that when you start having very strong negative feelings toward authority figures, there really isn't much you can do with that, aside from trying to sublimate that by writing, or by singing, or drinking or something . . . I mean, unless your parents are being horribly abusive. If you're talking about more subtle feelings of rebellion, subtle feelings of being penned in, etc., etc., you wouldn't have anywhere to go with these more subtle negative feelings. . . . It's not even about feeling positively, that's not the important thing—it's more, sort of, actions of obedience, and actions of love and caring, whether you feel that or not.

The ideal way for Koreans to deal with emotions, Jun maintained, was not to express or to explore them; in certain cases, it was not even to experience them. Instead, feelings were to be subjugated to socially condoned behaviors. This especially applied to negative emotions, such as anger. When such unacceptable feelings were experienced toward persons of higher rank in the hierarchy, Jun said, the culturally sanctioned way to handle them was to suppress them.

These culturally divergent constructions of introspection and emotion were supplemented by contrasting Korean and American constructions of the self. The Korean ideal of personhood that Jun described, in conformity with Confucianism, was one in which the actions of individuals were highly defined and constrained by their particular roles and statuses. As an example, Jun generalized about the differing behaviors of Korean and American parents.

> I think in America, parents are very clear that they are a separate person, that you know, "I am a person, I have needs." If it's the mother, it's "I am a mother, but I am also a woman, I have needs, I have sexual needs." . . . Now I think that in Korea, mothers very often don't show that they have a different identity than that of a mother, so it's just sort of like a mother who cooks and sacrifices. And sacrifices in the sense that if a kid needs something, the mother is always there with it, is always sort of listening, and always nourishing, giving food and washing and cleaning and taking care of you without any clear needs of her own. . . . It's almost like a symbiotic relationship where your mom is just your mom.

Further, it was Jun's understanding that in Korea,

> Your parents are constantly sacrificing so that you can do better in life. . . . Even if the parents don't have money, they will get loans that they will pay off for the rest of their life so that their kids can get married and have a good life.

Jun took pains to stress the reciprocity of sacrifice.

> Your end of the bargain is that you will comply with what few things that she [your mother] wants you to do. Since she is sacrificing one

hundred percent, if she asks you to do a couple of things, then you're supposed to be complying with those couple of things.

Those "couple of things" might include such pivotal life decisions as the choice of a spouse or, as in Jun's case, the choice of a career. Clearly, the interpersonal relationships Jun described did not privilege the requirements and rights of the individual, but were based instead on what she characterized as a system of mutual debt. Indeed, personal sacrifice was a recurrent motif of the stories she recounted about Korea.

> There are many, many cases of women who are widowed who didn't remarry because they wanted their children not to grow up with a stepfather—the idea being that in Korea, it was better to be a widow than to be a remarried woman when it came time for your children to get married. So that a lot of times, mothers would really sacrifice their sexual needs and their needs to be a woman, etc., etc., so that their kids could get married. Because, especially if it's a daughter . . . that this woman did not take two men into her bed, that it was just the one man, when he died that was it. So that—this is going a little far—but that she didn't transmit any promiscuity genes into her daughters.

If the above passage illustrated Jun's point about personal sacrifice in Korea, then it also illuminated a central feature of the Korean construction of the person. According to this construction, the immoral "genes" of reprehensible ancestors were transmitted to future generations. Their heirs had no escape from ancestral sins; instead, they were in danger of being genetically contaminated by them. This construction of the person produced family identities from which individuals were unable to detach themselves completely, as they were essentialized and internalized. As a result, the degree to which individuals could be differentiated from their parents and from their kin was limited.

In sum, according to Jun, Korean culture featured types of cognition, norms of emotional expression, and views of the self that diverged from those that she found characteristic of Americans. Because Jun's native culture discouraged both the individuation and the open expression of emotion that are among the primary objectives of psychotherapy, she might have been expected to avoid psychological treatment. Because it viewed character as determined by "genes," she might have been expected to doubt the possibilities of therapeutic change.

During her second sojourn in America, however, the dual identifications and the dual sense of self that had been forged during her first stay in the States were revived and reinforced. Jun began to think of herself not simply as Korean, but as bicultural.

> It's sort of like I inhabit a world that has two languages. It's a world that's sort of replete with symbolisms in both cultures. And so, in a way, I'm stuck always having to explain myself too much, and trying to explain myself at times to clarify for myself what all kinds of things mean, in whichever culture it is I'm trying to explain it to. So it's kind of a weird place to be.

Yet while being bicultural could conceivably have made Jun feel a part of both Korean and American cultural worlds, its effect on her was the opposite. Her experience was not one of dual belonging, but of a double marginality. Feeling at home in neither Korea nor the United States compromised her connection to both.

> My superego is split. . . . I have ideas about what people in my culture would think, but I don't really think that way. . . . For me, it's not that internalized. In a way, the only way one can function as a marginal being in two cultures is to have a very good sense of what's okay in both, but not to necessarily espouse those views for oneself. Sort of like again being a participant observer, where you're more of an observer and less of a participant. It's actually quite sad. I wish I were more of a participant.

This central problem in Jun's sense of self came into play when she considered entering psychoanalysis. She balked at the idea of working with a Korean analyst, convinced that he or she would be intolerant of difference, intolerant of human error, and authoritarian. More important, she feared that a Korean analyst would forbid her to voice thoughts and fantasies that were unacceptable in Korean culture, and would thereby reinforce her inclination to avoid confronting difficult material.

> For example, if I had a wish to have an affair, let's say, a Korean thera-
> pist would say that this idea is faulty, you shouldn't have an affair,
> and to help me implement ways to not have an affair. Or you know,
> try to control the impulse, if you will. When I have these longings,
> it's not that I really think I'm gonna act on them, it's more sort of try-
> ing to understand where these wishes come from. So I think that
> would be sort of one way in which it would be very uncomfortable
> to have a Korean therapist. . . . It is an impediment to exploration.

It was for these reasons that Jun chose to enter treatment with an American psychoanalyst. Her work with an American man, however, raised a different, and perhaps unforeseen, set of cultural issues. Because of the cultural differences between them, for example, she found it nec-essary to "explain too much" in sessions, describing even the most basic features of Korean culture and society to him so that he might under-stand her. But Jun soon realized that explaining things to her psycho-analyst did not necessarily clarify them. "It's sort of like trying to ex-plain a joke to someone who has no frame of reference, or who does not share the same reference. Where you have to try to explain the joke, and then it's not really funny anymore." The practice of "explaining too much" to her analyst not only entailed a loss of meaning for Jun, but also increased her distance from her own material. As a result, in her sessions she often experienced herself "not as one that's embedded, but as someone a little bit with a foot out the door."

Equally problematic for Jun were her reactions upon discovering that her American analyst would allow her to express thoughts and feel-ings that, according to Korean culture, should not have been voiced.

> I think that there are ways in which I think his [the analyst's] accep-
> tance of things and my cultural superego, as I like to put it, are not in
> accord with each other. Like I said before, again, this is not judgmen-
> tal. There's a part of me that's sort of thinking, well, this is scary. That
> there's this acceptance of these forbidden wishes is really scary.

That her analyst appeared to accept the "forbidden wishes" that Jun herself might have preferred to censor aroused such intense conflicts in her that she began to retreat from treatment.

> One central problem for me has been that I've missed a lot of sessions. . . . And I wonder whether that has something to do with the fear of allying too much with this person who's accepting of these forbidden wishes, and the fear of losing control of the forbidden wishes.

Jun also stayed away from treatment because she viewed it as an indulgence that had to be sacrificed to more important obligations. Indeed, personal sacrifice, which was a central motif of Jun's descriptions of Korean interpersonal relations, also emerged as a dominant theme of the Korean political landscape in which she had come of age.

> Nothing comes easily to people in my country. Everything has to be well thought out; moral stands on top of moral stands on almost everything, just because there are so many things to be morally outraged about. . . . In Korea, almost every breath you take, a lot of times you really have to take a stand, and have to make the decision to do it, or else you can't live with yourself. . . . I mean it really is at the level of, I might lose my job, I might lose my life, I might be tortured, but I need to take a stand because this is really wrong. So it's really again, you're really constantly questioning yourself, questioning your morals, your ethics, and who you are as a person's always being put to the test. . . . You're putting a lot on the line. Again, this is not easy to do, but if you live in my country, this is something that you are required to do for every moment of every day.

The risks of taking a stand in Korean society were not hypothetical to Jun. One of the more horrific stories about her kin that she had been told as a young girl concerned a relative who had been arrested for his political activism. During his lengthy imprisonment, Jun's relative was physically tortured. Following his release, he was refused employment and socially shunned.

Having learned that her relative's life had been destroyed as a result of his passionate political engagement, it was not surprising that Jun sought to avoid such a fate, the "seeds" of which might have been genetically transmitted to her. And having witnessed many other examples of personal devastation that resulted from lives of political commitment in Korea, it was perhaps to be expected that Jun preferred to remain uninvolved.

> I realize that in some ways when I was in Korea there was a very self-preservationistic aspect to being not committed because there are so many things where you have to take a stance. And in a way, not taking a stance, being very quiet, is really not laying very much on the line. Where if I were very vocal with the things that I wish for, if I were very vocal with my outrage, I could stand to lose a lot, and I didn't want to do that. . . . So when people say, "Well what do you think? Where do you stand on this?" In a way they're sort of like—I don't want people to know where I stand on this. . . . There is an incredible fear in being too out there, in being too visible.

Thus, it is clear that Jun's disengagement from Korean and American cultures was multiply determined; it was the product not only of a particular personal psychology, but of specific cultural, historical, and political experiences. Jun's decision to pursue graduate study in the United States was also multiply caused. More than a simple educational pursuit, it signified her need to rebel against the political engagement and personal sacrifice that Korean culture required of her. In coming to America, where "all you have to do is sort of live for yourself," Jun enjoyed a reprieve from her country's expectations. In addition, America offered her many opportunities that Korea could not.

> It's like, America is very seductive. It's a very rich culture, there's a lot of money—I mean, literally, there's a lot of money. There's also a lot of intellectual stimulation and richness. There's always the possibility of exploration here of all kinds of things. . . . So America's very seductive that way.

But although Jun clearly felt seduced by the United States, because she continued to carry her ancestors "very much in my mind," she declined to fully embrace American culture. Moreover, the distance that she maintained from American society was reproduced in her psychological treatment. Jun refused to give herself completely to her psychoanalysis; as she admitted, she kept "a foot out the door." For Jun, psychological treatment was fraught with conflict. Indeed, it was

> sort of like playing with a friend that your parents didn't want you to play with, where you value the friendship and you love this friend, but your parents say, "Don't play with this kid," because his parents are immoral, let's say. And playing with this friend gives a lot of pleasure, 'cause you're rebelling against your own culture, or against your cultural superego, your parents. But there's also sort of the fear, of well, what if I become like my friend? What if my friend's morals take over and I lose my moral uprightness, in which case then I'll have to give up my parents? I mean, you have to ultimately make a choice whether to stick with your friends or with your parents. And you have much more to lose if you lose your parents.

Jun's need to make a choice defined her psychological treatment. Loyalty conflicts were its dominant theme, as Jun felt attracted to the seductive identities, relationships, and opportunities that her host society offered, but wedded to the familiar demands and rewards of her native land. The contrast between the two was stark.

> It's almost like parents who are divorced. And you've got a rich dad who really doesn't care much about you, but you know if you went with this guy, you'll have the opportunity of a lifetime. Where you have this mom who's really poor, but who loves you deeply. And you can't abandon that mother.

This passage indicates the extent to which Jun's psychoanalysis replicated the contradictions that she lived daily as a result of her dual cultural identifications. Her treatment, rather than occupying a terrain of neutrality, was part of the American seduction, offering Jun clear alternatives to the mores and norms of her native culture. Nor was her psychoanalysis a simple seeking of personal understanding and growth. Instead, it provided a way for Jun to express her anger at her native society's demands and constraints, and a means of "rebelling against your culture, your superego, your parents." Psychoanalysis permitted Jun to realize wishes for individual expression and self-exploration that she believed would not have been tolerated in Korea, and to voice thoughts, feelings, and longings that would have been forbidden there. It also allowed her to reconnect with the passionate and artistic sides of her nature that her father had tried to eradicate. Psychoanalysis gave Jun the chance to participate in a relationship based neither on mutual debt nor on sacrifice; one in which she was able to experience herself as distinct from her kin and free of their "seeds."

But although psychoanalysis provided Jun with these pleasures, they retained an impropriety in her Korean eyes. Jun feared that to enjoy them would be to "lose my moral uprightness" and to "give up my parents"; in other words, it would be to lose what she most treasured. To avoid incurring such devastating losses, Jun removed herself from her treatment emotionally, firmly keeping "one foot out the door."

Jun's relationship with her analyst also mirrored her relationship with America. With him, too, she experienced a "fear of allying too much," and she therefore "distanced" herself from him. "I care about him very deeply and have enjoyed my sessions with him in all of this. I have internal discussions with him. . . . But I would never say that I cared about him, or would tell him about that." Perhaps the therapeutic relationship also represented for Jun—who was engaged to a Korean man—the fantasied but forbidden affair with an American man, which, if not resisted, would produce irrecoverable losses.

> My family would disown me. . . . If I married an American, I couldn't go back home. . . . All my extended family would miss me terribly. . . . And I also wanted to do something for my country. And staying in the States, that wouldn't be possible.

The transference therefore acquired cultural dimensions. Jun's analyst, like the country he represented, became an object with whom, for cultural reasons, she dared not become too intimately involved.

But it was not only that so many things American were seductive; it was that Jun was attracted to them. She flirted with America, and her psychoanalysis was part of her flirtation. Jun thus faced the task not only of resisting the American seduction, but of managing her attraction to it.

> It's very interesting, because when I came to the States I gained a lot of weight, like fifty pounds or so; twenty some kilograms. And I have a wardrobe full of very provocative clothes that I never wear. . . . There's a way in which I always want to hide my physical, provocative, attractive self from the world as well. . . . Even physically, I keep thinking, Why do I not want to come off as sexy? And again, it might have to do with forbidden wishes for a liaison with an American person. So if I'm too ugly or unattractive, I'm not gonna attract a kind of sexual provocation that otherwise I might attract.

In other words, Jun kept herself under wraps so that she would neither attract nor succumb to the seduction of the forbidden foreign object.

To further counter these temptations, Jun created a new fantasy of her relationship to America. Strikingly different from her earlier imaginings of rescue and romance in the arms of a blond, blue-eyed boy, this fantasy promised neither hope nor salvation.

> So my fantasy of the sort of the beginning of my end of my life would be, you know, to hook up with this really good-for-nothing American guy, have a lot of good sex, and then you know, leave grad school, can't find a job, the guy leaves me, I get AIDS or something—you know like some sort of weird sexually transmitted disease. And then I turn into like Madame X, become an alcoholic. . . . And then I end up with like, I'm 70 years old, I have no friends, I'm living in a dungeon-like place with my hair all sort of sticking up, and I'm cranky, and I'm a little bit crazy, and I have no money.

Thus, Jun's fears were clear; should she yield to the temptations of foreign objects, her life would be destroyed. Although she might casually flirt with psychoanalysis, because it was another American temptation, she ultimately had to resist it. Having been drawn to psychological treatment for reasons alien to her native culture—and perhaps, for reasons she only ambivalently embraced—she would not permit herself to participate in it fully. Given opportunities in treatment for self-expression, Jun routinely effaced herself; given opportunities for self-disclosure, she commonly concealed; and given opportunities for engagement, she frequently withdrew.

Psychotherapists are likely to find that many foreign patients resemble Jun, in that their English proficiency, skilled reproductions of American culture, and eager experimentations with Western identities obscure the fact that they are deeply psychologically identified with, attached to, and shaped by other cultures. Such patients are at risk of being constructed by their therapists as psychologically indistinct from mainstream American patients, and therefore as requiring no modifications in treatment. Yet Jun's experiences in psychoanalysis expose the limitations of standard clinical approaches in working with foreign and ethnic patients. Her account of her treatment suggests that Western psychotherapies that implicitly conceive of selves as culturally integrated may be ill-equipped to address patients with bicultural or multicultural identities. Such psychotherapies may be especially inappropriate in cases like Jun's, cases where the conflicts among various cultural identities continually make themselves felt, so that the very act of going to the therapist incites internal conflict. Moreover, Jun's treatment experiences suggest that clinical formulations that exclude sociocultural perspectives will necessarily produce clinical pictures that are culturally biased and partial. The fundamental features of Jun's treatment, including the transference, resistance, and therapeutic alliance, were multiply inflected with cultural, political, and social as well as psychological meanings. In the treatment of foreign and ethnic patients, such ostensibly "extrapsychic" factors require attention and analysis.

5

Confrontation: Maria

Maria, a Chicana and native Spanish speaker from East Los Angeles, underwent psychotherapy with a "very Anglo" psychotherapist in the Midwest. Maria's treatment was initially suffused by her previous experiences of ethnic discrimination, which resulted in her racialized hostility toward her therapist. This chapter considers the ways in which Maria's initial constructions—of her psychotherapist as the embodiment of white oppression, of psychotherapy as belonging to the Anglo world of privilege, and of English, the language of her psychotherapy, as "white-speak"—caused her to experience her therapy as a confrontation between warring cultural groups, and to try to dominate it by angrily resisting her treatment.

Maria's case, like Prakesh's, illustrates the complexities of intercultural psychotherapies that, from the patient's perspective, are mired in preexisting cultural antagonisms. But Maria's case, unlike Prakesh's, suggests that trusting therapeutic relationships can develop out of such adversarial beginnings. The ways in which Maria's gradual acceptance of her psychotherapist's whiteness mirrored her increasing tolerance of her own multiple cultural identities—including the Anglo voices within herself that she had previously denigrated and rejected—are examined here.

"THE CONQUEST"

Maria is a 29-year-old woman who identifies herself as a Latina and a Chicana. The youngest of four children, she was born in a "hood" hospital in East Los Angeles to Mexican parents. When she was only a few months old her family moved to Mexico, as her father found it difficult to make ends meet in Los Angeles. But as economic conditions were no better there, her family's stay in Mexico was short-lived; after a few years, her father returned his family to the United States.

When I asked Maria to tell me her earliest memories, she produced narrative after narrative detailing acts of political injustice and racism against Chicanos and against her family. In one such narrative, she described the East Los Angeles to which her family had returned after their stay in Mexico as a place of total chaos. This chaos followed a massive riot that had been precipitated by the police's violent disruption of peaceful protests by Chicanos and Latinos. Maria and her family returned to Latino neighborhoods around which fences had been erected, "supposedly protecting the community, but indeed, they were just enclosing us. So like when my father worked late, he couldn't get in, and he had to sleep out in the truck. And the guard was inevitably white."

Maria remembered the menacing presence of the white policemen who patrolled her neighborhood. She remembered her mother "going haywire" if her older brothers and sisters failed to return home by the eight o'clock curfew, and she remembered her family's nighttime ritual of "pushing all of this furniture in front of the door" to secure their project apartment, which had been broken into so often that "you needed the extra protection."

When Maria recounted these stories of oppression and discrimination against Chicanos, she raised systemic political and economic issues, issues that clinicians generally consider to be outside of the therapeutic frame (Chin 1993). Yet it was clear that these experiences had deeply marked Maria psychologically. The bitterness that she had first felt as a child of immigrants had endured, and her family's repeated experiences of discrimination in the United States had made her feel that she needed to arm herself aggressively against the violence of the outside world. "The way I see it is, if you grew up poor and Mexican in a large city, it was definitely a hostile place to be. You had no security, ever, outside of your family and your blood."

For Maria, a sense of self as a member of an oppressed and devalued minority group developed at an early age. "I remember the white kids calling us spics and wetbacks coming into our neighborhood. And we were told never to talk to white people." School, for her, was far from a respite from such pressures; instead, it was another site of insult. Spanish was both her native language and the only language spoken at home, but in school she was forbidden to speak it. "In school, the first thing they told you was 'Don't speak Spanish.' To my sisters and me, particularly, that meant, What are you saying? That my Mom isn't good enough?"

Maria's early experiences with mental health professionals were similarly full of humiliation and fury. When she was a child, she and her family had been subjected to "like one fucking stream of social workers," who would come to Maria's front door,

> go through our house, rummage in our cupboards, decide what we should eat, and then have the audacity to sit down, bring in the bilingual neighbor from next door or my oldest sister, and tell my mother how to raise us. . . . Because one, we continued to speak Spanish, and this was in L.A. and they didn't like that. And two, that we would fight to keep our language and our culture in school. . . . We'd all be really angry, we'd be like, "Screw you lady. Don't tell us what we can do." And my Moms just got pissed. She's a very mild-mannered woman, I mean she rarely raises her voice or anything, but she was pissed. I was like, "You better leave. Cause Moms is gonna go after you."

Perhaps it was to repair such demeaning early contacts with mental health professionals that Maria decided to become a social worker; at the time of these interviews, she was engaged in a social work doctoral program. And then, approximately two years ago, Maria decided to enter psychotherapy. In part, she thought that being a psychotherapy patient would inform her future work as a clinician. But additionally,

> I wanted it as a forum. I knew that there were several things I didn't understand about myself and about changes that had occurred in my life. And things traditionally, in my family, you just don't talk about. And that those did come up in my mind, and that they were concerns of mine, and that I wanted to work them through.

Maria had long delayed seeking treatment, because psychotherapy was "not something that's readily available to folks where I come from." As she explained, "Therapy in and of itself for a lot of people of color is a hangup. It's a huge privilege. It's a huge fuckin'—you know, just like, you have resources that most of your people do not have." But if Maria was concerned that engaging in psychotherapy would differentiate her from "folks where I come from," then she was also concerned about being culturally different from her psychotherapist. Maria had spent several years as the sole Chicana at a largely Caucasian university where her ethnicity was regarded as exotic. She worried that she would be equally alien to a Midwestern psychotherapist, and that, in consequence, she would be required to "explain myself and my beliefs and where I come from." Despite her reservations Maria decided to enter psychotherapy, choosing a therapist who offered low-fee treatments.

Maria recalled that she had been taken aback by her first sight of her psychotherapist, who was "an Anglo woman; *very* Anglo . . . she looks really light. . . . She's tall, very thin, very, very light skin. Blond, blue-eyed. Light eyed. . . . The first time I saw her, I'm like, 'Ho man! This is gonna be interesting'!" Having described her therapist as an Anglo, Maria immediately defined her own identity:

> Certain things are very common in my life. Academia is not. This is where I perform, this is not where I live. My life at home is real. My life in my apartment is real. My connections and my relationships are real. But the university life, my life as an academic, is not real, is not genuine. It's not my blood. It's not what I'll die for. It's not what

I'll kill for. And I know that those are very harsh words, but that's what I believe in; that there are certain things that I will protect to my death, and none of them are in my academic world.

Maria then described the "real" parts of her life in more detail.

There are many realities in my life that are not tolerated in this world. Like I do have gang affiliations. . . . And my *compadres*, they're all gang members. And they're not what you see on TV; they're old, they're what we call *veteranos*, veterans, they've all done long stretches of time. They've done time on the street and in prison, and they're no joke.

These *compadres*, whom Maria considered her "blood," had helped raise her, teaching her the rules of the street and incorporating her into their networks of protection.

So my mother would be doing laundry or cooking dinner and she'd send me out to play in front. And what I ended up doing was being the little kid who hung out with all the big-time *veteranos*, the big-time gangsters. And they protected me immensely. . . . So I had to fight on the streets, when people picked fights with me. But if I went down, I had not only my brothers and sisters, but these guys, who I learned later made it very clear; "If you go after her, you go after us." And nobody wanted to take on these guys.

Finally, Maria defined her academic career in terms of its benefits to her community, rather than in terms of its benefits to her. Like many of those who are part of disempowered sectors of society, Maria considered her personal accomplishments less important than the welfare of her community (Ewalt and Mokuau 1995). She was aware that this distinguished her from her fellow students.

I'm here because of my people. I'm here to service them and to take it back to my community. And a lot of the students that I try to share that with in this forum say, "Oh no, you can't do this for anyone else."

It's like, "Excuse me, fuck you and bullshit. You don't know what life is like on the other side."

In sum, in recounting her initial contact with her therapist, Maria emphasized three points. First, she experienced herself as split into two selves, one that she cherished as real and genuine, and the other—the self of the academy and of psychotherapy—that she denigrated as mere performance. Second, in Maria's view, she and her therapist inhabited worlds that were separate, distinct, and opposed. By locating her treatment in her therapist's world, she minimized its importance to herself. Third, Maria believed that because she and her therapist had such divergent, culturally determined value orientations, her therapist neither understood nor respected her world.

Clearly, accordingly to Maria's presentation, in her first encounter with her therapist she was shocked by their cultural differences. Maria's response to this was striking. Instead of seeking common ground, she renounced her academic self and experienced her Chicana cultural identity in its most extreme form. It was as if she found it necessary to differentiate herself from her therapist completely, and so she constructed her first psychotherapy session as a confrontation between an Anglo academic therapist and a Chicana gang member. By doing so, however, Maria established a therapeutic relationship of foreignness, mutual incomprehensibility, and mistrust.

It was apparent from Maria's initial portrait of her therapist that like many people of color, she was concerned about issues of coloring (Williams 1996). Indeed, in an earlier interview, she had described the skin and eye color of each member of her family in detail. They ranged from her dark-skinned, dark-eyed mother and very dark-skinned and green-eyed father to a brother who was very white-skinned and green-eyed; "he looks like a white boy." And then there was Maria.

I'm light-skinned. And a lot of my own patients have come in and said, "You're just like me." And my immediate reaction is "Fuck you. I am not like you. I am not white. I've never been white, I never want to be white." . . . The anger I have in being reduced to my skin color is very painful to me. . . . Even now when I go back to my neighborhood, a lot of people consider me white. . . . And I've never liked being white-skinned, I've never liked it. I always wanted to be dark-skinned like my mom, even since I was a little kid, I would stay out in the sun so I could get dark. And I've really hated how much I've lightened since I've been [here].

Indeed, if Maria's attention to skin coloring signaled her worries about her ethnic identification—especially as it was related to her therapist's ethnicity—then her construction of her therapist as an Anglo signified her racism. She recalled that as a teenager, her family had moved from the urban Mexican ghetto to the racially mixed suburbs, taking her from a high school where gang fights were common to a pristine place where she was the token Mexican. Although Maria was an honors student, she was placed in courses for those who spoke English as a second language, because the school had been informed that her first language was Spanish. Recalling this turn of events still infuriates her.

I hated going to that school with every bone in my body. People didn't look like me, didn't act like me, they couldn't understand what I was saying when I was trying to express myself sometimes. They didn't have my slang, they didn't have my experiences. . . . I hated them. I didn't have a single friend, I didn't like people, and to tell you the truth, I hadn't particularly liked white people before I went to that school, but I learned to hate them in that school.

These problems—which were problems not simply of cultural difference but of vigorous cultural antagonisms—plagued Maria's psychotherapy from its inception. It would not be extreme to propose that to Maria, the initial phases of her psychotherapy resembled less a meeting between two individuals than a confrontation between two hostile cultures. In therapy, Maria experienced herself not simply as a patient, but as "the Latina that's reacting to a white presence." Her therapist was neither a neutral nor a new object to her; rather, she was an Anglo who embodied Maria's history of white oppression. For Maria, therefore, the terms of the therapeutic relationship were clear; her therapist was not to be trusted.

> The only people I trust are those that are gonna die for me, and those
> are my *compadres* and my *familia*, my homeboys and my homegirls.
> . . . My therapist is only doing therapy with me for forty-five min-
> utes. These people are gonna die for me if they have to. And that's
> not a metaphor, that's reality.

Maria also believed that she and her therapist inhabited realities so
dissimilar that the distance between them was unbridgeable. Coming
from a background of poverty, she assumed that her therapist "had grown
up at least middle class, if not higher." She also assumed that her therapist had never had been subjected to the varieties of discrimination that
she endured in her day-to-day life. For example, while Maria was "still
followed by the cops when I go home," she believed that her therapist
had "never entered a roomful of people, just genuine everyday people,
and been looked at like she's gonna steal, or gonna threaten somebody,
or is unwanted." Maria's realities comprised her *compadres*' unlawful
activities as well.

> I mean, the phone calls I receive, the tightest relationships I have,
> are not about, "Hey, did you read this article?" You know, my phone
> calls are about, "Okay, where you at? Who's passin' by my way? How
> you doin' this week? How are the boys? Who got slammed?"

And Maria's realities included her own potential for violence.

> Violence is a real part of my life. . . . And I know that I know how to
> fight, and I know that I will use that if I have to. But sometimes it
> frightens me that I'm not incapable of certain things, particularly when
> it comes to my family. I'm like, "Anybody harms my family, I'm gonna
> kill 'em." And I'm not joking. This is not a joke. This is an actuality
> where I come from, that a lot of folks can't get here, especially folks
> who haven't experienced a life like mine. They don't understand that
> this is an actuality. It's not a threat, and it's not some boast or any-
> thing. It's just a fact.

But more important, Maria's realities included her ongoing role in gang affairs. Although she was careful to state that she was very, very rarely called in, there were occasions when she was asked to fulfill her gang obligations.

> My *compadre J*. can call me right now and say, "Okay, something came up, baby, you don't need to know the details. . . . So and so is arriving at such and such a place. Pick him up. He'll stay overnight and then take off." My only question is, "Is he trustworthy? Do I bring him to my house or somewhere else?" And he'll let me know. And that's the life I live.

While Maria acknowledged that her participation in such activities aroused considerable anxiety in her, she had long ago adopted culturally prescribed methods of defending herself against it.

> My *compadres* still expect me, and my position in the community is such, that I need to keep certain things at bay. Like anxiety, I need to keep at bay. Panic, it just has no place. . . . If I let fear in my life, it'll just crumble, it just has no place. . . . You learn not to react too much. You learn not to indulge in reacting too much. . . . If you indulge, you're gonna be overwhelmed. And there's just too much to be overwhelmed about.

Because she wanted to continue "not to react too much," Maria could not use her psychotherapy to examine her anxiety, but had to continue to "push it out." Further, because she wanted to remain involved with her community, Maria resisted her therapist's suggestion that she distance herself from her more dangerous realities. Maria's connection to her community was of primary importance to her, and to stay connected she was required her to carry out her *compadres'* requests. If she did not,

> the word would be that this is cowardice . . . that I'm what you call *leva*, that I'm not down, that I'm not trustworthy, I'm not honorable. . . . There's a lot of honor in this relationship, and for me to say no is

like somehow letting them down, disappointing them. And they've never disappointed me.

Moreover, Maria worried that while she could handle her obligations and realities, her therapist would find them overwhelming and would panic.

> I see her getting really worried. . . . I've seen my therapist sort of getting freaked out sometimes at the possibility of certain things happening, and I'm not particularly shocked by it. . . . You know, the reality of shit that happens; I mean threats, getting shot at, poverty, the realities of that. Fights, which is a very real thing for me.

Maria also considered herself to have been formed by the codes of the gang.

> A lot of my character issues are built on gang lifestyle. Like silence. Not talking about things. Just naturally censoring out information. You never, never specifically state things, or you're in a lot of danger of being caught by the cops, you know? . . . Everything's censored to some degree.

It was for all of these reasons that Maria justified her decision to keep her therapist out. This she accomplished by withholding from her therapist entire categories of information, ranging from specific family material about "some shit that went on when I was a kid" to "anything that's too critical of my mother."

Maria resisted letting her therapist "get into my world" for an additional reason: she had constructed two distinct worlds, and it was her desire that they remain separate. Maria understood this to be a common practice of those who, like her, had bicultural identities.

> We compartmentalize and fragment our world a lot, and that's what I do. And actually the thing that makes me most anxious in the world is joining the two worlds together. I don't like my *compadres* to see this [academic] side, and I don't like people on this side to meet them.

Indeed, any advance made by the therapist in the direction of the world on the other side was experienced by Maria as an invasion, and as "the conquest." Accustomed to social relations based on struggles for domination, and more specifically, experiencing the therapeutic relationship as re-creating the history of power asymmetries between Chicanos and Anglos, Maria constructed her relationship with her therapist along these lines, fending off the incursions she perceived.

After several months in psychotherapy, however, Maria's attitude toward her treatment began to change. Rather than continuing to exploit the differences between them in order to maintain postures of aggression and separation, she began to express ambivalence about the treatment alliance. For example, she voiced concerns that her therapist might misunderstand her. "I realize that a lot of what I do, a lot of my personality, is misconstrued by people in the academic world. And that includes my therapist."

In addition, Maria's wish to dominate the therapeutic relationship by frightening her therapist with tales of her *compadres* became tempered by her longing to see her therapist as an Anglo whom she could not cow. To determine how much information about her realities her therapist could tolerate, Maria began to test her.

> I tested her, for sure. I didn't flip out and start talking about my *compadres*—I mean, I'd mention them, and that these are guys that brought me up on the street, what have you—I didn't mention right away that most of them had been in prison for murder. I didn't mention that they have certain [gang] positions. I didn't mention too much about my personal family life or shit that goes on in my family. I gave that to her bit by bit. . . . I'd see how it would go, how she'd react.

Yet even as Maria's resistance to treatment lessened, the progress of her therapy was restricted by issues of language. Spanish, as the language of her family, was both "what we naturally go into" as well as the language in which Maria usually remembered the past; yet her therapy was a monolingual treatment in English. Maria found that when she translated her memories into English for her therapist, both their affective charge and their personal resonance faded.

It's like taking a memory, a very poignant memory, and making it go from color to black and white. The impression is there and it's very lasting and everything, but the vividness of it has been diminished. That's very much what it's like. I suddenly get a memory, it's very clear and very vivid, and it's all in Spanish. And then in order to have her understand it, I have to back off, understand it in another language, tell it to her, and by that time it doesn't have quite the same meaning to me at all. It's not as impassioned anymore. . . . It feels that it goes from occurring in my stomach to occurring in my head.

Undergoing therapy in English, in other words, blunted and intellectualized Maria's feelings. As Maria described it, speaking English in psychotherapy made her feel like a different person; it distanced her from her experiences, and to a large extent erased her Chicana identity.

I often feel that in English I'm telling stories that didn't really happen to me, even though it's been my life. Like I grew up with a whole bunch of gangs. And when I say it in English . . . it does feel a little dissociated. I know I was there. I know I lived it. I know what's been done, I know how things turned out. But it was all experienced as a Spanish speaking person. It was all experienced as a Chicana, and that's not necessarily what it is when I start speaking in English.

Speaking English in treatment thus allowed Maria to be "a lot more separate from the actual process" of psychotherapy. Maria soon began to find some advantage in this.

I think I utilize it, actually. I utilize it defensively. 'Cause it gives me a chance to stuff it down, to pause, and sort of rearrange things a little. So I know I use it in therapy, particularly like when she asks me a very provocative question. I'll think about it in Spanish, and my impulse is in Spanish, but then by the time it gets to English, I have this concise response that may or may not reflect what my initial response was.

But it was not simply that speaking English allowed Maria to feel detached; it posed the issues of translation in other forms as well.

Things just don't come out right in English oftentimes. I just feel that
I'm speaking and nobody's understanding what I'm saying. And I'm
trying to use the right words, but it's just not true, it's just not true in
what I'm saying.

Maria, in fact, deeply resented the translation process itself.

It's caged in anger, it's caged in hostility, both the hostility that I feel,
and the hostility I feel toward me—that is, that I feel others have
toward me. And that's often been how it's been presented to me; that
you *have* to, that you *have* to do this, you *have* to speak English, you
have to present yourself as an English speaker.

Translating for her therapist recalled for Maria her early experiences
translating for her mother, who spoke only Spanish. At those times, she
had mediated between the Anglo and Chicano worlds.

There were a lot of situations where we'd be in a store with my mom
and we all translated . . . and several experiences in which some white
person in back of us would make a comment about Mexicans and
how many kids they had, and that we're all on welfare. . . . And I would
see particularly the frustration on both ends. And oftentimes the
people who were using English would take it out on me, how frustrated they were. I remember at moments feeling very, I mean, having them make me feel humiliated.

Further, for Maria, English was not a neutral tongue. Rather, it was
an "evil" language that symbolized the oppression of Chicanos, and that
had been forced on her against her will.

I have this one memory of third grade—no it must have been second
grade. I couldn't say the word *squirrel*, and I still have to think about
it—we don't have a lot of s-q-u's in Spanish—this teacher, and I'm
being very generous in calling her that, sent me out of the room; I
mean, made me leave the room, because she couldn't tolerate my
mispronunciation! And I thought that was the cruelest thing to ever

to do to like a 6-, 7-year-old. And I never forgot it. My reaction, even though I didn't have the words, was like "You want me to say this? Fuck you. I'm gonna sit here, I'm gonna be quiet, and unless I can say it perfectly, I ain't saying shit." . . . Basically, the message to me was that I didn't deserve an education just simply because I couldn't say your goddam word? . . . So I learned really early to resent having to use this language. And I learned really early to resent having to present myself as a monolingual English speaker.

Maria's resentment extended to the unaccented English that she had felt pressured to acquire for scholastic purposes, and that she spoke in therapy.

This is what I call "whitespeak." . . . This is something that I had to learn, because when I spoke Chicano style, I would be sent out of class, and I would be told that I wasn't enunciating and I wasn't using words properly. . . . I do have an accent when I speak English; I have a "hood" accent. I have a "Chicana from the barrio" accent when I speak to my family, to my brothers and sisters and my homeboys. But here, I know better. If I speak like a Chicana, people will—it's like an amusing side-show, but it's not real. And they don't listen to what I'm saying, they're just too amused with the difference of my intonation.

In other words, the particular register of English that Maria spoke in therapy was trained and was suffused with negative associations. It gave her none of the comfort of her "Spanglish" or her "hood talk," other registers of English that signified her membership in a treasured group.

In East L.A. that's how we speak. That's how we recognize each other as coming from there. Sort of like in Spanish, every region has its own musical sort of tinge, and people can pick up where I'm from, and where my parents are from, given how we speak. . . . We can recognize each other immediately by the voice.

It was clear that for Maria, both Spanish and "hood" English were the languages of belonging and connection, while "whitespeak," the language of therapy, was the language of disconnection, oppression, and resentment. This, she believed, had slowed the progress of her therapy, and had added another dimension to her resistance.

> I think it limits my ability to work in the therapy. I also think it limits the amount of material my therapist has available to work with emotionally. . . . I mean, I was thinking the other day, even my resistance is very different. In English, when I don't wanna deal with something, I just say, "I don't want to." But in Spanish, it's *no lo quiero*, and just emotionally, it has a very different meaning. . . . There's a real depth. When you say *no lo quiero*, you feel, it, it's a real physical resistance. When I say, "I don't want to," I just feel dissociated, like I don't care, while *no quiero*, I care. I care. I don't want to, but I care.

But although her psychotherapy was problematic in many respects, Maria found that being in treatment with an Anglo therapist also afforded her novel opportunities. For example, she was able to explore painful childhood material and issues related to her experiences as an outsider in the university community—issues that she had found impossible to discuss with her family—with her psychotherapist. Maria also assumed that an Anglo therapist would be more likely than a Latina therapist to maintain the confidentiality of her disclosures. "I was very uncomfortable with the idea of taking my issues to a Latino in this area, because it's so confined. And they're so damn incestuous that I didn't think that was a good idea." In addition, although engaging in a monolingual English psychotherapy had undoubtedly slowed Maria's progress, it granted her the emotional distance she required to feel safe in her treatment. As a result, she was able to begin to address difficult issues when she felt ready to, without becoming flooded by intolerably intense thoughts and feelings. Maria acknowledged that had she spoken Spanish in therapy, she would have lost the shelter that a foreign tongue offered her. "It would be much more dangerous for me. Because I could see . . . being much more sucked into my inner world and what is actually going on."

Maria's increasing sense of comfort in her therapy was a clear consequence of her conviction that her therapist had made sustained efforts to understand her cultural background, even as she had challenged Maria's resistances to treatment.

> My therapist has taken a lot of time to understand my worldview. And she's challenged it, and she's not afraid to challenge it, and she's not been afraid to say, "You're full of shit." . . . And it helps me a lot in terms of being able to look at some issues and say, "What the fuck is going on here?"

For example, embedded in Maria's worldview was her Chicana sense of self. This was a self for which individuation was not a primary goal. It was also a self for which responsibility for family took precedence over individual achievement.

> To be highly individualized means I'm gonna be isolated, and I'm not gonna have the most important connections in my life. And to be highly individualized means I will never have a fulfilling relationship. . . . A lot of these issues have come up, and a lot of issues around my family, in terms of where I fit in in the family, and my responsibilities to them. And that's been hard for her to handle, I think. I think she got it, though, she got it after like the third time around, you know, issues of poverty. My sister's not rich, my sister's poor . . . and after the first couple times of saying, "You're not responsible for your sister," I'm like, "You don't know what the hell you're talking about," she's really been able to acknowledge that there's some things that I'm just not gonna change.

To the extent that her therapist "got it," Maria found therapy helpful. She credited her therapist with helping her to address many of the issues that had troubled her, ranging from her racism to her feelings of discomfort as a minority at the university. But at the conclusion of these interviews, Maria repeated her view that the divergent cultural histories of her therapist and herself had been, finally, insurmountable, and had substantially inhibited her treatment.

> Oftentimes I want to ignore that her color is part of it, that her cul-ture is part of it, but it is. . . . Somewhere, I don't know how, but it's

been communicated to me that you share these things only with people who are there, and who are somehow your blood.

Maria told me that she had communicated similar sentiments to her therapist. She recalled having told her,

> Let's get something straight. It's just never gonna happen completely.
> I mean, I trust you to some degree, but shit, you didn't birth me. If
> we break out in a war, I know which side I'm on, you know, and you're
> on the other side.

As these passages suggest, one feature of Maria's treatment that was especially complicated by the cultural differences between patient and therapist was the transference. At the inception of her treatment, Maria had constructed her therapist as a representative of an adversarial cultural group. While it might therefore be concluded that the transference had emerged the moment Maria laid eyes on her therapist, it might also be contended that Maria's initial reaction was not transference but racism, and that the development of a true transference was impeded by virtue of the therapist's being a foreign object to her. As Maria explained,

> One of the things I've been thinking about is that although I like her
> a lot as a person—I think she's a very nice lady—I don't particularly
> see her as anybody that's ever been in my life, as any figure in my
> life. There's nothing about her that remotely reminds me of a mater-
> nal figure, not any woman that I'd know, or anything like that. The
> only thing she really reminds me of is the people that I've met over
> here, and that's about it.

Maria's position as a therapist in training heightened her awareness of the extent to which, by various measures, she had resisted and sabotaged her psychotherapy. This was something about which she continued to experience internal conflict and frustration.

> The thing is that I do realize, and I do get pissed off at myself, at why
> am I limiting myself in this way if it's for my own good? And I know

what therapy can do. . . . I feel that as long as I keep doing this, my therapy will never go where it has to go. . . . It's a rough one, and I'm constantly in a struggle about it. Because it's not like it's bad shit, it's not like—you know, it's not like I'm hiding some deep-seated secret that's the cornerstone of my psyche and shit. It's just a natural thing. Like memories will come back to me, and I'm like, "You know, I really should tell her about that." And then I get there and I'm like, "I don't remember no more."

Maria's resistance, which she referred to as a "natural thing" was, in fact, largely a cultural thing. Conscious that withholding information would undermine her treatment, she continued to do so as a result of her identification with Chicano culture. Indeed, there were many ways in which the demands of psychotherapy were in conflict with the norms of her native culture. One required that she speak, the other that she remain silent, especially when in the presence of someone from the "other side." One privileged the individual, the other the family and the community. One valued personal integration, the other compartmentalization. And each embraced varying ethical standards.

But perhaps it can be suggested that as much as Maria denied it, her decision to remain in psychotherapy with a "white presence" signaled a desire to integrate the two worlds to which she belonged. Although I did not want to privilege my own interpretations over the explanations with which she provided me, I wondered whether Maria's original disaffection with her therapist was more complex than racism. Perhaps, in addition, Maria was ambivalent about her own multiculturalism. Certainly, she had chosen to pursue the educational opportunities that the Anglo academic world afford her; Maria's fears of differentiating herself from her *compadres* had not prevented her from seeking graduate training. And perhaps Maria's growing sense of trust and comfort in her treatment was not solely the result of her therapist's receptivity to her worldview. Perhaps it was also caused by Maria's nascent acceptance of the Anglo and academic voices within herself—voices that she had previously disowned and devalued. For as much as Maria employed a vocabulary of confrontation and difference to describe her psychotherapy and its white surround, she also expressed a wish for conciliation. Pained by the fact that "they" of the Anglo world misconstrued her, at the end of our interviews she voiced a clear desire that "they" might better understand her.

> Because it's so different, they'll assume certain things about me, given who I hang out with. But they're not seeing the other side of it, the other side that's really me, the caring, nurturing, connected side. They're seeing the shocking side. In the year, there's 364 days in which my *compadres* and I do nothing but hang out, talk, have a good time, take a walk, go around the block, go out to the park, what have you. That's what we do. And maybe one day of the year, that shit blows over and you gotta take care of business. But those 364 days are sort of put aside and not paid much attention to. And that's what I fear, that the whole picture isn't being seen, and people aren't always crazy.

6

Compartmentalization: Meena

Meena, a native of Bombay, India, sought psychotherapy for help in coping with severe marital discord. Her treatment, however, like the treatments examined in the previous chapters, was undermined by broad cultural incommensurabilities between herself and her psychotherapist. Not only did patient and therapist hold variant conceptions of selfhood, so that Meena's psychotherapy was addressed to a highly individuated self rather than to the relationally embedded self characteristic of her cultural background, but they also held such inequivalent cultural constructions of marriage, divorce, gender, sexuality, and emotion that Meena found it impossible to translate the Indian conceptual paradigms that shaped her experience of her marital problems from her native language of Marathi into English. In consequence, in her treatment, Meena faced the dilemma of how to present herself to her therapist. Should she present her Indian self to him, and risk that he misunderstand and stereotype her? Or should she present her therapist with a superficial, Westernized version of herself and use treatment instrumentally, to support her release from a difficult marriage?

Meena's negotiation of this dilemma is the subject of this chapter. We will see how Meena's attempts to compartmentalize her various cultural selves and to renounce her Indian identity helped her temporarily, but left her unprepared for the profound personal losses and cultural alienation that she was later to experience.

"THE CULTURE OF HIS WHITENESS"

Having recently completed her undergraduate studies, Meena, who was barely 20, had her heart set on going to the United States to pursue a graduate degree in literature. As a young woman from an upper middle class "somewhat Anglicized, but still fairly traditional Brahmin family," to do so required her family's permission. When Meena asked her parents for permission to study in America, her mother, uncertain of whether she should allow her daughter to go, traveled to another city to consult with Meena's grandmothers. Was this a proper thing for a young Indian woman of Meena's station to do? Meena's grandmothers were of one mind; they were certain that it was not. Their granddaughter was already past 20, they said, and her parents should be making every possible effort to find a man for her to marry.

Meena had, in fact, received several proposals of marriage since she had turned 18—and "very good proposals of marriage" at that. But her parents valued her education. Moreover, they preferred not to force her into marriage. And so they rejected Meena's grandmothers' advice, and granted her wish to study abroad. Meena told me that their decision was widely greeted with disbelief and horror. People would ask them, "Are you mad? Are you letting your 20-year-old unwed daughter go off to the West?"

It was the middle of the 1980s when Meena arrived in the West and entered graduate school at a large university. Three years later, she married an Indian man whom she had met there. But if marital harmony ever existed between them, it was brief; after only a few months of marriage, Meena realized that her new husband "made my daily functioning impossible."

My ex-husband held the threat of violence to my person so close around me at all times that I talked to nobody. . . . In some way my ex-husband had systematically cut me away and off from anybody that I might have been able to speak to. . . . He was the only person I talked to, his was the only perspective I got, on the things he did to me. . . . I felt like I was going mad.

Despite this description of her ex-husband's behavior, Meena had never considered him abusive. He was merely "pathologically jealous and pathologically possessive," and according to her family, this was insufficient cause for divorce.

When I grew up, I remember stories that my father used to tell me about his father and his father's relationship to his sisters—that's my father's sisters, so my grandfather's daughters. And he would say to them that there would only be a couple of conditions in which he would take you back—I mean, this is sort of the way marriage is seen—you give the girl away and you don't take her back. And one of the two conditions was if he ever laid a hand on you.

Although this threat of violence made Meena fear that she was "going mad," she felt that she had nowhere to turn. Bound by the Indian concept of shame, she was forbidden to disclose "this intensely personal thing" to anyone other than kin, and Meena had no kin in America.

[The concept of shame] is contained within the family. So in India, if I talked to my mother, I wouldn't be breaking the inside–outside divide; I'd be telling Ma. And if I told my aunt, I'd be telling my aunt, and I'm tied to her by blood.

Had Meena been in India when these difficulties occurred, she would have pursued the culturally sanctioned remedies that were available in her community.

> You have this sense of a community that can take care of these things,
> that you don't need to step out of the community. . . . I would have
> gone to my mother. And if my mother didn't know how to deal with
> it, my mother would have talked to my father's sister. Who, if she
> hadn't known how to deal with it, would have talked to another of
> my father's sisters.

While there was a small group of Indians at the university she attended, Meena did not feel that she could to turn to them for help; to do
so would have been to break the "inside–outside divide" and to experience great shame. Besides, Meena was certain that they would offer her
conventional Indian advice, and she didn't want to hear it.

> [They] would all pretty much give me the old down home line, which
> is, stay with your husband, that kind of stuff. . . . They would have
> either said stay in the marriage, or they would have said it was my
> fault, or some such homily.

Meena's American friends, who were unfamiliar with Indian constructions of marriage and divorce, provided equally unusable counsel.

> For them, the solution was a very quick one. . . . My friends would
> say, "Well, why don't you just leave him?" . . . They would automati-
> cally assume that it wouldn't be a problem for me to get a divorce.
> They would not understand that getting a divorce would entail my
> having to deal with very culturally determined concepts.

But an American colleague of Meena's who witnessed her "coming
apart at the seams" offered advice of a different sort; she recommended
that Meena seek psychological help. Meena, however, had come to the
West with significant prejudices against psychotherapy, which caused
her, at first, to recoil from it: "The idea that you would go to a psychologist—it's taboo!" When I asked Meena who might go to psychotherapy
in India, she replied,

> You go to a psychologist if you have mega-nervous disorders. . . . Like
> disturbed people. People who could not cope. Counseling always

seemed an expression of something psychologically wrong with a person. And I did not want to feel that there was something wrong with me.

In addition, for Meena, psychotherapy represented "the whole discourse of American psychobabble." Not only did therapy trivialize personal problems, but it signified to her the insecure boundary between the public and the private in American life, unlike in India.

> It seemed that there was always this excessive talk around what seemed to be really private issues. . . . There was no problem about, for instance, talking about sex on television, incest on television, so it just seemed very confused in some ways. . . . The whole idea of what was public and what was private had got completely muddled. . . . I've come to see that [for Americans] the concept of intimacy is peculiarly linked to distance. That you have the most intimate conversations with the most distanced person, and it was completely at odds for me.

Moreover, psychotherapy's focus on the isolated individual, which embodied American ideals of a distinct and separate self, conflicted with Meena's more inclusive sense of selfhood.

> When I talked to [American] people, [there was] that sense that they were individuals first and foremost, not members of a family—that there was an "I" there . . . that was in some ways distinguishable from things that I could not distinguish myself from.

In India, she explained,

> People have richer roles to their lives. They are not just that one individual. They're not just part of nuclear families. . . . It's being somebody in relation to other people. It's being somebody multiply in relation to others. Being somebody's older sister. Being somebody's younger sister. Being somebody's sister-in-law. Being somebody's brother-in-law's sister. Being the youngest niece, being the oldest

niece, being somebody's aunt—it removes you from being just the
"I" that is so dominant here.

An American therapist, Meena assumed, "would look at my divorce
as something happening to an individual," rather than as she saw it; as
something happening not just to her, but to her entire network of kin.
Meena's characterizations of herself and of her family suggest the familial self that Roland (1988) claims to be common among Indians. In
Roland's view, the familial self is embedded in family relationships, has
fused internal representations of self and other, and is primarily identified with the extended family. As such, it differs substantially from the
individualistic self that psychotherapy typically addresses. As Meena
stated,

> Psychotherapy was about *me. Myself*. I'm gonna look after *myself*. . . .
> I had nobody who was saying, "Well, how would your family react?"
> Nobody who felt that my mother's burden would be a burden for me.
> That my father's dishonor would be my burden. . . . There was noth-
> ing I saw [in American culture] that dealt with how families and gen-
> erations dealt with questions of shame, name, a family name that you
> would bring dishonor to, or you would besmirch. . . . I did not ex-
> pect somebody would actually understand.

And yet despite her reservations, Meena decided to enter psychotherapy. That she did so was the measure of her desperation.

> I just knew that I was in a really terrible situation. I did not want him
> to throw things at me. And I didn't want him to break chairs in which
> I was sitting or smash glasses near my ears. And I was just shit scared.
> I just knew that being in the house with him, I was terrified.

But it was also the case that certain cultural coincidences eased
Meena's way into treatment. For example, she had noticed similarities
between her Indian upper middle class morality, which demanded the
privacy of that which happened behind closed doors, and psychotherapy's promise of confidentiality. In addition, a product of her edu-

cational training was a certain social scientific belief in what a trained professional might accomplish. Meena imagined that at the very least, an American psychotherapist "would be able to yoke my narrative and keep it moving . . . so that I could perhaps do something like identify the problem." Meena hoped that an American psychotherapist might also offer her what those who were bound by her Indian cultural codes and by various family loyalties could not: objectivity. "Somebody objective and confidential would have no stake in me, and might be able to tell me whether I was in fact going mad, or whether I was correct to believe that some of these things were not right."

While a portion of Meena's initial resistance to psychotherapy was rooted in her view of it as a treatment for "disturbed people" with "mega-nervous disorders," her aversion to psychotherapy diminished once her American colleague reframed it as the treatment of choice for those who required situational help.

> My sense was that psychotherapy . . . helped you cope with a situation; not with fundamental character issues, or not with a fundamental strain of psychologistic formation, but with a situation. . . . And it made me feel that perhaps I would be able to get situational help, I would be able to get help on a day-to-day level.

And so Meena went to her first session with a particular situation in mind. Her presenting problem was her husband's pathological behavior, and her primary therapeutic objective was to rescue her marriage by curing her husband of it.

> At the time I know that I felt like I wanted to fix things. . . . That somehow by going to therapy I was going to change him. I think I felt that this was my last chance, that if there was even a chance that I could fix something in this marriage, that I had a sense of duty and obligation to try.

On her colleague's recommendation, Meena went to her university's student counseling services. There, she was assigned to a psychotherapist who was a white American man in his sixties. Meena immediately imagined that he viewed both her and her native country in very specific ways.

> I think he thought of me as this girl from an ancient culture who's trying to get away from a bad marriage, and I'm going to actually help her become more progressive in some ways. . . . I'm fairly sure that his conceptions of India were, you know, *Jewel in the Crown*, *Passage to India* conceptions. A land of, I don't know, dark-skinned, inscrutable Orientals who lived in this very, very hot, dusty land replete with tigers, elephants, and snake charmers, who spoke pidgin English at best. You know, timeless, ancient, deep souls, and just completely incomprehensible.

Convinced that her psychotherapist constructed her in these ways, Meena determined to prove his misconceptions to him. Doing so, however, exacerbated her predicament. On one hand, she thought it was important for her therapist to understand her Indian cultural identity. On the other hand, Meena wished to differentiate herself from what she assumed were her therapist's uninformed stereotypes of India. Indeed, from the inception of her treatment, Meena despaired of the possibility of presenting to her psychotherapist a version of herself that was both informed by her native culture and comprehensible to him.

> He had no clue. I had to start by almost telling him where India was on the map. . . . I had to do, where is India, what's India, what was my growing up like, what kind of parents, what situation, how traditional, what does traditional mean—I had to just lay out a frame for him that was brand new and had to, in some way, tell him that he had to put his stereotypical one aside.

Meena seemed to resent the fact that in her psychotherapy, she was required to perform "the same work that I had to do every day, day in, day out," as a foreigner in America. Although she found the task of cultural explanation exhausting, she labored in her treatment to ensure that her therapist would not reduce her to "this peculiar person who'd grown up in this peculiar way." As the therapy progressed, however, Meena became aware that her therapist "would sort of back away from" the material she presented about India. Like other foreign patients who stop presenting non-Western cultural material once they sense that their therapists have little interest in it (Kakar 1990), Meena began to omit Indian concepts that she feared her therapist would find perplexing or peculiar from her conversations with him, even when such concepts were central to her situation.

> We'd just get to an impasse, which we put in a sort of a bag of cultural difference. And I'd say, "Well, it's the way things are in India." And so he would steer me back to the individual. . . . He would say, "We'll let that be for now. Let's just talk about the problems you're having now."

As a result of their tacit agreement to disregard Indian cultural information, entire categories of material escaped therapeutic scrutiny. Meena's vacillating emotional states remained unexplored, for example, because despite her English fluency, she could not easily translate them from her native Marathi into English. The cultural surround of the Indian woman's sense of shame, which flooded Meena whenever she so much as imagined violating traditional Indian sexual mores, was similarly omitted from therapeutic discussions.

Meena also found herself confronted with the daunting task of conveying to her therapist the complexities of Indian constructions of marriage. She wondered whether her therapist had misconstrued her claim that Indian women sometimes tolerated marital violence, due to the absolute centrality of marriage to their lives. As she explained,

> There was a hierarchy of violence that one put up with. There were a lot of women that I talked to who would sort of say, "Yeah, he did that to me too. I didn't leave him." So that there was a lot that people were willing to put up with just to stay married, because of what marriage signifies. There are so many words that I can't even translate into English about the auspiciousness of the state of being married.

To make her therapist understand the "auspiciousness" of marriage in India had required Meena to convey Indian conceptual paradigms that

lacked American equivalents. For example, Meena tried to explain the
Hindi word *suhag*, which conveyed some of the transformative properties of marriage by embedding

> the actual, the physical acts of marriage, you know, like the ceremo-
> nial, ritual things. And then if you were to abstract from that a philo-
> sophical and phenomenological state of mind: that in fact, once you
> got married, you occupied a different state of mind, state of being,
> state of life. And that occupying that state of mind, state of being,
> state of life is desirable. . . . There are for women so many more sym-
> bols, colors you only wear when you're married, you know, things
> like that. Where once you enter that state, the home that you left,
> your mother's and father's home, is also an altered home for you, an
> altered space for you. . . . It's like even that space, which is physi-
> cally the same, is now a differently configured space.

Meena was not only skeptical that her therapist would understand
her cultural conceptions of marriage; given that he came from "a country where you've got a 54 percent divorce rate," she was equally doubt-
ful that he would comprehend the cultural meanings of divorce common to Indians of her sociocultural background. She tired of trying to
convince him that her family considered divorce a scandal, and that by
divorcing her husband she would damage not only her reputation, but
her family's reputation as well.

> It cast my family's morality into question. . . . [They] would have to
> go out in wider Indian society with everyone knowing that their
> daughter had gotten divorced. And they would have to deal with the
> judgment that would come down; that they sent this girl to America,
> Western morals had corrupted her, she married this nice Indian guy,
> and she divorced him. That this is precisely why we do not send our
> daughters to America.

Meena told her psychotherapist repeatedly that her family's reputation would suffer as a consequence of her divorce. Yet he continued

to advise her according to the precepts of Western individualism, even though this did not constitute her "way of being in the world."

> I basically got, "Well, what do *you* want to do? What do *you* think?" . . . Then it became, "Well, wouldn't your parents understand this? Well, wouldn't your family understand this?"

Initially, Meena bridled when her therapist suggested that she simply extricate herself from her culture, telling her,

> "Well, that's tradition. *You* don't have to live like that." Like it was something I could separate. Like, you know, "That happens in *your* culture." Like I could somehow, by stepping into America, be divorced from it.

But as her treatment proceeded, and as she abandoned the expectation that her therapist would "know me culturally," Meena began to find such separations advantageous. "I needed at least the momentary space in which I could do something artificially, like separate culture from me. . . . And for me, that sort of compartmentalization has always worked."

Meena also began to compartmentalize in another way. From her experience as a foreigner in the United States, Meena had learned the necessity of "talking to people about the things they will be able to relate to." She increasingly brought this method of compartmentalization into her treatment, translating herself and her difficulties into terms that she believed would be accessible for American psychotherapy. Indeed, the turning point in her therapy occurred when Meena relinquished her own construction of her husband's behavior and accepted her therapist's. She recalled a particular session in which she had described to her psychotherapist an incident that had occurred between herself and her husband the previous night.

> I said once [something] to the effect that, "We had a fight last night and glasses were broken." And he said, "What do you mean glasses

were broken?" And he would not let me leave it. He said "How did the glasses break? . . . Glasses do not break by themselves."

By continuing this line of questioning, Meena's therapist discovered that "glasses were broken" because Meena's husband had thrown them at her.

> And he said, "Do you believe that was right for him to do that?" And I said, "No, I don't think it was right for him to throw glasses at me, but he did not hit me." I had this sense that [my ex-husband] had not been, in some sense, violent with me. . . . Because hitting, to me, was [my ex-husband] taking his palm and slapping me across the face, or something like that. . . . And that was a breaking point for me because . . . I had never thought of [him] as violent; I'd only thought of him as pathologically jealous and pathologically possessive. And that terrified me.

In other words, the turning point in Meena's therapy came when she accepted the terms of the therapeutic discourse, when she adopted the voice of Western individualism, converted her material into terms comprehensible to her therapist, and accepted her therapist's representation of her ex-husband's behavior as violent. Meena explained that it was important to her that she and her therapist develop shared understandings of her predicament.

> He understood that I was traumatized, he just could not relate to why. And I needed to make him relate to why. And the only way I could make him relate to why was to accept his formulation of what constituted violence and then have him understand my relationship to my ex-husband as violent.

But adopting her psychotherapist's view of the world—and in particular, of her ex-husband's behavior—not only allowed Meena's therapist to understand her, it also served Meena instrumentally. For once she defined his actions as violent, she was, according to the criteria established by her grandfather, permitted to leave him.

That Meena employed her therapy in the project of marshaling the necessary support to end a difficult marriage is clear. But it was also true that Meena's treatment affected her in ways that she had not anticipated. For example, despite her therapist's unfamiliarity with the cultural dimensions of her difficulties, Meena found psychotherapy beneficial for the same reason many Western patients do: because she drew strength from the therapeutic alliance. Therapy not only provided Meena with a space to talk and with help in constructing a coherent narrative, but it also provided her with emotional support.

> I responded at that point less to the culture of his whiteness than to the strength of his kindness. . . . I would encounter, from this man, gentleness. . . . I was just so grateful that I had an objective, confidential voice that was telling me, "You're not mad. You're not nuts. This is terrible. I don't care what cultural context—no man should ever do this to a woman."

Therapy also provided Meena with a safe place in which to release her emotions, and with the sense that she was making progress. In fact, Meena came to appreciate "all of the things that I associate with American psychobabble."

> I got a lot of "What do *you* want to do, think about yourself as an individual, it's *your* life, what's good for *you*, separate yourself, make spaces for yourself"—all of the things that I associate with American psychobabble, I got. But they were useful then. . . . In some way, everything that I had previously been contemptuous of was helping me.

That Meena found psychotherapy beneficial was also linked to her having developed a positive transference to her therapist. Yet this did not occur immediately; her first reactions to him were highly unfavorable. Initially, Meena had felt put off by her therapist's position of power, which she referred to as "the culture of his whiteness." To Meena, "the culture of his whiteness" signified "an unexamined self-assurance. It's a degree of arrogant comfort in the world, that you don't actually have to adapt to anything. It's the assurance that everyone will adapt to you."

Despite Meena's obvious resentment of her therapist's cultural power, her positive transference to him was based, in part, on having experienced him as genuinely gentle and kind. But it was also the result of her having assimilated him to a particular Indian category of the person. For Meena, the defining characteristic of her therapist was his age, which evoked various culturally determined associations and assumptions.

> The fact that he was older helped because again, culturally, I took with me the sense that this is a much older man, and he'd lived through many summers. That he'd seen life, that presumably he'd seen his children go through some things, and that I was just going to try to relate to him as . . . a young kid. That in some sense, I was going to appeal to the wisdom of his years, if not his cultural understanding.

Meena also imagined that because of his age, he shared her appreciation of traditional things.

> The fact that I was traumatized by feeling like I needed to get out of something, that marriage was a lifelong commitment for me, I mean all of the old traditional things, I think these resonated with him . . . that he felt that he was dealing with somebody who, even if she was culturally completely foreign, was espousing things that I think he must have felt were part of a different era, but one in which he must have been a young man.

Indeed, it was as if her therapist's age had the effect of neutralizing his gender, so that intimate topics that she could never have broached with an Indian male she was able to discuss with him.

Further, as much as Meena was troubled by her therapist's inability to know her culturally, there were ways in which she welcomed his cultural ignorance. Because he was a non-Indian, "I could dump this stuff on him and he wouldn't even know why it would matter or anything like that. So it was somewhat safe." Her therapist was also someone whom she was able to experience as a new object, in that she could trust him not to hold her to her own culture's standards.

> I could in the space of that room express outrage at the ways in which I'd been treated, and not feel like somebody was going to say to me, "Well you made your bed and now you lie in it," which could have been an Indian response. . . . If I'd been talking to somebody Indian who'd understand that I didn't want to bring shame to my family, they would say, "Well, then, just grin and bear it."

But although Meena credited her treatment with having granted her immediate relief, she found its long-term effects highly disruptive. Certainly, as Meena acknowledged, the artificial separations that she had utilized in her psychotherapy had been beneficial. Implementing an individualistic sense of self and appropriating American conceptions of marriage, divorce, and violence had helped remove her from a marriage that she could no longer tolerate. Yet Meena's divorce, as well as her consequent rejections of her Indian "way of being in the world"—rejections that her psychotherapy endorsed—had serious repercussions for her. After ending her marriage, Meena experienced several years of extreme distress as she realized her new status as a divorced Indian woman. During these years, as the result of her divorce, she virtually cut herself off from her native country. Feeling betrayed by "somebody Indian, feeling betrayed by that community," she experienced an anger toward her country so unforgiving and complete that she fled from all things Indian, including the Indian parts of herself.

According to Meena, her psychotherapist had failed to help her anticipate these intensely painful and somewhat destabilizing developments. Perhaps because he had been unable to understand Meena's circumstances from her point of view—that is, from a point of view informed by particular cultural constructions of the self, of family, of sexuality, marriage, and divorce—he had insufficiently prepared her for the profound personal and cultural losses that she suffered as a consequence of her divorce. "I was breaking ties to India. . . . I was certainly breaking ties to a whole social upbringing that was influenced by ideas of *suhag* and *suhagen* that I'll never get back." When Meena realized that she had not only lost India, but that she would never completely adapt to American society, she entered an extended period of dual exile, a period characterized by severe emotional withdrawal and social isolation. Thus in virtually every respect, the compartmentalizations that had served and sustained Meena during her treatment boomeranged shortly afterward.

Given the obvious importance to Meena of exploring her indigenous conceptions of kinship, marriage, and divorce, and given her difficulties in doing so with an American psychotherapist, I asked her if she had ever considered consulting an Indian therapist. At first she responded,

> Had I been able to go to an Indian therapist, that would have been fabulous. I would not have had to spend so much time explaining. . . . I would not have had to explain why even the thought of leaving my ex-husband was producing that kind of trauma for me. . . . I would have got a lot more familial stuff. I would have got, you know, "What would your family think? . . . What would your brother think? What would this mean to your family's standing in the community? What would it mean to you as a representative?"

Upon further reflection, however, Meena concluded that working with an Indian therapist would have been impossible for her, because it would have violated the "inside–outside divide."

> An Indian therapist is still not my family, and Indian. So that would have felt very odd for me, because it would have been telling my family secrets to an Indian who was not my family. I would have been very nervous that this person knew my family. I mean, the Indian community of a certain socioeconomic formation is a very small one, and I would have been just terrified about that sort of disclosure.

Thus, although a culture-near psychotherapist would have better understood her trauma, Meena did not feel that this option was available to her.

As Meena's account of her psychotherapy demonstrates, as she participated in her psychotherapy she selectively employed the various cultural voices available to her. Meena candidly discussed her conscious appropriation of American discourses when they served her purposes. She used, for example, "a very American rhetoric," to justify her decision to enter treatment to her husband. "I said, '*I* don't know how to cope.' I couched it as *my* inability to deal with this; '*I* need some help.'" She used an American voice when she began treatment, framing her therapy as an attempt to isolate some of the problems as events to be dealt with, and once again when she ended it, invoking an American definition of violence to justify her decision to divorce her husband. Having entered psychotherapy with great reservations, she learned to speak its language in order to accomplish specific goals. Initially critical of psychotherapy's discourse of individualism, she employed it to exit her marriage. Despite her short-term gains, however, in Meena's final analysis, her therapy didn't work. Thus a central question raised by Meena's account of her treatment concerns how deeply psychotherapy penetrates when it is addressed to a version of the self that has been culturally and linguistically translated, and to a version of the self that has been presented to satisfy the particular Western requirements of the therapeutic situation.

7

Normalization: Yukiko

Yukiko, a young woman from Tokyo, Japan, entered psychological treatment to deal with the acute psychological distress that had been triggered by a rupture with her mother. Yukiko's culturally shaped understandings of what it meant to be different from others, and of what it meant to defy her parents—both of which were at the root of her anguish—apparently were foreign to her therapist, as were her conceptions of the self, of emotional expression, of interpersonal relationship, and of psychological dysfunction. Yet these and other culturally inflected conceptions remained unexamined within the therapeutic dyad.

Yukiko's account of her intercultural psychotherapy, like Meena's, illustrates the multiple cultural voices that are within many foreign and ethnic patients, and considers the emergence of particular voices in intercultural clinical encounters. In her psychotherapy sessions, Yukiko invoked both Japanese and Americanized cultural voices. Indeed, she employed her Western psychotherapy to differentiate herself from Japanese conventions and to express American ideals of selfhood even as she enacted Japanese modes of interpersonal relationship with her therapist. As the following account demonstrates, Yukiko found a measure of

needed support in the Western assumptions of her American psychotherapist, who validated behaviors that would have been considered
deviant and strange by Japanese traditional standards.

"A STRANGE JAPANESE"

Several years ago, when Yukiko was a young woman in her early twen-
ties, she became dissatisfied with her life in Japan. Neither her position as a corporate secretary in Tokyo nor her relationship with her
Japanese boyfriend held her interest, and she found herself longing "to
do something." What Yukiko decided to do was to go to the United
States to study marketing. Her aunt had lived and worked in a small
Midwestern town for more than twenty years, and her mother arranged
for her daughter to move in with her. After her arrival, Yukiko enrolled
in a local college. Several months later, she became romantically involved with a fellow student named Rob. When Yukiko's aunt learned
of her niece's relationship with Rob she was horrified, because, as
Yukiko relates, "Rob was younger than me, and he's American, and
my aunt didn't like that at all. She thought I wouldn't be happy married to somebody younger who doesn't have any job at all, and he's
American."

Indeed, Yukiko's aunt was so concerned about her niece's welfare
that she sent her back to Japan. When Yukiko arrived at the Tokyo air-
port she was met by her parents, and by the boyfriend whom she had
left behind in Japan. Yukiko's Japanese boyfriend "had a good education and a good job and stuff," and her parents had assumed that she
would marry him. They immediately told Yukiko that they, like her aunt,
disapproved of her relationship with Rob.

> I had a very big argument with my mother at the airport. Like she
> was really accusing me about, "What are you doing in America? I
> thought you went there to study, and now you got involved with some
> younger American boy!" And she was just accusing me for fooling
> around, not studying, and she was very upset.

In particular, what "upset" her parents was that "Rob does not have a job, he's just a college student, and he's American. And everything about him was just so upsetting to my parents, especially my mother."

That Rob was an American had extremely unfavorable resonances for Yukiko's parents. In their view, he was an unacceptable choice for a husband. Like many Japanese, Yukiko said, her parents held

> stereotypes about women who were married to an American or a foreigner, that those women be kind of wild type, or those interracial marriages don't last a long time, that kind of stuff, so maybe they didn't like that. . . . Especially the older generation has some stereotypes about all G.I.s. After the war, those G.I.s just played around with prostitutes or those women who try to make money by socializing with American GIs. So I think that some people think foreigners are just not serious and just play around with Japanese women.

Although Yukiko was aware that many other Japanese women would have ended a relationship to which their parents objected so strongly, Yukiko refused to break up with Rob. After a year of separation Yukiko and her American boyfriend were reunited in Tokyo, where they married.

Shortly thereafter Rob and Yukiko returned to the United States, where Rob resumed his studies and Yukiko went to work for a Japanese company. Yukiko knew that she had done something that was quite unusual by Japanese standards. Few Japanese, she said, "would just escape to get married with somebody like I did." Yukiko also recognized that these dramatic changes in her life coincided with her parents' divorce. Yukiko considered the divorce their problem, and wished to "escape from all these divorce things." She had long been aware of her parents' marital conflicts, and she supported their decision to divorce. At the same time, she was distressed by the dissolution of her parents' marriage. Yukiko explained that divorce was uncommon in Japan, and "pretty stigmatized, especially if you're a woman." She elaborated:

> Especially for my mother's generation, it's still unusual. And I think people just categorize divorced women as somebody who had a prob-

> lem. . . . But my mother is still struggling to get used to the fact that
> she's divorced. She isolated herself from everybody, her friends and
> her family and her grandmother. I think she's worrying too much,
> but she just thinks that everybody's embarrassed about her. So she
> doesn't socialize much anymore.

Yukiko acknowledged that the coincidence of her parents' divorce with her marriage to Rob and return to the United States had been difficult for her mother to bear.

> I think she felt like I betrayed her, like just left her in Japan, because
> she was getting divorced. I think she wanted me to be there. But in-
> stead I just took off and moved to the United States.

Previously, Yukiko and her mother had been very close. But after Yukiko and Rob married and settled in the States, her mother became so upset with her that she terminated their relationship.

> My mother was not talking to me at all. I tried to contact her, I used
> to write letters to her almost every week, or I sent pictures of Rob
> and me, like I wanted to tell her that we are happy together, so don't
> worry about me and stuff. But she didn't talk to me.

While Yukiko realized that she had done something unusual, when her mother cut off contact with her she began to worry that she had done something terribly wrong.

> I felt so guilty, even though I believed I made the right decision. I
> wanted to be with somebody who I loved. I didn't realize until I started
> living here that I must have done something terribly wrong, even
> though I didn't think I made the wrong decision. I don't know, I think
> the fact that she was not talking to me was a very difficult thing to
> accept. I tried, I tried hard to get our relationship back to normal.

Unable to repair her relationship with her mother, for the first time in her life Yukiko began to feel depressed.

Somehow I started getting so depressed and I didn't want to go to work, so I just stayed home sometimes, just laying on the couch and doing nothing. . . . I just feel like I'm not gonna be able to have just a normal life again. I just felt like so tired, and I didn't wanna do anything. I tried to read books sometimes, or I tried to watch TV or something, as I lay on the couch, but I didn't wanna do anything.

Yukiko "couldn't figure out what's wrong with me," yet she "knew that I couldn't stay on the couch for the rest of my life." When Rob's efforts to help her failed, he suggested that she consult with a psychotherapist, and Yukiko agreed.

I feel like I needed to do something. We used to live right next to a hospital, and I feel like, okay, maybe I should just go to the hospital and see somebody. If that's gonna help me getting out of this situation, maybe I should do it. . . . Maybe it's interesting to talk to somebody who's a professional, and maybe if she can tell me about what's wrong with me from an objective point of view, then I thought maybe that would help me.

Yukiko's willingness to seek psychological treatment was surprising, given that to have done so in Japan would have exacerbated her concerns about being strange. In her country, she said, "I think we kind of see somebody who goes to counseling as very strange—you have a very disturbed person psychologically. I think we kind of stigmatize people who go to counseling." Indeed, Yukiko recalled that she had approached the hospital's outpatient mental health facility with trepidation.

I was very nervous and I feel very strange about going to the psychiatric department which was on the ninth floor or the eighth floor in the hospital. First, I didn't wanna be seen by people. I'm going to the psychiatry department, I thought people might think I have a big problem, I'm very strange or something.

Despite such fears, Yukiko went to make an appointment with a psychotherapist. She was given a choice between two social workers, an

American woman who was available immediately and a Japanese woman who would be able to see her in two weeks. Yukiko expressed some reluctance about seeing the American therapist.

> I was a little bit worried about English. I thought maybe that the social worker is gonna have a hard time understanding me, or maybe I can't express my feelings well. And I was a little worried about how she would understand my feelings, me being a foreigner in America. I was a little bit worried that she wouldn't understand me struggling, adjusting to a different culture.

Yukiko maintained that she selected the American psychotherapist despite her misgivings because she did not want to delay her treatment. But there were other reasons she chose to work with the American. For one thing, she assumed that the American therapist would be unfamiliar with Japanese culture, and would therefore be more objective than the Japanese therapist.

> I really felt like I never can get a very objective opinion about my situation because everybody around me was getting very emotional and they're very subjective about what they think about my life. So I really felt like I needed to get out of those very subjective opinions. . . . She's from a different culture, and I thought she could be very objective about what I was going through.

An American therapist might also be more objective, Yukiko said, because she had received superior professional training. "I think I just believed that here psychology or social work, all those things, is more advanced here. So maybe she's more, how do you say—has advanced ideas about people's minds."

But in addition, it was clear that Yukiko did not feel comfortable discussing her difficulties with someone who was "in my group." Yukiko worried that a Japanese therapist would find her strange.

> If she was Japanese, I guess maybe I felt like I was exposing my embarrassment or shame, because I was doing something totally against Japanese traditional culture, or Japanese standards. So maybe I felt

like she would think I'm a very strange individual. I didn't want to get stigmatized by some Japanese person or social worker.

It seemed, in fact, that although Yukiko "wanted to think that I made the right decision," she too had begun to worry that her behavior was strange. Not only did Yukiko claim that she had violated Japanese norms by choosing a husband who was younger than she, unemployed, and an American, but she had also disobeyed her parents. Yukiko emphasized the importance of the Japanese concept of *oyakoko*, which defined children's primary obligation to be loyal and respectful to their parents. She knew that by disregarding *oyakoko*, she might have permanently damaged her relationship with her parents. After having been a "good daughter" all her life, which had required her to be obedient and to "behave in a ladylike manner," Yukiko suddenly found herself in danger of losing her parents because she had failed to find a husband who satisfied their expectations.

> I'm sure some people thought I was a very bad daughter because I was doing something against my parents' will. And I think a couple of older people told me, like my uncle and my aunt in Japan, that if I do something like that to my parents, then when I became a parent, maybe the same thing was gonna happen to me.

With these concerns in mind, Yukiko began psychological treatment. It was her initial expectation that her psychotherapist would give her some solutions, perhaps recommending that she go back to Japan and talk to her mother. Instead, her therapist

> just listened to me and she just kind of analyzed from her point of view: "That's what you say, Yukiko, but I think this way. So you don't need to feel so sad or feel responsibility about what you've gone through." So she kind of just gave me a different perspective, perception, about what's going on in my life.

For Yukiko, talking to someone about her problems was a novel activity. When she had felt "down" in Japan, she "didn't want to talk to anybody." In therapy, she also expressed her "true feelings" for the first time.

I don't remember much that she told me, but she just let me talk, and this was kind of nice, to kind of talk about my feelings, because some feelings I kind of repressed because I didn't want to make Rob worry about me too much, and I didn't like him to think that I'm regretting being here. So I think some of those feelings I never told Rob. So I think by telling those true feelings it kind of helped me through some things. . . . It was a big relief. . . . After I cry and after we finished the conversation, I felt kind of good, better than I was earlier.

But Yukiko was not only in need of relief; she was also clearly preoccupied by worries that she was different, unusual, and strange.

I was feeling somehow guilty about me doing something so unusual, you know, marrying somebody who's much younger than me, that kind of thing, and just moving from Japan to the United States—that's just kind of unusual. Not many people do that. So I was feeling like I must be very different from everybody else.

It is possible that some portion of Yukiko's sense of herself as different was rooted in her parents' divorce. Yukiko had described divorce as stigmatized in Japan. Given the more inclusive Japanese conception of the self, she might have experienced the stigma attached to her parents as a result of the divorce as extending to her.

To understand why Yukiko was so disturbed by the thought that other Japanese might find her unusual—indeed, many Americans would take this as a compliment—I asked her what it meant to be different in Japan. Yukiko explained that in Japan to be different held negative connotations, in part because it demonstrated disrespect toward parental authority and toward other Japanese traditions.

Different means it's rebellious, and just doing something against Japanese traditions. Like if I wanna please my parents, then I should have stayed in Japan and married my Japanese boyfriend. . . . I think usually Japanese children are taught to respect parents and try to listen to what your parents say to you, and I was doing something totally against it.

Further, those who were different in Japan risked being socially ostracized. Being different gave Yukiko "that feeling of not being part of the rest of the people. If you are different, you won't be able to share some of the values other people share. Then I won't be part of the group."

At one point during these interviews, Yukiko voiced a more positive construction of difference. "Somehow I feel like I was doing something very unique compared to other people. That was somehow a good feeling too, that I was doing something different." But she later made it clear that she had not completely internalized this view.

> I know that especially in American society it's kind of distinct to be different and unique. . . . Many teachers have been telling me good things—"You're different, you are so unique"—but I can't think that way. I'm always conscious about being different. So maybe, I don't know, that's coming from my Japanese background.

Clearly, Yukiko was caught between the conflicting valuations of difference that she attributed to American and to Japanese cultures. At times she tried to emulate those in American society who regarded difference as desirable and unique. Yet she was unable to completely divorce herself from the Japanese conception of difference, which suggested her as someone so strange and inferior as to be mentally ill.

> I thought maybe I was not emotionally stable or capable enough to have a normal, not a normal life, but an everyday life. . . . Everybody goes to work and has the everyday life. I was not able to go to work, and I was staying home, doing nothing, so maybe, you know, I was not functioning as well as normal people. So maybe I feel like I was really sick, mentally ill.

Given that Yukiko was so concerned about being different, perhaps the primary benefit to her of psychotherapy with an American therapist was hearing that her emotional reactions were natural and normal.

> My social worker was telling me, "You are doing such a hard thing that not many people do. So you don't need to feel bad about feeling

down, that's a normal reaction. You are doing such a hard thing, so don't feel bad about it." I thought that was very objective, her perception. It made me feel better, that maybe I'm not that crazy.

According to Yukiko, her American psychotherapist, because of her objectivity, was able to normalize her predicament in ways in which a Japanese therapist could not have. The American therapist was also able to reinforce behaviors for which a Japanese psychotherapist might have chastised Yukiko. "If you have traditional Japanese standards, then they'll say, 'You are causing a lot of pain on your parents and your family. You did something wrong.' I didn't want to hear that, I guess."

Yukiko also might have assumed that an American therapist would support her separation and individuation from her mother. Indeed, Yukiko's story suggests that immigration to the United States may facilitate the rejection of indigenous cultural norms and foster the development of autonomous selves, thereby promoting separation and individuation. For Yukiko, marrying Rob and settling in America "was my first big thing, being really against my mother."

My mother is very authoritative. And I think I have been following her rules until before I decided to be with Rob. And maybe all those feelings exploded when I decided to marry Rob, I guess. I really feel I have, to be with somebody I love. And I have seen that her marriage didn't succeed, didn't last. And I have seen as a little child that their marriage was falling apart, and they're fighting all the time. So I never wanted to have a marriage like that. That's part of my way of saying, "I don't want to be like you," maybe.

But perhaps it was inevitable that Yukiko's sense of being different would finally color her experience of psychotherapy as well. Yukiko imagined that her therapist had never treated anyone like her before. Once she began to experience herself as a troublesome patient, she lost faith in her therapist's ability to help her.

I'm sure that she didn't have somebody like me before, like some Japanese woman, so I thought maybe she worried about how to deal with me, maybe she was worrying about that. I'm sure she knows I need to be not treated, but dealt with in a different way from her other American clients. She needs to pay extra attention because of my language, and also I'm from a different culture and I'm living here. So maybe she needs to consider all those different things, which she doesn't need to do when she sees other American clients. . . . That's maybe kind of extra troubles for her.

Yukiko's view of herself as different also affected her conduct in therapy. To spare her therapist "extra troubles," she underreported the cultural aspects of her difficulties. But there was another reason Yukiko did not feel it was necessary for her to verbally detail her predicament. She sensed that her therapist already understood the cultural implications of her thoughts and feelings. For example, when I asked Yukiko whether she had explained to her psychotherapist the concept of *oyakoko* and the centrality of Japanese children's duty to obey their parents, both of which might have helped her therapist understand the cultural significations of her rupture with her mother, she answered, "I think I felt like she already knew that in Asian culture we feel more obligation to respect our parents' ideas. I think I sensed that she was already aware of that, that kind of thing."

By sparing her therapist the "extra troubles" of treating her, and by expecting her therapist to understand her thoughts and feelings without her having to voice them, Yukiko was enacting Japanese modes of relationship with her American psychotherapist (Roland 1996). Yet although she sensed that her therapist knew certain things about Asian culture, Yukiko offered no evidence that her therapist understood her cultural background; indeed, her accounts of her therapist's interventions reveal an insensitivity to Japanese culture. That she and her therapist actually held culturally variant constructions of the self, of emotion, of interpersonal relationship, and of psychotherapy was illustrated by Yukiko's discussion of crying. When I asked Yukiko whether she thought her therapist had fully understood how distressing her broken relationship with her mother was to her, she replied, "I think so, because I was crying when I was talking about it to her. So I hope she does." In this passage, Yukiko implied that she and her therapist constructed crying similarly; yet crying clearly held very different meanings for them. Yukiko continued,

> I think I knew that it was okay to cry in front of the social worker. I mean that was a very private space, and Kleenex was there right next to me. So I guess I kind of knew that it's okay to cry. And I think that I remember she was saying, "It's okay to cry."

While a patient crying in therapy might have been routine for Yukiko's psychotherapist, for her it was highly unusual. Indeed, Yukiko could not remember ever having cried in front of anyone before. Whether Yukiko's therapist knew this about her patient is impossible to ascertain; what seems clear, however, is that she and her psychotherapist neglected to discuss their culturally divergent conceptions of crying.

Yukiko and her psychotherapist also possessed culturally varying conceptions of Yukiko's condition. Although they both identified Yukiko as depressed, they had dissimilar understandings of the causes and symptoms of depression, and of its cure. For Yukiko, being depressed meant "I was not able to cope with the normal life everybody is able to cope with. Like maybe I'm not emotionally, psychologically capable, stable enough to function with society." In other words, in Yukiko's view depression referenced less a state of intrapsychic turmoil and emotional despair than a disturbance in the behavioral capacity to live a "normal life" and to "function with society." To overcome depression did not require the resolution of underlying internal conflicts or interpersonal issues, as it does according to psychodynamic views of depression, but rather the return to particular levels of activity that conformed to societal norms.

Further, Yukiko and her therapist differently constructed the central features of Yukiko's presenting problems. According to Yukiko her therapist had a "different perspective," and advised her that she didn't need to "feel so sad or feel responsibility." Yukiko, however, was grappling with the sheer horror of her betrayal of her mother and with her consequent disconnection from the larger Japanese social world.

Thus, as Yukiko and her therapist sat side by side week after week in an ostensible collaboration to relieve Yukiko's despair, they applied contradictory premises to the most central aspects of her case. Yukiko and her therapist viewed the self, the family, mental health, and interpersonal relationships from contrasting cultural perspectives. Their assumptions about each other also appeared to be shaped by their varying cultural subjectivities. But because these contrasting perspectives were never explicitly acknowledged, their effects on Yukiko's psychotherapy remained unexamined.

After several psychotherapy sessions, Yukiko began to feel that her therapist was "really not into talking with me." Perhaps it was difficult for Yukiko's psychotherapist to sustain an interest in a patient who sensed that the therapist already "knew things," and who therefore only hinted at her concerns; or perhaps Yukiko had indeed presented her therapist with unwanted "extra troubles." Yukiko's statement below, however, suggests that she sensed that her therapist was uninterested in her because her therapist had failed to provide her with the high degree of attunement that is central to Japanese interpersonal relationships.

> A couple of times I made an appointment after, I don't know what time, sometime in the late afternoon. So maybe she was tired, but I could tell she was not into listening to my talk. And sometimes I sensed that, and I didn't like that at all. She yawned a couple times, and I didn't like that at all, because I was maybe crying when I'm sitting here, and she was yawning. So I felt like, "Wow."

For reasons that Yukiko claimed not to understand, her therapist unilaterally decided to terminate her treatment. Yukiko suspected that her therapist had done so because she had lost interest in her. In any case, in Yukiko's view, her treatment ended before she was ready to leave it.

> I felt I was getting better, and I started going back to work and I was doing fine. So she thought, you know, maybe after the next couple of times we can stop seeing each other. So I felt like, Oh, well. . . . I was just worried a little bit that after I stop this maybe I was gonna be depressed again, that was my main concern.

When I asked Yukiko whether she had informed her therapist of her main concern and requested that the treatment continue, she said that she had not. It is possible that Yukiko had enacted the principle of *oyakoko* or some similar Japanese principle of relationship in the transference, one that, by mandating the respectful treatment of superiors, had obliged Yukiko not to challenge her therapist, but to defer to her authority.

In addition to having been compromised by unexamined cultural differences, Yukiko's treatment remained narrowly focused on her presenting problems and failed to address many other important concerns. One issue that was overlooked as a result was Yukiko's extreme unhappiness with her position as an outsider.

> I feel kind of sad because being here I'll never be American, but I'll be always a foreigner. And even when I go back to Japan right now, I'm not like a true Japanese anymore. Like I'm kind of very Americanized in some ways, and people sort of see me as a kind of a strange Japanese. So right now I feel that I'm not belonging to either of the two countries.

As Yukiko suggested, she had started to experience a shift from a "true Japanese" to a "very Americanized" sense of self. Not only had she begun to identify herself as a foreigner, but she frequently invoked the rhetoric of American individualism in her treatment in discussing the recent events in her life. For example, she characterized her parents' divorce as their problem, and she defied the principle of *oyakoko* by privileging her own life over her filial obligations to her mother.

> She's having such a hard time because she divorced my father. And after she started talking to me she told me that she's the one having such a hard time and I need to help her for what's happening to her. But I felt like I have my life too, you know. I actually have my own life. And I was very angry at her. She didn't try to understand me at all.

Yukiko's willingness to describe herself as depressed was another consequence of this shift to an Americanized self. I asked Yukiko if she had ever known any "true Japanese" who were depressed, and she replied,

> Not personally, but I think I have read about it or heard about it.
> . . . Like in Japan when you meet somebody and say "How are you
> doing?", you never say, "Oh, I'm down today." You try to be, "Oh
> I'm just fine" to be polite, I guess.

Americans, Yukiko said, were more honest about their emotions, and didn't mind saying, "Oh, I'm down, I'm depressed." Describing herself as depressed, then, corresponded to American rather than to Japanese norms governing the interpersonal presentation of self.

These alterations in her sense of self clearly entailed profound losses for Yukiko. The Japanese cultural values that had previously formed her sense of self had required her to be part of the group, to share some of the values other people share, and to "function with society." As a consequence of living as a foreigner in America, however, Yukiko became distanced from this group-based sense of self and attempted to adopt a self composed of "just me." But it was not only that Yukiko tried to embrace a more highly individualized, Americanized self; she also felt that she no longer fit into any group. Instead, Yukiko imagined that she was seen as a "strange Japanese" by other Japanese, and as a foreigner by Americans.

> Even if I stay here ten years, twenty years, I will always be consid-
> ered as a foreigner. And I don't think my Japanese accent will disap-
> pear, even when I have been here for thirty years or so. I feel like I
> would never be accepted as an American here.

If this statement expresses Yukiko's painful realization that she would never again belong to any group, then it also raises questions concerning her therapist's normalization of her behavior. For according to whose standards had Yukiko's behavior been normalized? Evidently, they were American standards; yet as Yukiko acknowledged, the United States was a foreign country, one to which she would never fully belong. Further, for Yukiko, the costs of being a "strange Japanese" were high. Yukiko's psychotherapist, however, had apparently failed to thoroughly explore with her patient the psychic consequences of her further differentiation from "true Japanese," nor had she seemed to recognize that her therapeutic interventions might exacerbate Yukiko's alienation from her native country.

With these considerations in mind, I was curious to learn how Yukiko had reacted to her therapist's interventions. I recalled that at the beginning of her treatment Yukiko had worried that she had done something terribly wrong to her mother, and that her therapist had assured her that she was not responsible for her mother's distress. When I asked Yukiko if she had believed what her therapist had told her, she replied, "Maybe not 100 percent, but I tried to believe it because I wanted to feel better. I wanted to get back to usual life, to function, to do daily routines. So I guess I tried to feel better."

Yukiko's account of her psychotherapy suggests that her psychotherapist had not, in fact, "considered all those different things which she doesn't need to do when she sees other American clients." Indeed, neither patient nor therapist seemed willing to undertake an open-ended and culturally informed examination of Yukiko's concerns. Yukiko clearly preferred to find quick solutions for her difficulties. "I think I was hoping that after I finish this, then we just go back to my normal life. Then we don't need to think about it." For her, being in psychotherapy remained stigmatizing, providing further evidence that she was strange. Although Yukiko voiced concerns about future depressive episodes, her return to normal life offered tangible proof that her current depression had been resolved.

If Yukiko had sought to limit the breadth and depth of her psychotherapy due to her cultural resistances to treatment, then it seems that her therapist had unknowingly complied. It may be that because they neglected to analyze the cultural differences between them, Yukiko and her therapist were unable to generate complex and culturally inflected understandings of the losses that Yukiko had incurred, of the shifts in her sense of self that had occurred, and of the suffering that she had endured.

Despite the intercultural problematics of Yukiko's psychotherapy, she found her treatment beneficial. She maintained that she valued her treatment for its normalization of her reactions, for its "relief effect," and for the opportunity it provided her to release her "true feelings" in a "private space" with an objective psychotherapist. After several therapy sessions, Yukiko, to her great relief, once again was able to "function with society." In fact, following her psychotherapeutic treatment, even Yukiko's relationship with her mother improved. Breaking nearly four years of silence, Yukiko's mother resumed communication with her daughter. As Yukiko told me, "I think she's really upset with me still about the fact that I did something so unusual. But she likes Rob very much."

8

Reconstruction: Rosa

Rosa's psychological treatment recalls previous subjects' intercultural psychotherapies in many respects. It too concerns a patient who was strongly identified with her ethnic group and with her native language, and who was antagonistic toward mainstream American society. Like Prakesh, Rosa, who was a Puerto Rican American, located her white psychotherapist within the dominant culture that had oppressed her ethnic group. Like Maria, she initially viewed her treatment as an opportunity to return the hostility that the white world had visited upon her. Constructing herself in terms of a series of cultural stereotypes, and imagining her "all-American" therapist as a hostile and powerful foreign object intent on destroying her, Rosa attempted to dominate her clinical treatment by rejecting her therapist's interventions, by refusing to participate in sessions, and by failing to show up for appointments.

Because Rosa's psychotherapy promoted Western ideals of selfhood, it exacerbated the contradictions she experienced between her American and Puerto Rican identities and intensified her fears of losing her core Puerto Rican self. Moreover, because her psychotherapy embraced Western conceptions of mental illness, of individual autonomy, and of emotional expression, it discouraged Rosa from expressing her distress in the contrasting terms of her indigenous culture. Yet despite these intercultural conflicts, Rosa was able to work through many of her preconceptions of psychotherapy and of her psychotherapist, and to use her treatment to begin to reconstruct her primary cultural identities.

"TARGET PRACTICE"

Rosa, who is in her early thirties, is a second year law student. The oldest child of parents who were born "on the island" of Puerto Rico, and who immigrated to the mainland of the United States as teenagers, Rosa was born and raised in New York City. As Rosa grew up in a Puerto Rican neighborhood on the city's Lower East Side, her first language was Spanish. Indeed, she did not learn to speak English until she went to kindergarten. Her parents have always addressed her in their native tongue.

After completing her undergraduate degree, Rosa entered a highly respected Midwestern law school. It was during her second year of study that Rosa began to worry that her circumstances had "pushed me over the edge." A number of situational difficulties marked Rosa's life at that time. Most distressing to her was the fact that her young son, who had lived with her during her first year of law school, had returned to New York to live with his father, from whom Rosa was divorced. Although Rosa recognized that she couldn't give him the care that he needed, she was anguished by their separation. In addition,

> For Puerto Ricans, children come first. And you as a mother, your main obligation should be your child. And the women not only in my family, but in his father's family, were pretty much not supportive. Every opportunity they had, they would tell me that I needed to rethink certain things.

Not only did Rosa feel pressured by her family to live up to Puerto Rican ideals of motherhood, but she felt pressured to excel in the extremely competitive environment of her law school.

When I came here, I was like, "You've gotta do this right. You've gotta do it perfectly, you can't fail at anything. You can't make one mistake, because if they see that, then that's it; your chances of doing what you wanna do or achieving the goals that you want to achieve are gonna be gone."

To add to these taxing circumstances, there were "issues with my family too, you know with my parents, and all this childhood stuff that seemed to be coming up. And so I think those three things just all kind of came together."

As a consequence, Rosa was having frequent anxiety attacks and feeling "totally, totally depressed." A friend of hers advised her to see a psychotherapist. At first Rosa refused to consider consulting a therapist, because it involved

> issues of taking family, personal things and sharing it with a stranger, which for me is something that I was taught not to do. I mean, you keep things within the family, and you keep things inside of yourself, and your problems are your problems, and only you can sort them out. Only you can take care of them, and no one else needs to know about it.

Not only would seeing a psychotherapist violate these family rules, but Rosa was convinced that it was a potentially dangerous endeavor. "You never know what they'll do with that kind of information. . . . [They might] use it against you, prevent you from achieving certain goals, jobs, career, things like that."

Yet despite her fears of sabotage and betrayal at the hands of a psychotherapist, Rosa told herself,

> "Well, you know, you can't do this alone anymore. You've hit rock bottom, and you've tried all the things that you know how to do, that may have worked for you in the past, that don't seem to be working for you now." So there was another voice inside me that said, "Well, you've got nothing to lose. You've got everything to gain." So I decided to do it.

Rosa decided to consult with a psychotherapist at a local social service agency. That she approached psychotherapy with great uneasiness was suggested by her determination to conceal her desperation from her therapist.

> It was, "Okay, I've gotta come here, [but] I can't let her know how messed up, destroyed, or broken up I am about certain things in my life." So even though I knew I was there to sort certain things out, the irony of it was that I went in there trying to posture that, "There are some things that are kinda messed up, but you know, I can handle them, I'll just share some things with you and mull it around, and I'll go home and poof, I'll take care of it."

In fact, Rosa approached psychotherapy with the intent to reproduce in her treatment the same boundary around personal issues and emotions that had been inscribed by her family.

> I still had set up a boundary in which, "Okay, you're there and I'm here, and there are just still some things that I'm not gonna let you know. There are just still some things that I'm not gonna talk about, and there's certain emotions that you're not gonna see."

It would have been difficult for Rosa to disclose her personal and emotional problems under ideal therapeutic conditions. But her need to protect herself by "not putting myself out there" intensified when she learned that the therapist to whom she had been assigned was white. Although Rosa had requested a therapist who was a woman of color, the local social service agency had had none available.

> So I went home and I thought about it, and I'm like, again, "What do I have to lose?" And I think a part of me was like, "Oh well, you know, we'll just do it," and didn't take it seriously, because she was a white woman.

Rosa imagined that her treatment would progress more smoothly were she in psychotherapy with a Puerto Rican therapist who, she believed, would have weathered difficulties that were similar to hers. She would quickly understand Rosa's predicament and get to the real root of the problems. Rosa imagined that her relationship with a Puerto Rican psychotherapist would be less one-sided than reciprocal; it would be a conversation between two women who were alike. Because her therapist was white, however, Rosa assumed that such conversations would be impossible, that her therapist would understand neither "the dysfunctional stuff with my family" nor her particular cultural background,

> in the sense of the time frame growing up, the early '70s, inner-city, being Puerto Rican. Being the first generation born on the mainland, being the first generation, my brother and I and my sister going on to college. And the tensions there with having to go home, back to New York, New York City, the Lower East Side, and all that stuff.

She also assumed that working with a white psychotherapist meant that she would have to undergo treatment in English, which was her second language.

> If the person doesn't speak Spanish, I will have to speak English. And some things, for me, I feel a whole lot more comfortable using certain Spanish words or phrases. So that for me, that became a barrier. Because I said to myself, "That means I won't be able to go in and just let it all hang out." And so that for me raised up a lot of issues of "Well, so then how beneficial is this therapy gonna be for you?"

More important was Rosa's belief that a woman of color would understand her current experience of culture shock in a hostile white environment, while a white psychotherapist would not.

> Coming here was just like, it was like going to a foreign country, it really felt like I was in a foreign country. And I think that in some ways a woman of color would have understood that complete invisibility with respect to gender and race and ethnicity. . . . I mean [people] thought I was mixed, biracial, whatever, and I got treated by black folks like crap, I got treated by white folks like crap, and I was just like, "As a Latina, where do I fit in this?"

Yet because Rosa also believed that she had "nothing to lose," she made an appointment to see a psychotherapist. "I was like, 'All right, you don't have a woman of color. What do you have in your spectrum of women?' And that's how I got paired up with Jan." Although Rosa thought that she had resigned herself to having a white psychotherapist, she was unprepared for her first encounter with Jan. In her eyes, Jan was "this image that we've all been bombarded with, that this is what you need to become: perfection." Moreover, to Rosa, Jan's perfection was culturally inflected. Jan was "like that all-American, Midwestern girl; blonde and tall, very feminine, very nice-looking white woman. And I'm like, 'This is what I need; to have the epitome of the American girl image right here in my face.'"

Constructing Jan as the all-American girl affected Rosa's orientation to her psychotherapy in various ways. It seemed to have the general effect of distancing her from her treatment.

> I really didn't take her seriously. Not that I thought she was an airhead or anything, but I'm like, "Oh boy, here we go . . . like oh boy, gotta be nice. She's gonna smile a lot, she's gonna be nice and cordial. I won't be able to curse and say 'shit' and all these other words. I can't be crass and crude." Because my image of her was that she was a nice, wholesome, American girl.

Sometimes, constructing her therapist as perfection caused Rosa to perceive herself as a collection of failures and flaws. At other times, it induced a competitive defensiveness in Rosa. For if her therapist were perfection, then "I can't just go in there and fall apart. You may be perfect, but I can be perfect too, in my ways. I know what I'm talking about; I'm not stupid, I'm not dumb." Further, competing with Rosa's idealization of Jan as perfection was a more acid view of her therapist as "a dragon lady," just like the other white women on campus.

> I've found them to be kind of vicious. And so at that point, I was just like, "Great, they'll smile at you and they'll stab you in the back." . . . I was just waiting, "Okay, when's that dragon lady gonna come out?"

Clearly, many of Rosa's various constructions of her therapist and of herself were culturally informed. In addition, these constructions were dialectically related to each other. For example, having envisioned Jan as the all-American girl caused Rosa to perceive herself as "a crazy, angry woman of color, inner-city, working class, and the negative baggage that comes with that." Rosa then assumed that her therapist shared this view of her, and that in Jan's eyes, "I was this ghetto kid just trying to make my way through this maze, and just couldn't cut it here at the university."

But it was Rosa's racialized construction of Jan that most deeply problematized her relationship to her therapist. For in Rosa's eyes Jan was white, and she had been taught never to trust whites.

> I got that from my dad since I can remember, as a small, small child. You don't trust white folks. They don't have your interests at heart, and all you can do is try and work situations to your own benefit. But you should never, ever trust them completely, because they'll stab you in the back.

Once Rosa had constructed Jan as white, Jan signified to her American society's mistreatment of Puerto Ricans.

> Here we are as Puerto Ricans in New York in a society that really doesn't want us and forced us to come here. My father would say, "New York sucks, the States suck, the American government sucks," on and on and on.

Such cultural constructions of herself and of her therapist initially shaped Rosa's responses to her treatment. Viewing herself as a member of an unwanted and disempowered ethnic group, and viewing her psychotherapist as a representative of the vindictive and "vicious" dominant culture, Rosa feared that her therapist would deliberately harm her. As a result, she determined to conceal her difficulties from Jan.

> Crying for me, especially in front of a stranger, especially in front of a white person, was just something like, it's taboo. You don't do that.

It's a sign of weakness; you're showing your wounds. You're making yourself vulnerable, and that's something that I think, indirectly, I was raised that you just—not with white folks you don't do that, because you don't know what they're gonna do. You can't let them know that you're in pain, especially if they've been the cause of so many things in your life. You can't give them that satisfaction.

She also determined to establish boundaries between herself and her psychotherapist.

It was just like certain boundaries, certain—I'll draw a line and we can play up until that line, and then I just won't cross, or I won't let her cross. So you know, it's like I gave her some, but not all.

But Rosa did not simply keep her therapist at bay. Rather, she endeavored to obliterate Jan's presence entirely by reducing her to a virtually inanimate "extra body."

In some ways I felt that, "Well I'll just go in there and talk about myself, for me, and kind of in a way not even include her as part of the process." I think what I had resigned myself to was kind of doing it the way I had done it, only here was an extra body—a white woman who I didn't take seriously, but I'll go through the motions.

Going through the motions, Rosa barely participated in her psychotherapy. She regularly arrived late for sessions, and sometimes missed sessions entirely without calling Jan to cancel them.

I'd be like, "Oh, whatever! I'm running late, so what!" I'd get really, like, "I'll get there when I get there." And some days, I'm like, "I don't wanna go, but I gotta go. I'll get there when I get there." And I know I pissed her off, and I think part of it was kind of, just maybe even to piss her off.

Perhaps Rosa was determined to make her psychotherapist feel as invisible and as powerless as she had felt living among nothing but white people. Certainly, she saw her psychotherapy as a microcosm of the hostile outside world. "I was acting out with her what I was going through with other white folks or white women and other people of color." But Rosa was not interested in re-creating the racial politics that defined her daily experience; instead, she sought to overturn them. That Rosa saw her psychotherapy as an opportunity to vent her rage at the white world was clear. "In some ways, Jan was the dummy, you know, that I would shoot and beat up and target practice with. This was my session, and I pretty much did what I wanted."

By transforming her psychotherapist into a "dummy," Rosa attempted to avenge the many wrongs that she felt whites had inflicted upon her.

> She was a white person, and in some ways I knew she was soaking this up. And so there was a sense of almost, like, healing for me, I think, in being able to do that. . . . I was like, "This was my therapy session, I'm paying for it, and so I'm in control, and she'll have to handle it. And if she doesn't like it, she can tell me, 'Well, I can't be your therapist anymore!'"

This passage suggests that if Rosa wished to do violence to Jan because of the healing it provided her, then she also fantasized about provoking Jan into an angry retaliation that would cause her to stop the treatment. Indeed, Rosa seemed determined to expose the "dragon lady" in Jan. But if Rosa was waiting for Jan to finally "stab me in the back," then she clearly was surprised by her therapist's reaction. For Jan did not metamorphose into the malignant white object that Rosa imagined her to be. Instead, she simply expressed her frustration with Rosa's resistances to treatment.

> I got a sense that she felt that I really wasn't working on myself in those sessions—all I did was come in there and whine, whine, whine, and complain, complain, complain—and that I really wasn't putting forth the effort to sort certain things out. And I saw that she got angry with me, and she said, you know, "You've kept me waiting," stuff like that. And I was like, "Oh, I've kept her waiting, okay." It was like

she threw a glass of cold water in my face, and I'm like, "Whoa, she talks back!"

While Rosa had anticipated that she would take pleasure in antagonizing Jan, her actual reactions were more complex.

> So I was like, "Okay, so she's not happy with my progress here, and I have mixed emotions about that, and so what!" And the other part was like, "Oh my God, now what does she really think about you? Does she think you're crazy, does she think you're a nut, does she think you need to be institutionalized?" So it was a mixed bag.

As Rosa suggests, a further aspect of her resistance to treatment stemmed from her worry that she was indeed a "nut" who needed to be institutionalized. Rosa apparently feared that if she were forthcoming in her therapy, her instability would be obvious to Jan. This piece of her resistance to treatment was fraught with the negative meanings that psychotherapy carries "for Latinos and Latinas."

> I remember my sister, she had some problems in school, and a guidance counselor suggested she go see a therapist. And my father was like, "She's not crazy, she's not crazy, she's not going anywhere!" Oh you know, "'F' those white people, they don't know anything about us, blah, blah, everything is go to therapy." And I think I believed that to a certain extent.

Psychotherapy, in Rosa's view, belonged to the world of oppressive and intrusive white people, and represented their sociopolitical power over Puerto Ricans. According to her father, psychological treatment had been inappropriately imposed on Puerto Ricans, perhaps as a means of social control.

But for Rosa, being in psychotherapy also meant "that I had to be really, really leaning toward that edge of craziness as opposed to being sane." While Rosa wished to conceive of her craziness as a natural response to the overwhelming environmental stressors she faced, she constructed her difficulties as intrinsic to her. In doing so, however, she employed Puerto Rican notions of mental illness. When I asked Rosa to explain these notions to me, she mentioned their two central categories, *padecer de los nervios*—literally, to suffer from nerves—and *loca*. She defined the first as the feminized condition of nervousness.

> I think in Puerto Rican culture, women are always portrayed as *las nerviosas*: always nervous, obsessing about things, not being able to be rational, not thinking straight, and always needing a man to kind of just get them back on track. You know, growing up . . . women were kind of demonized whenever they spoke out and said something about how they were feeling; "Oh it's all in your head, you're crazy, go see a doctor, here are some pills." It's kind of made into, like, this woman's thing, you know, women are always *padecer de los nervios*.

Loca, on the other hand, connoted a complex of unacceptable behaviors. A *loca*, Rosa said, was a female who had lost her mind, who didn't know what she was talking about, who had no common sense, and who was stubborn and hardheaded. A *loca*, in other words, referred equally to Puerto Rican women who were unstable, irrational, or independent. According to Rosa, *locas* invariably received the same type of response from males.

> The first reaction is like, "Ay, that's nothing, you're making a mountain out of a molehill," let's say, "You're just being a *loca*, just shake yourself up and do what you have to do." . . . "Oh, you're a woman, you're just being moody, just stop complaining, stop whining, just do what you have to do, just do it."

For Rosa, the concepts of *loca* and *nervios* were not mere abstractions. Rather, she had had wrenching firsthand experiences of them, as her mother had a long history of emotional problems.

> I remember my mom, my mom had a nervous breakdown when I was about 4 or 5 and again when I was like 8. And so then hearing my father, whenever my mother kind of stood up for herself; "Oh, you're crazy, go see a shrink, *tu es loca*," just, you know, "Get outta here."

But Rosa's mother was not the only *loca* and *nerviosa* in the family; Rosa's father had often used these terms to describe her.

> It's funny, growing up my father would say that, "*Tu es nerviosa*," that I was nervous. And it's funny, because that's something that he always claimed about my mother, *padecer de los nervios*, that's why she couldn't think straight, that she was crazy.

Further, Rosa had clearly internalized such views of herself. For Rosa, being independent was associated with being crazy; she was convinced that she was "just a *loca*, a *nerviosa*." Thus, unbeknownst to Jan, Rosa understood her presenting complaint in Puerto Rican terms, as *nervios*. As she explained,

> I had reached the ultimate level of *nervios*—you know there are different levels, this is the way I saw it—in which, I'm out of control. So one of the initial things that drove me to therapy was, well, you're really out of control. You can't even control your nervousness now.

Rosa's sense of how to best address the problem of her *nervios* was also culturally determined. Certain that others would castigate her for her weakness, her solution was to hide it.

> It would bubble up and . . . I was always kinda stuffing it in, 'cause, you know, that was a part of me that I couldn't show anybody, 'cause it was the ultimate sign of weakness, and I couldn't show that. I wasn't raised to allow that part of me to be out there, or to be accepted.

Rosa's understandings of her emotional difficulties in Puerto Rican terms, however, undermined her participation in treatment. The constructions of psychological disturbance and cure that she attributed to Puerto Rican culture contradicted those of psychotherapeutic theories. For example, Rosa explained that Puerto Rican culture discouraged emotional expression, not only because it was an unacceptable show of weakness, but because it demonstrated an intrinsic, and therefore unchangeable, female flaw. Rosa accepted the Puerto Rican view that her *nervios* would never be eradicated. What she desired from psychotherapy was not an investigation into the causes and meanings of her *nervios*, but a method for their containment.

> What made me go see someone was that I felt that I couldn't control this nervous condition that I had, and I had to talk to someone so I could just stuff it back in its nice little space inside of me and just leave it there. . . . Just sew myself up and keep on going.

The conventional theories of psychotherapy, however, caution against the repression of anxieties, and recommend that they be uncovered and aired. Rosa feared that this process would cause the ruin of everything that she had achieved.

> Just let me control it, 'cause you can't see what's really inside of me. 'Cause if you do, you're gonna think it's the most disgusting, most craziest, out of control thing in the world. And you won't know what to do with it, and you'll probably get scared, and then—I don't know how somebody else will react. Would they be violent, would they suggest that I need to be institutionalized?

If Rosa's initial treatment goal was to simply control her nervousness, however, Jan's confrontation of her was a turning point that caused her to conceptualize her therapy differently. For Rosa evidently concluded that her treatment would be pointless unless she suppressed her native views of *nervios* and accepted those of her psychotherapist.

> I went in there thinking therapy was one thing, and Jan had her own conception of it. . . . I think there was a battle there, about how the therapy was gonna go. And it's not that she won out; I think that I realized that I was wasting my time if I was just gonna dance around certain things and just always had my face up, that facade up. That it would be totally counterproductive.

This confrontation with her therapist also caused her to reconstruct Jan.

I still couldn't have been bothered with white women as a group, and
didn't trust them as a group. I saw Jan as the exception, I really did. She
didn't reinforce certain stereotypes I had, at least in our therapy sessions, of white women. She wasn't judgmental. She wasn't pushy. She
wasn't domineering. She wasn't cutthroat. But at the same time, she
wasn't the nice little all-American white girl who needs to be seen and
not heard. When she had something to say, she said it, and when she
wanted to push me on certain things, she did. So I grew to respect her
a lot, I grew to respect her a whole lot. But I still saw her as an exception.

Once Rosa had reconstructed Jan as an exception rather than as a representative of a domineering and cutthroat group, the therapeutic alliance
improved. Collaborating with Jan and her Western vision of psychological dysfunction and healing, Rosa experienced a productive period of
therapy, during which she benefited from symptomatic relief and from
a deeper understanding of her conflicts and anxieties.

But after several months of treatment, Rosa decided that further
psychological progress depended on her returning home to New York
City. She found it impossible to resolve long-standing family issues from
such a distanced place.

> Even though I felt that I had made a lot of progress on certain things,
> it was still very external to me. It felt like I needed to be home to kind
> of work out some of this stuff. I had to get in touch with a part of me
> that was so inside of me that I had to go back to my family and kind
> of deal with certain things.

Rosa also found it difficult to explore certain issues with Jan because
her psychotherapy was conducted entirely in English, and she could only
express certain parts of herself in Spanish. "Spanish in some ways really
speaks to the real who I am, deep, deep, deep down inside. I don't think
I can translate that, I really don't." Moreover, Rosa wished to reattach
herself to cultural things that formed a core of her sense of self.

> I think what I needed to recapture in my life was cultural things that
> I loved; the language, and certain ways of being, that for me since I

can remember as a little girl, I felt was trapped inside of me. That one day I realized "Wow, this is who I am, this is a very core part of who I am." And so I needed to go back to that for a while.

It is striking that once Rosa realized "who I am," she could no longer make use of the psychotherapy that had brought her to this realization. Perhaps this was because the sense of self that her psychotherapy had fostered contrasted with the sense of self that was trapped inside her, and that she longed to recapture. Indeed, when Rosa described herself, she referenced two distinct and divergent cultural selves: a "very core" self that had formed in her childhood, and a secondary self that had developed out of her later experiences as a law school student, and as a patient of psychotherapy, in a site of cultural displacement.

That Rosa experienced these cultural selves as in conflict with each other was apparent. Her psychotherapy encouraged her to be emotionally expressive rather than restrained, active rather than passive, and independent rather than submissive, qualities that, according to her view of Puerto Rican culture, defined her as a *loca*. Rosa clearly valued these qualities and desired to maintain them, but not if it required her to relinquish her core connections. Interpreted from this perspective, it seems that Rosa needed to return to New York City not only to recapture her indigenous culture following her separation from her home, but to discover whether she could integrate her newly proactive and autonomous sense of self with the Puerto Rican ways of being that formed her core.

> I had to kind of go back into the niche or the role that I was in, and kind of work with that and play with that. But not just being a person or something that was just sitting there that was being acted upon, but also being very, very conscious and very, very aware, and also being very much a part of what was happening. Because I, too, was making choices, and I, too, had an impact on my other family members too.

After several months in New York City, Rosa returned to law school to complete her degree. While she had been in New York, she had kept in touch with Jan with the intention of resuming treatment with her when she returned to school. But although Rosa credited her psychotherapy with helping her see and work through numerous issues at home, when she resumed her weekly psychotherapy sessions she felt removed from them. Once again, she was conscious of the cultural gap between herself and her therapist, and once again, as a result, she withheld personal material from Jan.

> I think in those months that I went back home and then had to come back and explain to Jan what happened, [it] was difficult in some ways, because it just couldn't be translated. It was something that was very deep and profound. . . . I think music for me became like a metaphor in the months I was there. And I just knew she didn't understand what that meant, because it's just a culture I came from in which music is who we are, it's how we express ourselves, it's how we tell our stories and our history, and that was really important for me. And so I don't remember even saying much about that to her.

Although Rosa continued to attend psychotherapy, she was more keenly aware of its limitations.

> We could only talk about things on certain levels, and then after that, it just couldn't go any farther. So I could talk about my family and my experiences almost in a . . . how can I put it, in a clean way, in a really kind of just, I don't know, what's the word? I guess I couldn't be raw about certain things. The rawness of my experience of course I couldn't bring in on certain levels, because I just couldn't translate that, the fullness of all the experiences.

It is conceivable that once she had reconnected with her Puerto Rican identity, Rosa felt alienated from the Westernized identity that had been strengthened by her psychotherapy with Jan. She became increasingly frustrated with her therapist's distance from Puerto Rican culture, considering it an obstacle to her treatment.

> I shouldn't have to sit down and bang my head to try to explain something to someone when the only way they can know it is by walking

in my shoes, and the likelihood of her doing that was probably zero at that point. And so I was like, "Well, I can't keep talking to her about it, and talking to myself about it, I need more." And she just couldn't take me there.

Thus, although she acknowledged that she had previously benefited from psychotherapy, Rosa concluded her treatment much as she had begun it, feeling culturally disconnected from her therapist and doubting psychotherapy's value to her.

Rosa's psychotherapy was characterized by three distinct phases. There was an initial phase of battle, in which she overtly challenged her therapist and resisted her psychotherapy largely because saw Jan as a representative of the white world. This was followed by a middle phase of collaboration, in which Rosa distinguished Jan from other white women, accepted her conception of psychological treatment, and cooperated in establishing a therapeutic alliance. The third and final phase was one of frustration and disengagement, in which Rosa withdrew from her psychotherapy with Jan because she couldn't translate the cultural meanings and experiences that were most profound to her.

In Rosa's psychotherapy, the divergent cultural worlds of patient and therapist did not present insurmountable obstacles to treatment, and yet they contributed to its termination. Clearly, many of the experiences and conceptions that determined her sense of herself were foreign to Jan. According to Rosa, there was scant possibility of Jan ever "walking in [my] shoes." In other words, for Rosa, there was little chance that Jan would ever grasp the contingencies of her life.

Rosa had entered psychological treatment conceptualizing her troubles in Puerto Rican terms. In her eyes, she was a *loca* who had "reached the ultimate level of *nervios*." Yet although Rosa held such culturally determined understandings of herself and of her psychological state, during her year and a half of psychotherapy she neglected to convey these Puerto Rican constructions of her difficulties to her therapist, so that they never became the subject of therapeutic inquiry. It is conceivable that a cultural psychotherapy—oriented toward the systematic examination of Rosa's indigenous ideologies of psychic functioning—would have helped avert the therapeutic impasse that restricted Rosa's treatment, and finally brought it to a close.

Part III

Conclusion

9

Constructing a Cultural Psychotherapy

CULTURE IN THE CLINIC

How might the six interviews analyzed in Part II inform the clinical treatments of foreign and ethnic patients? The central lesson of these interviews, and their primary challenge to standard psychotherapeutic views, derives from their finding that human psychologies are culturally as well as individually constituted, and that as a result, the psychological is inevitably cultural. Specifically, these interviews contradict conventional clinical constructions of psychological dysfunction in terms of Western and universalizing therapeutic discourses and diagnostic categories. In addition, they contest clinical perspectives that reduce foreign and ethnic patients' discussions of cultural material, including alternative cultural metapsychologies, to resistances to, or defenses against, psychological treatment. As the interviews presented in Chapters 3 through 8 demonstrate, the specific cultural formations of foreign and ethnic patients, as well as the cultural differences between them and their therapists, deeply and continually shape psychological treatments.

In stating that the psychological is inevitably cultural, I do not mean to suggest that all persons of the same nationality or ethnicity are psychologically identical. Nor do I claim that all foreign and ethnic patients from a particular cultural background experience emotional difficulties and psychological treatments in exactly the same way. As I argued in the introduction to Part I, there is extensive intracultural variation in individual psychologies. Due to disparities in gender, age, ethnicity, and social class, among other factors, individuals from similar cultural backgrounds internalize and reproduce cultural norms and ideals in idiosyncratic ways. Intracultural variations in individual subjectivities and behaviors are magnified among those who migrate across ethnic and national borders, as do many of the foreign and ethnic patients who enter psychotherapy in the United States. Such persons typically piece together their divergent cultural worlds and experiences, creating person-specific cultural identities that have been characterized as "hybridities" (Bhabha 1994, p. 2). Yet it is also clear that the various assumptions, worldviews, values, ideals, and norms that many foreign and ethnic patients have internalized, and that have shaped their psychologies, differ significantly from the Western ones that are embedded in standard psychotherapies. Thus, while I do not propose that all Indian men will respond to personal difficulties or to psychological treatment as Prakesh did, or that all Mexican-Americans will construct themselves and their psychotherapists as Maria did, I do claim that foreign and ethnic patients' particular cultural backgrounds deeply affect their senses of self and their subjectivities, and so must be seriously considered in their psychological treatments.

This chapter presents the general themes of the six intercultural treatments presented in Chapters 3 through 8. These chapters illustrate the cultural dimensions of intercultural treatments in several ways. First, they demonstrate that because both parties involved in psychological treatments have particular cultural histories and identities, and because both occupy specific cultural positions, psychotherapeutic encounters are inevitably cultural encounters. Second, these interviews show that although the standard theories of psychotherapy have traditionally constructed such central psychotherapeutic concepts as presenting problems, transferences, countertransferences, and resistances to treatment as phenomena that are exclusively psychological, such clinical phenomena also embody particular and significant cultural meanings and functions. Third, these interviews illustrate that anthropology's cultural approaches to the self, to emotion, to development, and to language offer clinicians new ways of conceptualizing and accessing the culturally organized lived experiences and subjectivities of foreign and ethnic patients. In addition to examining the general themes that emerged from this research, this chapter raises new questions about intercultural treatments that require further study. In its final sections, this chapter suggests specific, culturally informed approaches to intercultural psychotherapies.

Cultural Presenting Problems

Although the standard theories of psychotherapy do not construct them as such, the research presented in Chapters 3 through 8 demonstrates that all presenting problems are cultural. One way in which the presenting problems of the subjects interviewed here were cultural was in their content. Embedded in the presenting problems of every subject were culturally specific conceptions of self, of others, of relationship, and of emotion. For example, Yukiko's opening complaint, which contained the anguished narrative of her estrangement from her mother, provides a Japanese account of filial obligations, or *oyakoko*, and of the harsh penalties that may befall those who fail to honor them. This presenting complaint cannot be fully understood if it is divorced from its Japanese context and assimilated to Western conceptions of separation and individuation in late adolescence. Only by viewing it within the matrix of culturally configured family relationships and culturally distinctive, relationally embedded selves might a Western therapist grasp what this problem meant to Yukiko. The marital crisis portrayed in Meena's initial complaint provides another clear example of the culturally specific content of presenting problems. Meena's marital crisis took shape in response to particular Indian constructions of self, marriage, divorce, shame, and dishonor. For Western therapists to comprehend the complex meanings and implications of Meena's predicament requires them to understand such cultural constructions.

The contents of these subjects' presenting problems were also cultural in that they embodied specific cultural metapsychologies. Most of these subjects entered psychotherapy with indigenous conceptions of emotional instability and repair, conceptions that differed significantly from their psychotherapists' Western ideologies of psychological dysfunction and cure. Prakesh, for example, did not experience his condition as one of an internal dysphoria, or depression, but as one of external trouble, or *mushkil*—a situation that, in his view, clinical treatments could not remedy. Other subjects appeared to have plural cultural metapsychologies, and to conceptualize their distress from both indigenous and Western perspectives. Yet even when subjects entered psychotherapy characterizing themselves and their difficulties in terms of the standard categories of Western psychiatry, the ways in which they employed these categories diverged in important respects from their conventional psychiatric significations. Unbeknownst to their therapists, these subjects had invested these standard categories with culturally specific meanings. Thus, Rosa's representation of her difficulties to her therapist as "anxiety attacks" masked the fact that she also experienced her psychological distress, and herself, in terms of the Puerto Rican categories of *loca* and *nerviosa*. Similarly, Yukiko's descriptions of herself to her therapist as "depressed" concealed that fact that she understood depression in Japanese terms, as involving disturbances in public functioning, social conformity, and belonging—factors that, moreover, defined the terms of psychological recovery.

A further cultural dimension of these subjects' presenting problems concerned their formal properties. Most subjects entered treatment presenting externalized, isolable, and situational complaints—a damaged ear, a jealous husband, an estranged mother—for which they sought immediate and practical solutions. As a rule, they demonstrated little interest in examining underlying psychological patterns and processes or in pursuing open-ended or exploratory treatments. Meena's claim that she had sought clinical treatment to rectify her desperate situation rather than to explore fundamental character issues typified both the forms these subjects' presenting problems assumed and their limited expectations of psychotherapy.

For these subjects, such concrete and circumscribed approaches to treatment were multiply determined. Certainly, as discussed in the in-

troduction to Part I, their approaches were shaped in part by the socializing functions of preliminary clinical procedures, which inclined these
subjects to eliminate indigenous cultural ideologies and narrative detail
from their presenting complaints. Moreover, all of these subjects were
from segments of societies in which the practice of psychotherapy was
uncommon. According to their reports, in their home communities
psychiatric treatments were provided only to those who were severely
disturbed, and mental disorders were viewed as causing family embar-
rassment and shame. As Meena explained, for Indians of her cultural
background to seek psychological help was taboo. Jun claimed that
Koreans who underwent mental health treatments risked jeopardizing
their families' social positions, while according to Yukiko, Japanese who
engaged in psychological treatment were stigmatized. Given their negative views of both psychological disability and psychological treatment,
it is unsurprising that many of these subjects defined their presenting
complaints as delimited, external problems, and that they sought quick
and concrete remedies for them.

But in addition, these subjects were keenly aware of the cultural
divergences between themselves and their therapists in worldviews and
experiences. Their sensitivities in this regard shaped their presenting
problems as well. Many subjects feared that because their therapists were
unfamiliar with their cultural backgrounds, they would misunderstand
and misjudge them. Prakesh expressed the concern that his therapist
found his cultural background peculiar and deprived; Maria worried that
her therapist condemned her *compadres'* activities. Like Meena, who
refused to be reduced to an inscrutable and exotic specimen of alterity,
such considerations discouraged these subjects from incorporating indigenous categories and concepts—even those that were central to their
difficulties—into their presenting problems.

Cultural Transferences

In Chapter 1, I expressed my skepticism regarding the universality of
the classical transference concept, a concept that suggests that patients
experience their therapists as persons with whom they had early and

primary relationships. On the basis of my interviews with the subjects of this research, it is difficult to determine whether they developed transferences to their therapists in the classical sense. Yet it is clear that they established "modernist" (Cooper 1987, p. 77) versions of transferences; that is, they formed specific constructions of their psychotherapists, developed distinct feelings about them, and enacted particular types of relationships with them in their clinical sessions.

Like presenting problems, all transferences are cultural as well as psychological. That tranferences have escaped being comprehended as such is largely due to the fact that most psychotherapies involve patients and therapists of culturally similar backgrounds. Under conditions of cultural similarity, therapist and patient are likely to share basic assumptions about persons, about the mind, and about reality. They are also likely to share cultural assumptions about relationships, similarly defining normal and expectable patterns of interaction. When patient and therapist share cultural conceptions of relationships, the cultural nature of transference virtually disappears; rarely does it create complications for the treatment. In such cases, differences in patterns of relationship are constructed as psychological, and are ascribed to variations in individual subjectivities and histories. Only in intercultural treatments does the cultural nature of transference clearly emerge.

Transferences are necessarily cultural because, as these interviews demonstrate, the interpersonal experiences, internalized objects, senses of self, and relational patterns that constitute transferences are culturally shaped. In each case examined in this research, various cultural features of transferences were elaborated. Indeed, a primary finding is that its subjects were incapable of conceptualizing their therapists as either culturally decontextualized or culturally neutral objects. Instead, they constructed them as fully culturally contextualized persons with particular cultural characteristics who belonged to specific segments of American society.

In some ways, the transferences that developed in these six intercultural treatments resembled those that commonly emerge in psychotherapies between culturally similar patients and therapists. These subjects' transferences tended to be multilayered and ambivalent. Often they were fluid, shifting in substance and in emotional valence as the treatments progressed. Like transferences in same-culture psychotherapies, the transferences that the subjects described were dialogically engaged with their various and evolving experiences of themselves.

Yet the transferences described by the subjects differed in many respects from those that are common in same-culture treatments. For example, athough their precise features varied from subject to subject, most of the cultural transferences that emerged in the beginning phases of these treatments were negative. In these cases, subjects' encounters with therapists from different cultures evoked the feelings of alienation and estrangement that previously have been reported (Basch-Kahre 1984). Such feelings found expression in these subjects' constructions of their therapists in terms of their irreducible alterity. Most identified their therapists as members of diametrically opposed cultural categories. Rosa, who saw herself as Puerto Rican, experienced her American therapist as white, while Maria, who identified herself as a Chicana, constructed her therapist as Anglo. In like fashion Meena, who considered herself non-Western, related to her therapist as a Westerner, and Prakesh, who described himself as a member of the Third World, viewed his psychotherapist as First World. Clearly, these subjects constructed their therapists not as culturally neutral individuals, but as the representatives of particular cultural groups. Because their experiences with these groups tended to have been unfavorable, their initial transferences to their therapists were predominantly negative.

Further, many of these subjects experienced their therapists not simply as the other, but as the enemy. When previous contact between the subjects and the groups within which they situated their therapists had been malignant, as was the case for Maria and Rosa, negative transferences containing intense racial and ethnic prejudices and stereotypes immediately surfaced. Subjects who experienced such hostile negative transferences transformed the clinical consulting room into a replica of the larger social environment, reenacting their daily racialized battles within it. Thus Rosa, who constructed her therapist as white, turned her psychotherapy into a microcosm of her struggles with the white world. When patients constructed the sociopolitical relationships between their cultural groups and those to which they assigned their therapists as adversarial, as did Prakesh and Maria, hostilities and competitions that were grounded in cultural antagonisms saturated the transference.

The positive transferences that emerged in the early phases of treatment also tended to embody stereotyped cultural forms and meanings. Commonly, they were based not on therapists' personal attributes, but on their professional categories and roles. The positive transferences that Yukiko and Meena experienced early in their treatments, for example, were derived from their constructions of their American therapists as objective and professionally trained. Accordingly, foreign and ethnic patients from cultures in which less individualized notions of the person predominate might be expected to develop stereotyped, role-centered transferences to their psychotherapists. Patients from hierarchically ordered societies—those in which interactions with persons of professional status are likely to be governed by specific cultural prescriptions—might also be expected to experience their therapists primarily in terms of their professional roles.

The precise cultural composition of their transferences strongly affected the ways in which the subjects of this research conducted themselves as psychotherapy patients. Typically, these subjects' cultural transferences defined the parameters of therapeutic encounters by determining whether they should disclose or conceal particular emotional reactions, personal and family information, and cultural detail. Because Rosa initially experienced her therapist as a powerful and sadistic white, for example, she refused to show Jan her anguish and withheld important emotional responses and material from her. Similarly, because Jun constructed her psychoanalyst as a sexually permissive American man who would encourage her forbidden wishes, she hid her sexual fantasies from him. But other subjects found that constructing their psychotherapists along Western lines facilitated disclosures that would have been impossible to make in the presence of a culture-near psychotherapist. For example, by differentiating her therapist from Indian categories of maleness, she effectively neutered his gender. As a result, she was able to discuss sexual topics with him that she could never have broached with an Indian man. Similarly, by constructing her therapist as objective, Yukiko set her apart from traditional Japanese standards and perspectives. She thus was able to confide in her therapist without fears of being considered strange.

As their intercultural psychotherapies evolved, many of the cultural transferences described by these subjects underwent transformations. Substantive shifts in transference commonly occurred in the middle phases of treatment. In some cases, positive transferences emerged when the subjects experienced improvements in their condition, and when they felt that their therapists genuinely were concerned about them. All of the positive transferences that developed here entailed subjects' reconstructions of their therapists, which tended to transcend initial cultural stereotypes and to minimize cultural antagonisms and differences through the identification of common ground. For the first time in treatment, therapists were accorded an individuality that distinguished them, to some extent, from their larger cultural groups. Rosa, while continuing to experience her psychotherapist as white, reconstructed Jan as an exception to the white women she knew. Maria, while continuing to regard her therapist as an Anglo, redefined her as a rare, trustworthy Anglo. Preexisting positive transferences deepened; some took on particular indigenous cultural forms. For example, as Meena's positive transference to her therapist grew to extend beyond an appreciation of his social-science skills she reconceptualized him in Indian terms, viewing him as someone who possessed wisdom because he had "seen many summers." The research reported here suggests that without such movement away from rigid cultural stereotypes, intercultural psychotherapies are likely to stall early in treatment, as was the case for Prakesh.

A further finding of this research, however, was that negative cultural transferences frequently resurfaced in the final phases of psychotherapy. As subjects gained confidence in their therapists and revealed more intimate material to them, intense feelings of cultural opposition and estrangement were reignited, causing them once again to retreat from their therapists. In the later stages of her treatment, Maria regained the sense that because her therapist was not her "blood," she could never fully let her in. Rosa came to the similar conclusion that because her therapist would never "walk in my shoes," she would never be able to grasp her core. Reexperiencing their therapists as diametrically opposed others, some subjects concluded that such cultural differences constituted insurmountable barriers to further therapeutic progress. Rather than attempting to overcome these differences, they terminated their treatments.

The transferences described by the subjects were also cultural in that they embodied specific non-Western models of relationship. Reconstructing her therapist as a wise elder, Meena reproduced Indian relational patterns in which a young woman might seek help and comfort from her seniors. Relying in part on nonverbal exchanges of feeling and mood with her therapist, Yukiko employed Japanese modes of interpersonal communication and interaction. Cultural dimensions of transferences such as these pose challenges to therapists who conduct intercultural treatments. Although they could not be certain, both Meena and Yukiko maintained that their therapists appeared to have been unaware of the cultural models of relationship that they had enacted in their sessions. This research thus raises questions regarding the consequences for intercultural treatments when patients develop cultural transferences whose foreign characteristics and relational obligations are unfamiliar to their therapists, and that therefore cannot be apprehended or analyzed.

Cultural Countertransferences

Therapists' countertransferences affect the progress and outcomes of all psychotherapies, including—and perhaps especially—those in which psychotherapist and patient are culturally dissimilar. Although countertransference reactions remain an undertheorized area in intercultural clinical practice, recent clinical research has described the various "ethnocultural countertransferences" (Comas-Diaz and Jacobsen 1991, p. 392) that can develop when therapists treat patients from other cultures. Recent research indicates that psychotherapists often feel ill at ease in treating patients from other cultures. Common countertransference reactions include experiencing feelings of guilt and aggression toward foreign and ethnic patients, and reducing them to cultural stereotypes. Some therapists disapprove of such patients' cultural beliefs, practices, and politics; in a few cases, psychotherapists have refused to treat foreign and ethnic patients whom they have found extremely unreachable or antagonistic (Foster 1996b, Gorkin 1996, Moskowitz 1996). While such studies are informative, they fall short of drawing the conclusion that all countertransferences are cultural.

Because this research was designed to examine the treatment assessments of patients rather than psychotherapists, the therapists who treated these subjects were not interviewed, and an informed discussion of their cultural countertransferences is precluded. Thus we cannot know for certain how Rosa's therapist experienced her patient's angry confrontations, how Yukiko's therapist reacted to her patient's frequent silences, how Jun's analyst responded to his patient's emotional disengagement, or how Meena's therapist felt about treating a patient whose emotional vocabulary and cultural concepts fell outside of his grasp. Based on these subjects' reports of their psychotherapies, however, we are familiar with many aspects of their treatments. We know that in all six treatments, there were significant differences between patients and therapists in cultural formation, in native language, in metapsychology, in patterns of relationship, and in treatment expectations. We also know that most of these subjects acted out in their treatments; they withheld information and concealed affects, deliberately provoked their therapists, and subjected them to longstanding cultural antagonisms. These subjects' reports of their treatment give us the sense that they were challenging patients—in Yukiko's words, that they presented their therapists with "extra troubles."

In light of these subjects' reports, some preliminary observations about cultural countertransferences can be made. This study supports the view that psychotherapists who treat patients from other cultures are likely to experience countertransference reactions that differ from those they experience when treating patients from similar cultural backgrounds. In intercultural treatments, therapists' early countertransference reactions can be expected to contain unexamined cultural prejudices and stereotypes. Moreover, the unfamiliar presenting problems, senses of self, family configurations, cultural concepts, metapsychologies, and forms of interaction that psychotherapists routinely encounter in intercultural treatments are likely to produce countertransference feelings of disconnection, discomfort, and frustration—feelings that can deprive therapists of their usual clinical bearings and compromise their clinical skills.

Therapists who conduct same-culture treatments have discovered that analyzing their countertransference reactions deepens their understanding of their patients' psychological worlds. These benefits extend to intercultural treatments as well. Psychotherapists who experience countertransference feelings of disapproval, estrangement, or incompetence when treating foreign and ethnic patients might interpret such feelings as indicators of differences between themselves and their patients in cultural assumptions and ideologies, rather than as evidence of their patients' psychopathology. Therapists who feel frustrated by the difficulties in establishing clinical alliances with foreign and ethnic patients might understand such difficulties in light of divergent patterns of relationship and communication rather than as signs of either party's relational deficits. By providing critical insights into patients' culturally colored internal worlds and interactive patterns, the analysis of cultural countertransferences can enrich intercultural psychotherapies.

Cultural Resistances

Freud (1924) identified the analysis of patients' resistances to change as a central task of psychoanalytic treatment. According to classical psychoanalysts, resistances are grounded in patients' unconscious early childhood conflicts and are intrapsychic in origin and operation. As psychoanalytic theories have evolved over the years, these views of resistances have been challenged. Recent conceptions of resistances, especially those that are grounded in two-person models of treatment, construct resistances as jointly created by patients and clinicians, rather than as produced and experienced intrapsychically by patients alone (Boesky 1990). Although such reformulations offer expanded conceptions of resistances, they continue to construct resistances to treatment as psychological phenomena. Neither classical nor newly revised conceptions acknowledge the cultural nature of resistances. As a result, they cannot account for the resistances to treatment described by the subjects of this research.

That resistances to psychological treatment, like presenting problems, transferences, and countertransferences, are cultural, embedding culturally specific meanings and motivations and taking particular cultural forms, was clearly demonstrated by this research. In part, these subjects' resistances to treatment were the consequences of their cultural metapsychologies, which, in most cases, were unrelated to psychotherapy's ideologies of psychic disturbance and repair. Just as Americans who fall ill when traveling abroad are apt to mistrust the diagnostic skills, healing capabilities, and remedies of local curers, most of the subjects of this research lacked faith in Western psychological treatments. Meena initially saw no causal link between discussing her problems in therapy and gaining psychological relief. Even as she entered clinical treatment, she dismissed psychotherapy as "psychobabble." Stronger reservations about psychological treatments were expressed by Prakesh. In his view, psychotherapy was unconnected to the workings of the human mind. Instead, clinical treatments were "quackery" and their practitioners were "charlatans."

These subjects' resistances to treatment were further determined by the application of indigenous cultural rules governing interpersonal interactions to their psychotherapeutic encounters. In many cases, such cultural rules tightly constrained the contents and recipients of subjects' self-disclosures. Meena, for example, initially restricted her disclosures due to the "inside-outside divide" that forbids Indians of her background from confiding in persons outside of the family. When Jun concealed her "forbidden wishes" from her analyst, she was applying Korean prescriptions that prohibit the expression of illicit sexual desires. And when Rosa erected a boundary that obstructed the flow of information between herself and her therapist, she enacted Puerto Rican strategies preventing fluid interactions with whites. Indigenous cultural conventions also restricted the ways in which subjects communicated with their psychotherapists. Yukiko's nonverbal interactions with her therapist typified Japanese patterns of communication that privilege the empathic sensing of thoughts and feelings rather than their verbalization, especially in hierarchical relationships (Roland 1996).

Foreign and ethnic patients' resistances to treatment not only take particular cultural forms and embed particular cultural meanings, but also serve culturally specific ends. This research suggests that patients in intercultural treatments frequently resist psychotherapy because they perceive it as a threat to their indigenous cultural identifications. In the view of these subjects, psychotherapeutic engagement constituted an unacceptable yielding to Western influences. Some subjects worried that if they became fully engaged in their clinical treatments, their indigenous cultural allegiances would be weakened. Others feared that if they became emotionally involved with their therapists, they would overidentify with their therapists' foreign cultures and lose touch with their home communities. Clearly, their cultural resistances to treatment served to protect their indigenous identifications from therapeutic—and therefore from Western—tampering. To keep these indigenous identifications intact, and to stave off nascent cultural loyalty conflicts required them to reject psychotherapeutic interventions and to distance themselves from their therapists.

Further, cultural resistances to treatment reflected these subjects' deep concerns about power imbalances in the therapeutic relationship. This research suggests that issues of analytic power and authority are magnified in intercultural psychotherapies. Indeed, in characterizing their therapeutic relationships, the subjects commonly described starkly asymmetrical relations of power. Most of them located their psychotherapists within the sociocultural groups that had dominated their indigenous communities. In consequence, when Maria constructed her therapist as Anglo and herself as Chicana, and when Rosa identified her therapist as white and herself as Puerto Rican, they referenced not only opposing ethnic allegiances but histories of political antagonism as well. Similarly, when Prakesh referred to his therapist as First World and to himself as Third World, and when Meena identified her therapist as Western and herself as non-Western, they invoked not only divergent national affiliations but their native India's history of colonial domination by the West. Firmly attaching their psychotherapists to Western structures of power, these subjects experienced them as the dominant partners in the therapeutic relationship.

For many of these subjects, not only their psychotherapists but the discipline of psychotherapy itself embodied Western structures of hegemony. In Rosa's view psychotherapy belonged to the world of white people, and its occasional entry into her Puerto Rican neighborhood signified the unwelcome intrusion of whites. Maria associated psychotherapy with the social workers who, in her childhood, had invaded her family's house to "rummage in our cupboards, decide what we should eat" and "tell my mother how to raise us." Having endured such early experiences of humiliation, and having since relegated psychotherapy to the Anglo world of privilege, Maria worried that by engaging in psychological treatment she was betraying her community. Indeed, for many of these subjects, to participate in psychotherapy was to revisit personal and collective experiences of subjugation, and to reinscribe Western domination.

Such perceptions of psychotherapy and of their psychotherapists nourished these subjects' cultural resistances to treatment. Seeking to escape Western hegemony, many of them struggled to take control of their therapeutic encounters. Jun exercised some measure of control in her sessions by withholding pertinent information from her analyst and by frequently canceling her sessions. Prakesh quietly sabotaged his treatment by reframing it as English language instruction. Others more overtly displayed cultural resistances to treatment. Some subjects were openly hostile to their therapists. By turning their therapy into "target practice," in Rosa's words, they effectively stalled their treatments. Rejecting Western metapsychologies, they did not define themselves as patients with underlying psychological problems. Rather, they viewed themselves as persons who had been affected by physical ailments, by family conflicts, by social discrimination, by cultural displacements, and by political oppression.

Some subjects consciously chose to participate in the Western discourse of psychotherapy in limited ways. Unlike Maria, who demanded that her therapist understand her worldview, these subjects concluded that mutual understanding between themselves and their therapists was contingent on their accepting conventional therapeutic perspectives. Meena observed that it was necessary to adopt the rhetoric of psychotherapy because her therapist was incapable of, and finally uninterested in, seeing the world from her point of view. And as Rosa explained, unless she withdrew from the battle between herself and her therapist about "how the therapy was gonna go," her treatment would be totally counterproductive.

Freud (1924) contended that the patient's rejection of psychoanalysis, in and of itself, constituted a resistance to treatment. As the result of this narrow view of resistances, which continues to this day, foreign

and ethnic patients' difficulties with particular elements of the therapeutic frame are reduced to individual defensive operations or to personal psychopathology. While individual factors do come into play, clinical perspectives that ignore the cultural meanings of resistances are
bound to be counterproductive in intercultural treatments. This research
indicates that foreign and ethnic patients have little motivation to embrace
forms of psychological treatment that contradict indigenous ideologies of
self and of mind, that violate cultural norms governing self-disclosure,
that jeopardize cultural identifications, and that, moreover, are associated
with Western domination. Clearly resistances must be reconceptualized,
so that the analysis of their cultural features and functions becomes an
integral component of intercultural treatments.

ANTHROPOLOGY IN THE CLINIC

In the sections above I have argued for cultural understandings of traditional psychotherapeutic concepts, understandings that more accurately
represent the dynamics of intercultural treatments. In the sections below,
I maintain that anthropological perspectives make essential contributions to our constructions and understandings of the foreign and ethnic
patients who undergo mental health treatments. In particular, I examine the ways in which cultural anthropology's approaches to the self, to
human development, to emotion, and to language inform our analyses
of intercultural treatments and provide us with new insights into clinical material.

Cultured Selves

It is primarily through its conceptions of the self as culturally constructed, and therefore as variable across cultures, that cultural anthropology enriches our understandings of intercultural psychotherapies. As
discussed in Chapter 2, based on their extensive ethnographic research
on the self in widely divergent cultural contexts, many cultural anthropologists have concluded that selves are differently organized, bounded,

motivated, related, and experienced across cultures. According to these relativistic conceptions of the self, Western selves that possess distinct self–other and self–environment boundaries, that have an internal locus of control, and that strive for personal autonomy, mastery, and achievement (Geertz 1973) represent no more than one possible version of the self.

Despite the fact that the "self-contained individuals" (Sampson 1988) described above are relatively rare in the human population, these are the selves that standard psychotherapies take as their subject, and that they hold as their ideal. This research suggests, however, that psychological treatments that privilege such conceptions of the self are poorly positioned to serve foreign and ethnic patients who, like these research subjects, experience themselves in ways that contradict Western notions of selfhood. The subjects described selves that were differently bounded and individuated than Western selves. Often their self–other boundaries were indistinct, so that self, family, and community representations, identifications, and interests were fused. As Meena observed, although the Americans she knew thought of themselves as individuals first and foremost, she found it impossible to conceive of her desires, motivations, and concerns as separate or separable from those of her family. Yukiko similarly distinguished Japanese selves, which were part of the group, from American selves, that were composed of "just me." Further, the subjects described selves which devalued the independent action, self-expression, and self-assertion that Western selves commonly prize. Jun portrayed Korean selves as embedded in cultural systems of mutual debt. These systems, in her view, required sacrificing personal wishes, repressing feelings of rebellion, and upholding family and community expectations in order to preserve social harmony. This research suggests that some foreign and ethnic patients whose native cultures value social conformity and the welfare of the collective are likely to reject, or at best to feel ambivalent about, psychotherapy's emphasis on personal autonomy and differentiation.

The selves that these subjects described further diverged from Western conceptions of the self regarding ideologies of personal agency and control. Western selves are commonly constructed as active agents that seek to exercise mastery and control over others and over their environments (Cushman 1990, Geertz 1973, Landrine 1992). For Westerners the arena of personal control encompasses the self, so that most aspects of functioning are viewed as internally regulated. In addition, because they are constructed as possessing a fundamental plasticity, Western selves are viewed not as biologically determined and fixed but as capable of substantive change; indeed, they are considered to be capable of refashioning their most basic characteristics and identities.

Notions of therapeutic progress and change are, to a large extent, contingent on the idea that alterations in the self are possible. Some of the subjects, however, saw themselves as fundamentally unchangeable. When Jun explained the genetic transmission of "seeds" from one generation of Koreans to the next, she described a cultural ideology of individual formation by means of which moral character and mental stability were innately predetermined and unalterable. When Rosa defined being a *loca* and suffering from *nervios* as intrinsic elements of the female condition, she represented them as irremediable parts of herself. Because both Jun and Rosa understood central aspects of themselves to be inherent, inherited, and fixed, they had little faith in the possibilities of therapeutic change. Foreign and ethnic patients who conceive of the self as intrinsic and unchangeable are likely to have limited expectations of treatment. Many such patients may enter treatment seeking to acquire defensive strategies of coping and containment rather than fundamental personal change.

But psychotherapy not only embodies Western ideologies of the self in its theory, it also actively promotes them in its practice. When clinicians encourage their patients to function autonomously, to separate from their parents, to become more assertive and expressive, or to pursue their self-interests, they are inviting them to enact Western ideals of selfhood. Although clinicians might not conceptualize their interventions as such, the subjects were clearly aware of their therapists' advocacy of Western cultural selves. Both Meena and Maria recalled, with some resentment, that their therapists had repeatedly pressed them to distinguish themselves and their interests from those of their families. Other subjects expressed gratitude for such therapeutic interventions. Rosa, for example, claimed to appreciate Jan's support of her independence and assertiveness, as this facilitated her transformation from "something just sitting there being acted on" into an active and internally directed self.

The clinical questions that arise when psychotherapists acknowledge cross-cultural variation in the construction of the self are further complicated by the fact that many individuals who speak more than one language, and who have resided in more than one culture, conceive of themselves as composed of multiple cultural selves. Jun claimed to have a bicultural self. Yukiko distinguished her Americanized self from her true Japanese self, and Rosa, Maria, and Meena, respectively, described a core self, a real self, and a way of being in the world that differed from the selves that they presented to their therapists. While it has been contended that all inhabitants of ethnically diverse societies possess multiple cultural selves as a result of their ongoing exposures to other cultures (Erickson 1997), it might be presumed that multiple cultural selves are most keenly experienced by those who, like these subjects, continually negotiate conflicting cultural realities in their everyday lives.

It is possible that some of those who conceive of themselves as composed of multiple cultural selves experience these selves as complementary. Perhaps under optimal circumstances, such selves provide a multiple consciousness that, like the "double-consciousness" described by DuBois (1903, p. 5), is a fount of personal creativity and strength. But those who claim that their multiple selves contain divergent cultural assumptions, ideologies, and values frequently experience internal contradiction, competition, and disharmony. Multiple cultural selves that were highly conflictual were described by most of the subjects, as exemplified by Jun's portrayal of her bicultural self as split between contradictory standards of morality and sexuality. Indeed, most of the subjects struggled to achieve a sense of balance among these selves; it is plausible that such struggles brought them into psychotherapy.

The multiple cultural selves that these subjects described typically comprised both the selves that were firmly embedded in their native cultures, and the Westernized selves that were born out of their contact with mainstream American society, or with the larger Western world. According to their reports of their therapies, these subjects presented different cultural selves to their therapists at varying points in their treatments. As in other kinds of intercultural interactions, indigenous cultural and ethnic identifications were often intensified in treatment (White and Lutz 1992). Some subjects, having constructed their psychotherapists as particular cultural stereotypes, then located themselves in response to such constructions, presenting their therapists with extreme versions of their indigenous selves. Accordingly, having idealized her therapist as a "perfect" American, Rosa presented herself as a "crazy, angry woman of color." Having perceived her therapist as an Anglo and an academic, Maria portrayed herself as a Chicana gang member. And having characterized his therapist as an overconsuming, wasteful member of the First World, Prakesh identified himself as a morally superior member of the Third World.

If these subjects' presentations of their various cultural selves were sometimes dialogically related to their cultural constructions of their psychotherapists, then at other times they were dialogically related to how they imagined their psychotherapists had culturally constructed them. For example, Meena maintained that once she sensed that her therapist viewed her as one of the "dark-skinned inscrutable orientals" who came from "a land populated by snake charmers," she deliberately displayed her command of English and enacted a more Westernized version of herself in order to dispel the Indian stereotype that she imagined her therapist had formed of her.

The subjects' presentations of particular cultural selves served additional purposes as well. Just as some patients who are multilingual choose to undergo psychotherapy in a second language in order to shelter themselves from the intense emotions summoned by their native tongue (Amati-Mehler et al. 1993), some of these subjects presented their therapists with nonnative cultural selves in order to defend themselves against the primary emotions that were embedded in their indigenous selves. Accordingly, Yukiko's presentation of an Americanized self to her psychotherapist served the purpose of distancing a true Japanese self that might have felt shamed by her disobedience to her parents and devastated by her mother's rejection of her. Subjects sometimes foregrounded their Americanized selves in treatment in order to accomplish specific goals that violated the standards and values of their native cultures but of which, in their estimation, their American therapists would approve. Enacting Americanized selves for their therapists thus facilitated both Meena's divorce from her pathological husband and Yukiko's separation from her powerful mother. For subjects like Jun, psychological treatment provided welcome opportunities to experiment with, or perhaps to solidify, emergent Western selves possessed of a greater individuality and autonomy.

Unlike those subjects who realized some benefit from expressing Westernized selves in their treatments, other subjects feared that their core or real selves, which in their view had already been weakened by their residence in a foreign setting, were further endangered as the result of their participation in psychotherapy. In their treatments, these subjects experienced pressures for cultural assimilation and for transformations of the selves that were most embedded in their native cultures. Many of them presented culturally stereotyped versions of themselves to their therapists in order to fend off unwanted therapeutic invasions. To fortify their indigenous cultural selves, Rosa and Maria portrayed themselves, respectively, as a ghetto kid and as a street kid.

It is clear that the subjects, as the result of having internalized multiple cultures and worldviews, experienced themselves as containing plural, contradictory, and separate cultural selves. In their accounts of their treatments, they depicted each self as a distinct, discrete, and nonoverlapping entity, and they described their skills in compartmentalizing and in selectively presenting particular cultural selves. Yet it is likely that selves such as these, which are culturally complex, are in fact more nuanced, fluid, and interrelated. They may exist on a continuum rather than as separate entities, and they may be experienced simultaneously rather than sequentially. Further research is necessary to better understand how the internalization of multiple languages and cultural systems of meanings affects the self.

At the same time, however, it is clear that Western views of the self as unitary, internally cohesive, and consistent across contexts require reconsideration. Clinical constructions of multiple, disjunctive, and contradictory selves as necessarily pathological (Akhtar 1984), which are founded on these views, also require revision. Cultural conceptions of selfhood offer psychotherapists alternatives to conventional psychological understandings of the self. Some such conceptions contend that the Western ideal of the cohesive, integrated self is an illusion (Ewing

1990) and that persons universally acquire multiple, conflicting, and shifting selves that are grounded in the contradictory values and assumptions that all cultures contain. Other such conceptions propose that hybrid identities (Bhabha 1994) naturally develop in persons whose lives span multiple cultures and languages. Persons with such identities frequently benefit from opportunities to inventively combine received community traditions with newly encountered cultural material. But because some continually perceive reality from plural perspectives, they suffer from the feelings of cultural marginalization and alienation that afflicted Jun.

When cultural conceptions of the self are applied to intercultural psychotherapies, they provide therapists with new ways of understanding foreign and ethnic patients. Unlike Western ideologies of unitary selves that dominate contemporary clinical theory and practice, these conceptions of selfhood normalize the conflicting and shifting selves of foreign and ethnic patients. In addition, they indicate that the integration of the self, which is a frequent psychotherapeutic aim, may be an inappropriate objective in intercultural treatments. For foreign and ethnic patients, the integration of the self may constitute an unattainable Western ideal that, moreover, may entail the loss of valued cultural identifications and ties. It also may represent the imperative to culturally assimilate, which they reject.

Cultural conceptions of the self not only challenge the relevance of standard psychotherapeutic goals to the treatment of foreign and ethnic patients, but also identify new directions for intercultural clinical practice. Rather than seeking to repair disunities and contradictions in the self, these conceptions of selfhood suggest that intercultural psychotherapies explore the histories, interrelationships, contextualizations, and meanings of the multiple cultural selves that patients experience. Accordingly, they draw attention to the precise circumstances under which foreign and ethnic patients present such various, culturally distinct selves in clinical encounters. Given that Rosa, Maria, and Meena claimed to have presented their therapists with selves that diverged from their core or real selves, therapists might seek to understand why some foreign and ethnic patients conceal their indigenous selves in therapy; they might also explore how such concealments affect intercultural treatments. Questions such as these merit further investigation.

Cultural conceptions of selfhood also direct clinical attention to the ways in which foreign and ethnic patients manage conflicts among what they experience as contradictory cultural selves. Some such patients may idealize aspects of their Westernized selves and denigrate their indigenous selves. Others, like Maria and Prakesh, may do the opposite. For although Maria and Prakesh clearly valued the educational and professional opportunities offered by the Anglo or First World, they had difficulty accepting their internalizations of aspects of these worlds. In their clinical treatments it is important for foreign and ethnic patients to acknowledge and explore their various and conflicting cultural selves. The inability to tolerate particular cultural selves, the internal discomfort that results from discrepant cultural values and assumptions, and the consequent experiences of cultural marginality and isolation pose central psychological questions that require therapeutic consideration.

Finally, cultural conceptions of the self draw clinical attention to the potential benefits of fluid and shifting selves. What are the possible advantages of multiple consciousnesses? How can psychotherapy help foreign and ethnic patients not to escape their double vision (Bhabha 1994), but to derive new strengths, pleasures, and abilities from it? The means by which some individuals successfully come to terms with internal cultural diversity and conflict also warrant further investigation.

Comparative Human Development

As discussed in Chapter 2, the psychological theories that inform clinical theory and practice generally conceive of human development as grounded in biological processes. Positing that development results from the human organism's physiological maturation, these theories, and the research they have spawned, have generated an abundance of developmental norms. Although these norms embody Western developmental categories and ideologies of the self, and although they are based primarily on research with Western subjects, psychology has constructed them as universal. By privileging Western developmental schemes, such universalizing perspectives overlook the role of culture in human development. They fail to acknowledge that culture ascribes forms, meanings, and objectives to development by organizing the life span around culturally defined phases, concepts, milestones, and tasks, and that developmental paths vary across cultures.

This research challenges the psychological assumptions of uniformity in development that underlie clinical theory and practice—and that inform intercultural clinical treatments—and supports anthropological views of development as culturally shaped. The problems and concerns that the subjects presented to their therapists were shaped by culturally specific developmental goals, expectations, and contexts. Commonly, these subjects referred to developmental objectives that differed from those that standard psychotherapeutic theories construct as normative. Yukiko, for example, described the pivotal role that the concept of *oyakoko*, which defines Japanese expectations of filial behavior, played in her development. She explained that she had tried to be a good daughter, conforming to her parents' desires rather than gratifying her own. Yukiko's extreme anguish at having disobeyed her mother by marrying Rob reflects the centrality of *oyakoko* in her development. Similarly, Meena's adolescent development was organized around the auspiciousness of marriage, and around the necessity of acquiring the skills that would permit her to perform wifely duties and tasks. The North Indian concept of *suhag*, which invokes a complex of specific ideologies, behaviors, and statuses surrounding marriage, helped orient her as a girl toward the singular goal of wedlock. That the concept of marriage had figured so prominently in her development, and that being a wife had defined her as a successful woman in North Indian eyes, compounded Meena's difficulties in leaving her husband.

Further, although developmental psychology has conceptualized separation and individuation as the main thrusts of both infant (Mahler et al. 1975) and adolescent (Blos 1979) development, for none of the subjects were they primary developmental objectives. Not only did attaining adult status entail cultural expectations that diverged from the prototypical Western quests for personal identity, independence, and achievement, but autonomous actions often brought punishment and stigma. Rosa was expected to do as her father told her. When she showed flashes of independence, her family criticized her behavior as aberrant, undesirable, and *loca*. Yukiko was bound, even as an adult, to obey her mother. When she disobeyed her by marrying Rob, her mother severed relations with her for several years, and Yukiko was marked as strange. Jun was also expected to comply with parental directives, and worried that certain violations of them, such as marrying an American man, might cause her parents to disown her.

For these subjects, development did not comprise a series of progressive movements away from society, but a series of progressive movements into it. Adulthood did not represent the culmination of lifelong processes of separation and individuation; rather, it represented the culmination of lifelong processes of social attachment and interconnection, and made them more fully social beings with newly strengthened group identifications, ties, and responsibilities. Accordingly, Maria voiced her commitment to serving her community, while Jun expressed the desire to "do something for my country."

The subjects also detailed the distinctive cultural contexts within which their early development had occurred, contexts that invariably were differently configured from those assumed by Western developmental norms. Many subjects described their early development as having been embedded in relational matrices that went beyond their immediate or extended families, encompassing larger social groups. Maria spoke of an upbringing that had occurred on the street and that was structured by her *compadres*, the surrogate family that protected her and taught her the codes of the barrio. Jun's conception of her family, in "going back generations," included distant Korean ancestors. Meena's sense of self developed within an extended family whose members were so intertwined that Meena's decision to leave her husband dishonored her kin. Because such variations across cultures in family composition and organization structure children's early relationships and environments in particular ways, producing divergent developmental expectations and experiences, they are an important topic for exploration in intercultural psychotherapies.

Cultural Emotions

Cultural anthropologists maintain that persons from different cultures define and experience their emotions in markedly divergent ways. Their ethnographic accounts portray the multiple varieties of emotional experience that exist across cultures. To extend this relativistic construction of emotions to intercultural clinical theory and practice is to suggest that in intercultural treatments, patient and therapist are likely to have varying, culturally shaped assumptions about and histories of emotions. Specifically, they are likely to differently configure the nature, meanings, and functions of particular emotions, the causes of emotional responses, the avenues for their expression, and the strategies for their management.

Such relativistic constructions of emotions contribute to our understandings of the intercultural treatments presented in Part II. First, the emotions that many of the subjects reported having experienced in the course of their psychotherapies conformed not to Western emotional concepts but to categories of emotion that were indigenous to their native cultures. Meena claimed that the emotions she experienced in response to her marital crisis, such as the Indian woman's sense of shame, corresponded to emotion words in the Indian languages of Marathi and Hindi rather than to English ones. These emotion words were embedded in North Indian notions of appropriate female sexual behavior and derived their affective power from such contextual associations. Because Meena's therapist was unfamiliar with her emotional vocabulary and with the specific cultural world in which it was embedded, Meena found it extremely difficult to convey her emotional experience to him.

Second, the subjects sought to manage their emotions in ways that conflicted with therapeutic assumptions. None of them entered treatment with the view that emotional release was psychologically pivotal to improvements in their condition or in their functioning. Nor did they construct emotional expression as beneficial in and of itself. Rather, they entered psychotherapy with clear preferences for native cultural strategies of emotion management that called for the suppression of emotions in distinctive ways. Jun maintained that for Koreans, expressing negative emotions such as anger toward parents and other authority figures was unacceptable. Such emotions were to be denied, repressed, or sublimated "by writing or by singing or drinking." As Jun explained, Koreans placed importance on exhibiting respectful behaviors and on fulfilling social obligations; the feelings underlying these actions were considered unworthy of attention.

Third, some subjects described culturally specific ideologies of emotional causality that determined the ways in which they conceptualized and managed their emotions. Because Rosa viewed her emotions as caused by her gender—an aspect of herself that she had no power to change—she experienced her feelings as frighteningly out of control. Fearing that she was crazy, and that those to whom she revealed her emotions would think that she needed to be institutionalized, Rosa's general strategy was to conceal and to contain her emotions—in her words, to "stuff it back in," to "sew myself up and keep on going." Although Rosa entered psychotherapy in search of more effective means of emotional containment, her goals in this regard were opposed to her therapist's. Indeed, Jan sought to reframe Rosa's emotions as normal, as understandable, and as controllable, and to help Rosa accept and express them.

This research also indicates that emotional responses that appear to be universal assume variant roles and meanings across cultures. Crying, for example, which might be configured as a pancultural emotional response, has markedly divergent meanings for persons of different cultural backgrounds. As Yukiko's account of her treatment suggests, she and her American therapist constructed crying in very different ways. Yukiko recalled that her therapist had told her that it's okay to cry, and Yukiko observed that "Kleenex was right next to me" throughout her psychotherapy sessions. Yet Yukiko described her native Japan as a society in which to reveal personal sadness and distress to another was viewed as impolite. For her to have cried in the presence of another was clearly an extraordinary event, and one whose particular meanings required analysis.

While Yukiko accepted her therapist's invitation to cry in psychotherapy, Rosa rejected similar opportunities. If Yukiko had felt more comfortable crying in front of someone who was not from her home community, then for Rosa the opposite was true; for her, it was taboo to cry in front of a white person. In Rosa's view, to cry in Jan's presence would be to expose weakness in front of someone white, who might exploit any vulnerability she revealed. For Rosa, then, crying was not simply an emotional behavior, but one with sociopolitical implications.

When therapists treat patients whose cultural backgrounds are similar to theirs, they and their patients are likely to share assumptions regarding the nature, meanings, and causes of emotions. They are also likely to share a sense of the range of possible events in people's lives, and of the potential emotional reactions to any given circumstance or occurrence. But as relativistic constructions of emotions suggest, and as this research demonstrates, Western psychotherapists and their foreign and ethnic patients differently configure acceptable and expectable emotional responses. Further, because emotions are grounded in shared cultural meanings, therapists who treat foreign and ethnic patients are less able to predict how such patients will react emotionally to the events of their lives. Just as Meena's therapist seemed not to have anticipated the rage she came to feel toward all things Indian, or her traumatic sense of loss upon her separation from Indian society, therapists who work with patients whose cultural backgrounds differ from theirs may have difficulty anticipating the nature and extent of their emotional responses. The close exploration of culturally specific emotions is therefore an integral component of intercultural psychotherapies.

Culture, Language, and Translation

Anthropological perspectives on language draw our attention to the linguistic features of intercultural treatments. Together with clinical studies of language use in psychotherapy, these perspectives point to the problems experienced by patients who undergo psychological treatment in a language other than their native tongue. Like many foreign and ethnic patients who are treated by American therapists, every subject of this research underwent psychotherapy in a nonnative language. For all of them English was a second—in Meena's case, a third—language, yet all of their psychotherapies were conducted exclusively in English. As they faced psychotherapists who knew neither their native language nor their culture, the problems of translation were primarily theirs, in that it was incumbent upon them to make their difficulties comprehensible to their therapists. For this to occur required these subjects to perform multiple levels of translation.

If the first level of translation was essentially linguistic, requiring them to find the precise words for their problems in a language that to them was foreign, then the second level of translation was conceptual, requiring them to explicate native ideologies of emotional distress in English so that their American psychotherapists might grasp them. Indeed, for these subjects, translation entailed converting entire, culturally specific conceptual paradigms into English. Most subjects reported that the near impossibility of generating adequate descriptions of indigenous concepts of affect, development, selfhood, and experience undermined their treatment. Prakesh, who realized that his therapist would never "get" what he was saying, made his treatment a source of personal amusement. Rosa, who found herself incapable of translating what was most profound to her, emotionally withdrew from her therapist. And Meena, who felt that she could not possibly convey Indian constructs of marriage, divorce, and sexuality to her American therapist, finally erased such material from her sessions.

A further level of translation involved a shift in register. Translating from the vernacular into standard English was the task of Maria and Rosa, who were from ethnic groups within the United States, and who had grown up speaking nonstandard versions of English. Even after having translated her clinical disclosures from her native Spanish into English, and from Chicana cultural categories into terms she thought her Anglo therapist would comprehend, Maria felt that it was necessary to translate her "hood talk" into standard English—into what she called "whitespeak"—so that her therapist would not regard her as "an amusing sideshow."

In support of previous clinical findings, this research illustrates that patients who speak foreign languages in psychotherapy find it difficult to express themselves emotionally (Russell 1988), and that they are more distanced from the early memories that are encoded in their native tongues (Javier 1995). It also supports prior findings that some foreign and ethnic patients choose to undergo treatment in a second language in order to protect themselves from experiencing intense primary affects—in Maria's words, to avoid being "sucked into my inner world"—and in order to remove issues and conflicts that are highly charged from therapeutic scrutiny (Amati-Mehler et al. 1993). As this research shows, translation can result in the dilution of emotional reactions in session, and in the dissociation of affect from clinical disclosures, contributing to a net loss of personal resonance in intercultural treatments.

But if the subjects interviewed here sometimes instrumentally employed the distancing effects that occurred when they spoke English to ward off intense affects in treatment, this research also demonstrates that the processes of translation themselves can alter emotional dispositions. As these subjects translated their disclosures into non-native languages in treatment, they reported the emergence of other cultural selves with distinct personal and emotional textures. Rosa, for example, experienced different cultural selves when she spoke Spanish and when she spoke English. Although she described her Spanish-speaking self as sensitive and kindhearted, when she spoke English, as she did in treatment, she experienced a self that was strong and willful. But as Rosa explained, this translated, English-speaking self—the self of her psychotherapy—was an inauthentic facade.

Further, this research suggests that there is a politics of translation that carries its own affective charge. The subjects not only attributed specific political and emotional meanings to the various languages they spoke, but in many cases they equated translation from their native languages into English with betrayal. When they spoke English in psychotherapy, issues of cultural identity and of Western hegemony were inflamed. For some, to define themselves in the language of psychotherapy was to discredit indigenous psychological knowledges and to embrace Western structures of domination. Prakesh quite pointedly refused to label himself as suicidal and depressed, referring to his condition as *mushkil*. For Prakesh, Maria, and others, speaking English in treatment aroused powerful and conflicting emotions as it was simultaneously the language of education and professionalization, which they valued, and the language of colonialism and oppression, which they deplored. Although Maria had used her English competence to advance her academic career, speaking "whitespeak" in therapy linked her treatment to childhood experiences of Anglo derision and discrimination, even as it intensified her fears of becoming disconnected from her home community. For many foreign and ethnic patients, speaking English in psychotherapy may reinforce the power asymmetries they experience in being treated by a member of the dominant culture. Because acts of translation can arouse overwhelming feelings of personal resentment and sociopolitical subjugation, the meanings of translation must be explored in intercultural treatments.

THE BENEFITS OF CROSS-CULTURAL TREATMENTS

As the preceding sections make clear, the subjects frankly described the ways in which working with psychotherapists from different cultural and linguistic backgrounds had hindered their psychological treatments. Yet they also claimed to have found their psychotherapies beneficial. Even those subjects who initially conceived of psychotherapy unfavorably, as taboo or as "psychobabble," as well as those who initially had difficulties with its nondirective methods, individualistic orientation, and emphasis on personal expression, reported some therapeutic gains. Yukiko and Meena, who before entering treatment had considered the activity of exploring intimate personal issues with a total stranger unthinkable, both claimed to have profited from it. Rosa, who had entered psychotherapy in search of specific practical strategies for containing her emotional volatility, reported that Jan's nondirective approach "gave me a voice."

Among the features of psychotherapy that these subjects identified as curative were the sense of release and space to talk that it offered. Many subjects credited their psychotherapies with having given them a forum for exploring matters that they could not discuss with their families—things that, in Maria's words, "you just don't talk about"—and they reported having benefited from the open-ended conversations that their therapists had facilitated. Echoing Fairbairn's claim, since quoted by Guntrip (1975), that the remedial possibilities of clinical treatment lie not in its analytic insights but in the personal relationship between patient and analyst, these subjects cited the healing properties of their therapists' kindness, trustworthiness, and concern. Prakesh alone reported that his therapist's unfamiliarity with his native language and culture had completely obstructed his treatment. All the other subjects developed somewhat sustaining relationships with their therapists—at least for some portions of their treatments—despite their divergent cultural backgrounds.

Indeed, those subjects who claimed to have benefited from their therapists' objectivity, were referring, in fact, to their therapists' lack of knowledge about their native cultures. These subjects claimed that they had found some advantage in working with psychotherapists who, being culture distant, were unaware of their indigenous mores and norms. Yukiko, for example, was relieved that her therapist did not see her transgressions through Japanese eyes, and that she therefore did not find her different or strange. Meena derived a similar comfort from her therapist's unfamiliarity with her cultural codes; in her view, this rendered him incapable of evaluating her, and of advising her, as she imagined that someone from her background would have. Because their therapists had little sense of what constituted normative or moral conduct in their home communities, most of the subjects did not feel judged by their therapists, and were spared from experiencing intense feelings of shame in their treatments.

But while the subjects claimed that they prized their therapists' openness and objectivity, perhaps what some truly appreciated were their therapists' Western assumptions and values. Indeed, some subjects actively sought therapeutic validation of thoughts, wishes, and behaviors that would have been disparaged or condemned in their native cultural contexts, but that conformed to psychotherapy's Western ideologies of separation, of individualism, and of autonomy. Jun, for example, assumed that her American analyst would support her desires for self-expression and self-determination, just as Yukiko expected her therapist to encourage her separation from her mother. Foreign and ethnic patients who enter psychotherapy wishing to become more independent and individualistic, to experiment with other ways of being, or to escape traditional moralities and controls, are likely to appreciate their American therapists' "objective" validation of actions, fantasies, and desires that their home communities discourage.

TREATMENT IMPLICATIONS

In addition to identifying some beneficial aspects of intercultural clinical treatments, this research suggests specific ways in which such treatments might be enhanced. Specifically, it emphasizes the need for psychotherapists to become further acquainted with the workings of language and culture: with their characteristic categories, features, and functions; with the ways in which they shape psychological functioning; with the methodologies for their exploration in the clinical consulting room; and with the psychological ramifications of linguistic and cultural change.

Listening for Culture

Clinicians who work with patients from other cultures encounter individuals with wide ranges of knowledge about, and experience with, mainstream American society. Some foreign and ethnic patients who seek psychotherapy are new to the United States and are unfamiliar with its linguistic and cultural patterns, while others are quite fluent in mainstream American language and culture. When such patients present Westernized selves in treatment, their therapists may overlook the cultural differences between them. In these cases, the culturally specific features of patients' presenting problems, selves, developmental histories, emotional experiences, transferences, and resistances may remain outside the frame of therapeutic inquiry.

This research suggests that regardless of their familiarity with, or integration into, mainstream American language and society, foreign and ethnic patients carry aspects of their indigenous cultural worlds into their psychotherapies; yet it also suggests that for a variety of reasons, many such patients neglect to reveal these worlds to their psychotherapists. As discussed above, many foreign and ethnic patients are quick to sense their psychotherapists' discomfort with unfamiliar cultural material, and to delete such material from their therapeutic conversations. Moreover, the English words that such patients employ in treatment to describe themselves, and their relationships, emotions, developmental histories, and psychological states, often are imperfect—and sometimes impoverished—translations of indigenous cultural categories and terms. Such translations further distance foreign and ethnic patients' other cultural worlds.

For intercultural treatments to become more effective, patients' indigenous cultural material must be returned to the therapeutic arena. How might clinicians gain access to such important material, material that their patients have deliberately omitted, or that has been lost in translation? Just as psychotherapists who work with Western patients have learned to listen selectively to therapeutic disclosures, closely attending to the particular categories of material that they believe to be suffused with essential psychological resonances, therapists who work with foreign and ethnic patients must learn to listen selectively for material that is saturated with indigenous cultural significations. By identifying the particular categories that contribute to the cultural construction of human experience, anthropologists help orient clinicians toward the types of material that require close attention in intercultural treatments.

These categories include culturally specific conceptions of the self and of its psychological functioning, developmental paths, emotional worlds, and linguistic experiences. As previously discussed in this chapter, these aspects of human experience are tremendously variable across cultures. In consequence, when foreign and ethnic patients present their self-experiences and interpersonal relationships in treatment, their therapists have the opportunity to attend to their specific cultural configurations. Similarly, when such patients describe their psychological functioning, psychological states, and emotional reactions, their therapists can listen for distinctive cultural features and meanings. Indications of particular developmental paths in foreign and ethnic patients might emerge through descriptions of the household compositions, kinship structures, and family relationships within which their development unfolded, or they might emerge through mention of culturally specific developmental ceremonies, markers, and norms. In addition, given the psychic binds of translation itself, therapists might pay attention to foreign and ethnic patients' feelings about speaking a foreign language in treatment. And given the marginal status of psychotherapy in many of their home communities, therapists might also listen for indications of their discomfort in undergoing psychological treatment.

Finally, this research demonstrates that foreign and ethnic patients are deeply affected by their migrations across domestic and international cultural boundaries. For many such patients, the struggles of adapting to new sociocultural surrounds negatively color their perceptions of their treatments and of their therapists, restricting therapeutic disclosures. Not only do migrations pose significant psychological challenges (cf. Akhtar 1995) that require clinical examination, but also they are situated within particular socioeconomic conditions and structures of power. Often they involve experiences of political oppression and social discrimination. Listening for foreign and ethnic patients' stories about their migrations into, and relationships with, mainstream American society allows psychotherapists to examine the social and political factors that have played formative roles in their psychological histories, but that commonly are excluded from therapeutic consideration.

Asking about Culture

Extending cultural inquiry into the psychological clinic requires not only that therapists learn how to listen for cultural material, but also that they learn how to explore it in treatment. Psychotherapists, traditionally, have not been so inclined. In contrast with anthropologists, who have embraced the concepts and techniques of psychoanalysis to deepen their understandings of other societies and of other selves, psychologists have resisted the reciprocal enterprise of integrating anthropological theories and methods—specifically, their relativistic perspectives and ethnographic techniques—into clinical practice. Throughout this book I have advocated the undoing of these resistances, contending that when American therapists treat patients from other cultures, the parameters of the clinical encounter must expand to encompass explorations of patients' indigenous languages and cultures.

To expand the parameters of clinical encounters is to engage in a commonly practiced, but uncommonly acknowledged, endeavor. As Pine (1990) has observed, it is an unofficial fact of clinical life that clinical methods are regularly adapted to suit the needs of particular patients. To suit the needs of foreign and ethnic patients requires that psychotherapists open other spaces—spaces of cultural formation, experience, and expression—as topics of therapeutic interest and intervention. Intercultural treatments therefore require psychotherapists to conduct clinical interviews that are ethnographically informed.

Anthropological research, or more precisely, ethnography, has been described as the practice of "thick description" (Geertz 1973, p. 6), the object of which is "first to grasp and then to render" (p. 10) other cultural worlds. Through their interpretations of culturally specific categories and structures of meaning that are public, thematically consistent, and to some degree shared within particular cultural contexts, anthropologists have sought to convey the native's point of view (Geertz 1973, 1983). Anthropologists who conduct ethnographic research characteristically take up residence among the people they study, learn to speak their native languages, and participate in their daily lives in order to grasp the character of their lived experience. Clearly, conducting intercultural treatments is a different kind of endeavor. In some respects, it is the inverse of ethnography. Psychotherapists work with foreign and ethnic patients who are extracted from their native cultural contexts, who inhabit, albeit often temporarily, the psychotherapist's cultural surround, and who, as a rule, speak the psychotherapist's language rather than their own in their clinical sessions.

Yet clinical work might be construed as ethnographic in its elicitation of thickly described patient narratives, which, when regarded from culturally informed perspectives, allow psychotherapists to grasp the culturally specific nature of their patients' lived experience. As in ethnography, these narratives may be read as texts that reveal the underlying structures of meaning that inform observable behaviors; as in ethnography, their latent content is subject to professional interpretation. Because ethnography entails suspending preconceived constructions of reality and listening for difference across cultures, intercultural clinical work can acquire additional ethnographic qualities by investigating the ways in which foreign and ethnic patients' narratives are shaped by their particular cultural assumptions and experiences. By adapting ethnographic techniques for use in the psychological clinic—by cultivating an openness to listening for and to asking about particular examples of cultural difference—therapists have the opportunity to explore the various cultural categories and structures of meaning that significantly shape their foreign and ethnic patients' lived experience and psychic worlds.

Introducing ethnography into the psychological clinic violates the conventional therapeutic wisdom. Specifically, it contradicts the clinical consensus that constructs patients' discussions of cultural material as defenses against inner psychic lives (Akhtar 1995), and that constructs therapists' explorations of cultural material as distractions from patients' fundamental needs (Comas-Diaz and Jacobsen 1991, Devereux 1958). I would argue, however, that to introduce ethnography into the psychological clinic is to support emergent psychological theories that construct culture and mind as mutually influencing and inseparable (Shweder 1990). I would further argue that to introduce ethnography into the clinic is to support contemporary clinical theories that propose the equal distribution of clinical authority and power, and that configure clinical treatments as the therapist's learning from the patient (Casement 1985).

How might therapists learn from their foreign and ethnic patients in intercultural treatments? Given, as discussed in previous sections, that such patients often have hybrid cultural identities, which they commonly experience as multiple cultural selves, how might psychotherapists learn about and evaluate foreign and ethnic patients' various subjectivities and cultural worlds? More importantly, given their propensity to present Westernized versions of themselves in treatment—especially in reaction to the perceived demands of clinical encounters—how might therapists conduct ethnographically informed interviews through which foreign and ethnic patients' indigenous cultural perspectives emerge?

Therapists might begin by eliciting their foreign and ethnic patients' life histories—a classic ethnographic activity. Such accounts provide therapists with opporunities to investigate their patients' culturally specific formative events, and the culturally particular ideologies of self, of emotion, and of experience with which they are linked. Therapists might also ask foreign and ethnic patients to describe typical life cycles in their home communities (Marcus and Fischer 1986). Such descriptions are likely to introduce the culturally specific developmental norms and expectations that structured patients' early lives into the treatment. When therapists employ such techniques, techniques that are characteristic of "person-centered ethnographies" (LeVine 1982, p. 293), they encourage their foreign and ethnic patients to bring the indigenous cultural constructs and categories that shaped their subjectivities and histories into the clinical domain, so that they might inform subsequent therapeutic discussions. These basic ethnographic techniques also permit foreign and ethnic patients to help organize therapeutic discourse around experiences and concepts that are of significance to them, rather than having this organization predetermined by Western psychological assumptions and ideals.

Employing ethnographic techniques of inquiry can also deepen therapists' understandings of foreign and ethnic patients' presenting complaints and symptomatologies. When foreign and ethnic patients present with suicidal ideation, for example, therapists need to get a sense of the cultural patterning of suicide—of its usual precipitants, meanings, and prevalence—in their home communities. Therapists might ask their patients whether any relatives, friends, or acquaintances from home have attempted suicide. They might explore how and why such persons tried to take their own lives. Therapists might also ask their patients what they would have done—including to whom or to what they would have turned—had their suicidality emerged at home. Cultural information of this kind can help therapists more accurately assess and treat foreign and ethnic patients' suicidality.

Ethnographic investigations generally include linguistic components. When patients undergo psychotherapy in a nonnative language, it is important for their linguistic histories, as well as their attitudes toward the language that they speak in treatment, to be thoroughly explored (cf. Foster 1996a). In addition, the meanings, interpersonal implications, and normative contextual associations of the indigenous terms and concepts that foreign and ethnic patients spontaneously employ in intercultural clinical conversations require examination. Alternatively, when such patients attach English labels to their presenting problems, primary emotions, and psychological states in treatment, it can be instructive to ask them about the native language terms they would apply to such problems, emotions, and states. Therapists might then ask their patients to identify other contexts or situations to which these terms refer. Through such linguistic inquiries, key metapsychological concepts and ideologies often emerge. Had Prakesh's psychotherapist investigated the Bengali terms that he applied to his predicament, he might have grasped Prakesh's construction of his condition as external and situational. Not only would this have brought Prakesh's psychotherapist closer to his patient's experience, but it would have facilitated the exploration of their culturally divergent metapsychologies.

Incorporating ethnographic perspectives within the therapeutic frame is not without its strains. As this research indicates, foreign and ethnic patients who prefer to keep indigenous cultural material outside the clinical arena might resist ethnographic explorations. Some might feel, as Meena did, that their therapists' ethnographic queries configure them as peculiar, exoticized objects. Others might resent explaining too much to their therapists, as Jun did. But this research also suggests that many foreign and ethnic patients will view their therapists' efforts to learn the particularities of their cultural worlds as respectful acknowledgments of difference, as expressions of genuine interest and concern, and as antidotes to otherwise dominant Western psychotherapeutic discourses.

Incorporating ethnographic perspectives into psychotherapy also makes demands on psychotherapists, requiring them to acquire new cultural sensitivities and skills. This newly cultural psychotherapy asks psychotherapists to question their own culturally determined selves, emotions, values, and assumptions, to recognize the specific cultural positions that they occupy, and to be willing to discuss the effects of their varying cultural subjectivities with their patients. It also requires them to critically consider the relevance of Western psychotherapeutic objectives and agendas to the foreign and ethnic patients they treat.

But incorporating ethnographic perspectives into psychotherapy has its limits. Anthropologists continually struggle to grasp the subjective experiences and psychic realities of those whom they construct as "other." Increasingly, they characterize their understandings of other cultures as incomplete and partial. The ethnographic possibilities of intercultural psychotherapies are even more severely limited. There are limits to how much therapists can learn about their foreign and ethnic patients' cultural worlds when intercultural treatments are conducted in a site, and in a language, of displacement. There are limits to how much therapists can learn about their patients within the space of a clinical hour, or within the frame of short-term or once-a-week treatments. And there are limits to how well foreign and ethnic patients can articulate cultural assumptions and ideologies that frequently are automatic, habitual, and taken for granted.

But despite these strains and limits, ethnographic efforts are worthwhile. Exploring reciprocal cultural stereotypes and varying cultural assumptions and psychologies lessens the chances that therapeutic impasses will develop and that counterfeit psychotherapies (Welles 1993) will occur. Investigating foreign and ethnic patients' formative cultural experiences and foundational cultural constructs facilitates access to primary affects, early experiences, and indigenous identifications, and illuminates important aspects of their lives. And examining culturally determined metapsychologies and presenting problems undermines the Western privilege and authority that are deeply engrained in traditional clinical theory and practice. Employing ethnographic perspectives in the clinical consulting room thus works to foster therapeutic rapport and to deepen intercultural psychological treatments.

Questions for Further Inquiry

In addition to indicating theoretical and methodological directions for future intercultural treatments, this research raises questions about such treatments that require further consideration. One set of questions concerns the potential obstacles to intercultural psychotherapies. Might some foreign and ethnic patients experience the cultural differences between themselves and their therapists as presenting insurmountable barriers to treatment? Under what conditions might they find the problems of translation so onerous, the politics of the clinical consulting room so invidious, and its metapsychologies, values, and assumptions so foreign as to preclude effective psychotherapy? A second set of questions concerns how the multiple cultural selves that foreign and ethnic patients experience are articulated and organized. How are emotions, cognitions, subjectivities, and memories distributed across them? How do they interface and interact? Are the selves that develop early in life more primary and enduring, or otherwise distinct, from those that develop later? How do therapeutic interventions that are addressed to a particular self affect other cultural selves?

Future research on intercultural psychotherapies might consider whether patients' erection of uncrossable boundaries between themselves and their therapists replicates the sociocultural and political conflicts that have marked their experience, as well as the profound internal conflicts that separate their differentially realized and valued cultural selves. If, in fact, the rigid interpersonal boundaries that some foreign and ethnic patients establish between themselves and their therapists can be interpreted as mirroring divisive external and internal experiences, then the softening of these boundaries might represent their attempts to reconcile, and to accept, their divergent cultural worlds.

Many psychotherapists wish that the space of clinical treatments might be imagined, as it was in Freud's time, as free of external impingements. Many wish that it were a place of pure psychological process, a place unencumbered by political, historical, socioeconomic, and cultural realities. As this research illustrates, however, the clinical consulting room is a space suffused with the historical, political, and sociocultural circumstances that patients bring to psychotherapy. When patients have experienced the traumas of political oppression, colonial subjugation, and socioeconomic discrimination, these realities, too, pervade the space and shape the dynamics of clinical encounters.

As the processes of globalization intensify, intercultural clinical encounters become everyday occurrences. Once clinical consulting rooms are inhabited by psychotherapists and patients who are differently culturally positioned and configured, therapists will require new ways of exploring the interactions between culture and their patients' psychologies. Under these clinical conditions, cultural inquiry becomes an essential component of the therapeutic project. When explorations of culture are omitted from intercultural psychological treatments, opportunities for therapists to conceive of individuals as both psychologically and culturally constituted, and for culturally dissimilar therapists and patients to create the shared understandings on which successful clinical treatments depend, are lost. But when such explorations are made an integral piece of intercultural psychotherapies—and especially, when they are combined with understandings of presenting problems, transferences, resistances, selves, emotions, and developmental paths as cultural as well as psychological—these treatments can be enriched. When the analytic attitude is combined with the ethnographic attitude, the foundations will be in place for a cultural psychotherapy.

References

Abbasi, A. (1996). *Hate and envy in interracial-intercultural context in therapy.* Paper presented at the Michigan Psychoanalytic Society 21st Annual Symposium, Detroit, April.

———— (1997). *When worlds collide in the analytic space.* Paper presented at the 1997 American Psychoanalytic Association winter meetings, New York, December.

Abel, T., Metraux, R., and Roll, S. (1987). *Psychotherapy and Culture.* Albuquerque: University of New Mexico Press.

Abu-Lughod, L. (1986). *Veiled Sentiments: Honor and Poetry in a Bedouin Society.* Berkeley: University of California Press.

———— (1991). Writing against culture. In *Recapturing Anthropology: Working in the Present*, ed. R. G. Fox, pp. 137–162. Santa Fe: School of American Research.

———— (1997). The interpretation of culture(s) after television. *Representations*, Summer, pp. 109–134.

Adams, M. V. (1996). *The Multicultural Imagination: "Race," Color, and the Unconscious.* London: Routledge.

Akhtar, S. (1984). The syndrome of identity diffusion. *American Journal of Psychiatry* 141(11):1381–1385.

——— (1995). A third individuation: immigration, identity, and the psychoanalytic process. *Journal of the American Psychoanalytic Association* 43(4):1051–1084.

Amati-Mehler, J., Argentieri, S., and Canestri, J. (1993). *The Babel of the Unconscious*. Madison, CT: International Universities Press.

Applegate, J. (1990). Theory, culture and behavior: object relations in context. *Child and Adolescent Social Work Journal* 7(2):85–100.

Astuti, R. (1998). "It's a boy," "it's a girl!" reflections on sex and gender in Madagascar and beyond. In *Bodies and Persons: Comparative Perspectives from Africa and Melanesia*, ed. M. Lambek and A. Strathern, pp. 29–52. New York: Cambridge University Press.

Bakhtin, M. M. (1981). *The Dialogic Imagination: Four Essays by M. M. Bakhtin*, ed. M. Holquist. Austin: University of Texas Press.

Basch-Kahre, E. (1984). On difficulties arising in the transference and countertransference when analyst and analysand have different sociocultural backgrounds. *International Review of Psychoanalysis* 11:61–67.

Battaglia, D. (1990). *On the Bones of the Serpent: Person, Memory and Mortality in Sabarl Island Society*. Chicago: University of Chicago Press.

Behar, R. (1993). *Translated Woman: Crossing the Border with Esperanza's Story*. Boston: Beacon.

Benedict, R. (1934). Anthropology and the abnormal. *Journal of General Psychology* 10:59–92.

Bettelheim, B. (1990). *Freud's Vienna and Other Essays*. New York: Knopf.

Bhabha, H. (1994). *The Location of Culture*. New York: Routledge.

Blos, P. (1979). *The Adolescent Passage*. New York: International Universities Press.

Bock, P. (1980). *Continuities in Psychological Anthropology*. San Francisco: W. H. Freeman.

Boesky, D. (1990). The psychoanalytic process and its components. *Psychoanalytic Quarterly* 59:550–584.

Bowlby, J. (1958). The nature of the child's tie to his mother. *International Journal of Psycho-Analysis* 39:350–373.

Brazelton, T. B. (1977). Implications of infant development among the Mayan Indians of Mexico. In *Culture and Infancy*, ed. P. H. Leiderman, S. Tulkin, and A. Rosenfeld, pp. 151–187. New York: Academic Press.

Brenner, C. (1974). *An Elementary Textbook of Psychoanalysis*. New York: Doubleday.

Briggs, J. (1970). *Never in Anger: Portrait of an Eskimo Family*. Cambridge: Harvard University Press.

Casement, P. (1985). *Learning from the Patient*. New York: Tavistock.

Caton, S. (1986). Salam tahiyah: greetings from the highlands of Yemen. *American Ethnologist* 13:290–308.

Chin, J. (1993). Toward a psychology of difference: psychotherapy for a culturally diverse population. In *Diversity in Psychotherapy*, ed. J. Chin, V. De La Cancela, and Y. Jenkins, pp. 69–91. Westport, CT: Praeger.

Cohler, B. (1992). Intent and meaning in psychoanalysis and cultural study. In *New Directions in Psychological Anthropology*, ed. T. Schwartz, G. White, and C. Lutz, pp. 269–293. New York: Cambridge University Press.

Comas-Diaz, L., and Jacobsen, F. (1991). Ethnocultural transference and countertransference in the therapeutic dyad. *American Journal of Orthopsychiatry* 61(3):392–402.

Cooper, A. (1987). Changes in psychoanalytic ideas: transference interpretation. *Journal of the American Psychoanalytic Association* 35:77–98.

Crapanzano, V. (1992). *Hermes' Dilemma and Hamlet's Desire*. Cambridge: Harvard University Press.

Cushman, P. (1990). Why the self is empty: toward a historically situated psychology. *American Psychologist* 45(5):599–611.

Daniel, V. (1984). *Fluid Signs: Being a Person the Tamil Way*. Berkeley: University of California Press.

Devereux, G. (1958). Cultural factors in psychoanalytic therapy. *Journal of the American Psychoanalytic Association* 1:629–655.

Doi, T. (1981). *The Anatomy of Dependence*. Tokyo: Kodansha International.

——— (1984). Psychotherapy: a cross-cultural perspective from Japan. In *Mental Health Services: The Cross-Cultural Context*, ed. P. Pedersen, N. Sartorius, and A. J. Marsalla, pp. 267–279. Beverly Hills: Sage.

Draguns, J. (1985). Psychological disorders across cultures. In *Handbook of Cross-Cultural Counseling and Therapy*, ed. P. Pedersen, pp. 55–62. Westport, CT: Greenwood.

DuBois, W. E. B. (1903). *The Souls of Black Folk*. New York: Modern Library, 1996.

Dwyer, D. H. (1978). *Images and Self-Images: Male and Female in Morocco*. New York: Columbia University Press.

Erickson, F. (1997). Culture in society and in educational practices. In *Multicultural Education: Issues and Perspectives*, ed. J. A. Banks and C. A. McGee Banks, pp. 32–60. Boston: Allyn & Bacon.

Erickson, F., and Shultz, J. (1981). *The Counselor as Gatekeeper: Social Interaction In Interviews*. New York: Academic.

Ewalt, P., and Mokuau, N. (1995). Self-determination from a Pacific perspective. *Social Work* 40(2):168–176.

Ewing, K. (1990). The illusion of wholeness: culture, "self," and the experience of inconsistency. *Ethos* 18(3):251–278.

Fairbairn, W. R. D. (1941). A revised psychopathology of the psychoses and psychoneuroses. In *Essential Papers on Object Relations*, ed. P. B. Buckley, pp. 71–101. New York: New York University Press, 1986.

——— (1943). The repression and the return of bad objects (with special references to the "war neuroses"). In *Essential Papers on Object Relations*, ed. P. B. Buckley, pp. 102–126. New York: New York University Press.

Flegenheimer, F. (1989). Languages and psychoanalysis: the polyglot patient and the polyglot analyst. *International Review of Psycho-Analysis* 16:377–383.

Foster, R. P. (1996a). Assessing the psychodynamic function of language in the bilingual patient. In *Reaching Across Boundaries of Culture and Class: Widening the Scope of Psychotherapy*, ed. R. Perez Foster, M. Moskowitz, and R. A. Javier, pp. 243–263. Northvale, NJ: Jason Aronson.

———— (1996b). What is a multicultural perspective for psychoanalysis? In *Reaching Across Boundaries of Culture and Class: Widening the Scope of Psychotherapy*, ed. R. Perez Foster, M. Moskowitz, and R. A. Javier, pp. 3–20. Northvale, NJ: Jason Aronson.

Foucault, M. (1963). *The Birth of the Clinic: An Archaeology of Medical Perception*. New York: Pantheon.

———— (1980). *Power/Knowledge*. Sussex, England: Harvester Press.

Freud, S. (1900a). *The Interpretation of Dreams*. New York: Avon, 1965.

———— (1900b). *The Psychopathology of Everyday Life*. New York: Norton, 1965.

———— (1905). Three essays on the theory of sexuality. *Standard Edition* 7:125–143.

———— (1912). A note on the unconscious in psychoanalysis. In *A General Selection from the Works of Sigmund Freud*, ed. J. Rickham, pp. 46–53. New York: Doubleday, 1989.

———— (1913). *Totem and Taboo*. New York: Norton, 1950.

———— (1915). *General Psychological Theory*. New York: Macmillan, 1963.

———— (1920). *Introductory Lectures on Psychoanalysis*. New York: Norton, 1966.

———— (1924). *A General Introduction to Psychoanalysis*. New York: Pocket Books, 1970.

———— (1940). *An Outline of Psychoanalysis*. New York: Norton, 1969.

Friedman, L. (1988). *The Anatomy of Psychotherapy*. Hillsdale, NJ: Analytic Press.

Fromm, E. (1941). *Escape from Freedom*. New York: Farrar & Rinehart.

Geertz, C. (1973). *The Interpretation of Cultures*. New York: Basic Books.

———— (1983). *Local Knowledge: Further Essays in Interpretive Anthropology*. New York: Basic Books.

———— (1984). Anti anti-relativism. *American Anthropologist* 86:263–278.

Gehrie, M. (1979). Culture as an internal representation. *Psychiatry* 42:165–170.

Good, B. (1992). Culture and psychopathology: directions for psychiatric anthropology. In *New Directions in Psychological Anthropology*, ed. T. Schwartz, G. White, and C. Lutz, pp. 181–205. New York: Cambridge University Press.

————— (1994). *Medicine, Rationality and Experience: An Anthropological Perspective*. New York: Cambridge University Press.

Good, M. J., and Good, B. (1988). Ritual, the state, and the transformation of emotional discourse in Iranian society. *Culture, Medicine and Psychiatry* 12:43–63.

Goodenough, W. (1976). Multiculturalism as the normal human experience. *Anthropology and Education Quarterly* 7(4):4–7.

Gorkin, M. (1996). Countertransference in cross-cultural psychotherapy. In *Reaching Across Boundaries of Culture and Class: Widening the Scope of Psychotherapy*, ed. R. Perez Foster, M. Moskowitz, and R. A. Javier, pp. 159–176. Northvale, NJ: Jason Aronson.

Greenberg, J., and Mitchell, S., eds. (1983). *Object Relations in Psychoanalytic Theory*. Cambridge: Harvard University Press.

Greenson, R. (1949). The mother tongue and the mother. *International Journal of Psycho-Analysis* 31:18–23.

Grosskurth, P. (1987). *Melanie Klein: Her World and Her Work*. Cambridge: Harvard University Press.

Gumperz, J. (1972). Introduction. In *Directions in Sociolinguistics: The Ethnography of Communication*, ed. J. Gumperz and D. Hymes, pp. 1–25. New York: Holt, Rinehart & Winston.

Guntrip, H. (1975). My experience of analysis with Fairbairn and Winnicott. *International Review of Psycho-Analysis* 2:145–156.

Gupta, A., and Ferguson, J. (1992). Beyond "culture": space, identity, and the politics of difference. *Cultural Anthropology* 7(1):6–23.

Hardman, C. (1981). The psychology of conformity and self expression among the Lohorung Rai of East Nepal. In *Indigenous Psychologies: The Anthropology of the Self*, ed. P. Heelas and A. Locke, pp. 161–180. New York: Academic.

Harkness, S. (1992). Human development in psychological anthropology. In *New Directions in Psychological Anthropology*, ed. T. Schwartz, G. White, and C. Lutz, pp. 102–122. New York: Cambridge University Press.

Hartmann, H. (1958). *Ego Psychology and the Problem of Adaptation*. New York: International Universities Press.

Heelas, P. (1986). Emotion talk across cultures. In *The Social Construction of Emotions*, ed. R. Harre, pp. 234–266. Oxford: Blackwell.

Herdt, G. (1990). Sambia nosebleeding rites and male proximity to women. In *Cultural Psychology: Essays on Comparative Human Development*, ed. J. Stigler, R. Shweder, and G. Herdt, pp. 366–400. New York: Cambridge University Press.

Herron, W. (1995). Development of the ethnic unconscious. *Psychoanalytic Psychology* 12(4):521–532.

Hollingshead, A., and Redlich, F. (1958). *Social Class and Mental Illness: A Community Study*. New York: Wiley.

Horney, K. (1937). *The Neurotic Personality of Our Time*. New York: Norton.

Jahoda, G. (1993). *Crossroads Between Culture and Mind*. Cambridge: Harvard University Press.

Javier, R. A. (1995). Vicissitudes of autobiographical memories in a bilingual analysis. *Psychoanalytic Psychology* 12(3):429–438.

Javier, R. A., and Rendon, M. (1995). The ethnic unconscious and its role in transference, resistance, and countertransference: an introduction. *Psychoanalytic Psychology* 12(4):513–520.

Kakar, S. (1985). Psychoanalysis and non-Western cultures. *International Review of Psycho-Analysis* 12:441–448.

——— (1990). Stories from Indian psychoanalysis: context and text. In *Cultural Psychology*, ed. J. Stigler, R. Shweder, and G. Herdt, pp. 427–445. New York: Cambridge University Press.

——— (1997). *Culture and Psyche: Collected Essays*. Oxford, England: Oxford University Press.

Kaplan, A. (1993). *French Lessons*. Chicago: University of Chicago Press.

Kennedy, S., Scheirer, J., and Rogers, A. (1984). Our monocultural science. *American Psychologist* 39(9):996–997.

Kirschner, S. (1996). *The Religious and Romantic Origins of Psychoanalysis*. New York: Cambridge University Press.

Klein, M. (1935). A contribution to the psychogenesis of manic-depressive states. In *Essential Papers on Object Relations*, ed. P. B. Buckley, pp. 40–70. New York: New York University Press.

Kleinman, A. (1980). *Patients and Healers in the Context of Culture*. Berkeley: University of California Press.

Kleinman, A., and Good, B. (1985). Meanings, relationships, social affects: historical and anthropological perspectives on depression. In

Culture and Depression: Studies in the Anthropology and Cross-Cultural Psychiatry of Affect and Disorder, ed. A. Kleinman and B. Good, pp. 1–42. Berkeley: University of California Press.

Kleinman, A., and Kleinman, J. (1985). Somatization: the interconnections in Chinese society among culture, depressive experiences, and the meanings of pain. In *Culture and Depression: Studies in the Anthropology and Cross-Cultural Psychiatry of Affect and Disorder*, ed. A. Kleinman and B. Good, pp. 429–490. Berkeley: University of California Press.

Kohut, H. (1971). *The Analysis of the Self*. New York: International Universities Press.

——— (1977). *The Restoration of the Self*. New York: International Universities Press.

——— (1984). *How Does Analysis Cure?* Chicago: University of Chicago Press.

Koss-Chioino, J., and Vargas, L. (1992). Through the cultural looking glass: a model for understanding culturally responsive psychotherapies. In *Working with Culture*, pp. 1–22. San Francisco: Jossey-Bass.

Kuhn, T. (1962). *The Structure of Scientific Revolutions*. Chicago: University of Chicago Press.

Kurtz, S. (1992). *All the Mothers Are One: Hindu India and the Cultural Reshaping of Psychoanalysis*. New York: Columbia University Press.

Lacan, J. (1977). *Ecrits*. New York: Norton.

Landrine, H. (1992). Clinical implications of cultural differences: the referential versus the indexical self. *Clinical Psychology Review* 12:401–415.

LeVine, R. (1982). *Culture, Behavior and Personality*. New York: Aldine.

——— (1990). Infant environments in psychoanalysis: a cross-cultural view. In *Cultural Psychology: Essays on Comparative Human Development*, ed. J. Stigler, R. Shweder, and G. Herdt, pp. 454–474. New York: Cambridge University Press.

Levy, R. (1973). *Tahitians: Mind and Experience in the Society Islands*. Chicago: University of Chicago Press.

——— (1994). *Psychoanalysis and the nonmodern*. Paper presented at "Psychoanalysis among the Disciplines" conference, University of Michigan, Ann Arbor, November.

Lichtenberg, J., Lachmann, F., and Fosshage, J. (1992). *Self and Motivational Systems: Toward a Theory of Psychoanalytic Therapy.* Hillsdale, NJ: Analytic Press.

Littlewood, R. (1990). From categories to contexts: a decade of the "new cross-cultural psychiatry." *British Journal of Psychiatry* 156:308–327.

Lock, M. (1998). Deconstructing the change: female maturation in Japan and North America. In *Welcome to Middle Age! (And Other Cultural Fictions)*, ed. R. A. Shweder, pp. 45–74. Chicago: University of Chicago Press.

Lutz, C. (1988). *Unnatural Emotions: Everyday Sentiments on a Micronesian Atoll and Their Challenge to Western Theory.* Chicago: University of Chicago Press.

Magnarella, P. (1991). Justice in a culturally pluralistic society: the cultural defense on trial. *Journal of Ethnic Studies* 19(3):65–84.

Mahler, M., Pine, F., and Bergman, A. (1975). *The Psychological Birth of the Human Infant.* New York: Basic Books.

Mannheim, B., and Tedlock, D. (1995). Introduction. In *The Dialogic Emergence of Culture*, pp. 1–32. Chicago: University of Chicago Press.

Marcus, G. E., and Fischer, M. M. (1986). *Anthropology as Cultural Critique: An Experimental Moment in the Human Sciences.* Chicago: University of Chicago Press.

Markus, H., and Kitayama, S. (1991). Culture and self: implications for cognition, emotion and motivation. *Psychological Review* 98(2):224–252.

Mead, M. (1928). *Coming of Age in Samoa.* New York: Dell, 1968.

Mitchell, S. (1993). *Hope and Dread in Psychoanalysis.* New York: Basic Books.

——— (1997). *Influence and Autonomy in Psychoanalysis.* Hillsdale, NJ: Analytic Press.

Modell, A. H. (1984). *Psychoanalysis in a New Context.* New York: International Universities Press.

Morley, J. (1991). Perspectives on English for academic purposes. In *Linguistics and Language Pedagogy: The State of the Art*, ed. J. Alatis, pp. 143–166. Washington, DC: Georgetown University Round Table on Language and Linguistics.

Morones, P., and Mikawa, J. (1992). The traditional Mestizo view: implications for modern psychotherapeutic interventions. *Psychotherapy* 29(3):458–466.

Moskowitz, M. (1996). The end of analyzability. In *Reaching Across Boundaries of Culture and Class: Widening the Scope of Psychotherapy*, ed. R. Perez Foster, M. Moskowitz, and R. A. Javier, pp. 179–193. Northvale, NJ: Jason Aronson.

Muensterberger, W. (1969). Psyche and environment: sociocultural variations in separation and individuation. *Psychoanalytic Quarterly* 38:191–216.

Nanda, S. (1994). Hijras: an alternative sex and gender role in India. In *Third Sex, Third Gender: Beyond Sexual Dimorphism in Culture and History*, ed. G. Herdt, pp. 373–418. New York: Zone Books.

Nandy, A. (1995). *The Savage Freud*. Princeton, NJ: Princeton University Press.

Obeysekere, G. (1990). *The Work of Culture*. Chicago: University of Chicago Press.

Ogden, T. (1994). *Subjects of Analysis*. Northvale, NJ: Jason Aronson.

Ortner, S. (1996). *Making Gender: The Politics and Erotics of Culture*. Boston: Beacon.

Pine, F. (1990). *Drive, Ego, Object and Self*. New York: Basic Books.

Proctor, R. (1991). *Value-free Science? Purity and Power in Modern Knowledge*. Cambridge: Harvard University Press.

Rabin, H. (1995). The liberating effect on the analyst of the paradigm shift in psychoanalysis. *Psychoanalytic Psychology* 12(4):467–481.

Renik, O. (1993). Analytic interaction: conceptualizing technique in light of the analyst's irreducible subjectivity. *Psychoanalytic Quarterly* 62:553–571.

Rogler, L., Malgady, R., Costantino, G., and Blumenthal, R. (1987). What do culturally sensitive mental health services mean? The case of Hispanics. *American Psychologist* 42(6):565–570.

Roland, A. (1988). *In Search of Self in India and Japan*. Princeton, NJ: Princeton University Press.

——— (1996). *Cultural Pluralism and Psychoanalysis: The Asian and North American Experience*. New York: Routledge.

Rosaldo, M. (1983). The shame of headhunters and the autonomy of the self. *Ethos* 11(3):135–151.

Rosaldo, R. (1989). *Culture and Truth: The Remaking of Social Analysis.* Boston: Beacon.

Rosen, L. (1985). Intentionality and the concept of the person. In *Criminal Justice*, ed. J. R. Pennock and J. W. Chapman, pp. 52–77. New York: New York University Press.

Rouse, R. (1991). Mexican migration and the social space of post-modernism. *Diaspora* 1(1):8–23.

Russell, D. (1988). Language and psychotherapy: the influence of nonstandard English in clinical practice. In *Clinical Guidelines in Cross-Cultural Mental Health*, ed. L. Comas-Diaz and E. Griffith, pp. 33–68. New York: Wiley.

Sabin, J. (1975). Translating despair. *American Journal of Psychiatry* 132(2):197–199.

Saleebey, D. (1994). Culture, theory and narrative: the intersection of meanings in practice. *Social Work* 39(4):351–359.

Sampson, E. E. (1988). The debate on individualism. *American Psychologist* 43(1):15–22.

——— (1989). The challenge of social change for psychology. *American Psychologist* 44(6):914–921.

Schafer, R. (1992). *Retelling a Life: Narrative and Dialogue in Psychoanalysis.* New York: Basic Books.

Scheper-Hughes, N. (1990). Mother love and child death in northeast Brazil. In *Cultural Psychology: Essays on Comparative Human Development*, ed. J. W. Stigler, R. A. Shweder, and G. Herdt, pp. 542–565. New York: Cambridge University Press.

Schwartz, T. (1978). Where is the culture?: personality as the distributive locus of culture. In *The Making of Psychological Anthropology*, ed. G. Spindler, pp. 419–441. Berkeley: University of California Press.

——— (1992). Anthropology and psychology. In *New Directions in Psychological Anthropology*, ed. T. Schwartz, G. White, and C. Lutz, pp. 324–349. New York: Cambridge University Press.

Shostak, M. (1981). *Nisa: The Life and Words of a !Kung Woman.* Cambridge: Harvard University Press.

Shweder, R. A. (1990). Cultural psychology: What is it? In *Cultural Psychology: Essays on Comparative Human Development*, ed. J. W. Stigler, R. A. Shweder, and G. Herdt, pp. 1–43. New York: Cambridge University Press.

———— (1993). Cultural psychology: Who needs it? *Annual Review of Psychology* 44:497–523.

———— (1998). Introduction: Welcome to middle age! In *Welcome to Middle Age! (And Other Cultural Fictions)*, pp. ix–xvii. Chicago: University of Chicago Press.

Shweder, R. A., and Bourne, E. (1984). Does the concept of the person vary cross-culturally? In *Culture Theory: Essays on Mind, Self and Emotion*, ed. R. A. Shweder and R. A. LeVine, pp. 158–199. New York: Cambridge University Press.

Slote, W. (1996). Koreans abroad in therapy. In *Cultural Pluralism and Psychoanalysis: The Asian and North American Experience*, A. Roland, pp. 187–198. New York: Routledge.

Small, M. (1998). *Our Babies, Ourselves*. New York: Doubleday.

Smith, J. (1981). Self and experience in Maori culture. In *Indigenous Psychologies: The Anthropology of the Self*, ed. P. Heelas and A. Locke, pp. 145–159. New York: Academic.

Spindler, G. (1978). *The Making of Psychological Anthropology*. Berkeley: University of California Press.

Stern, D. (1985). *The Interpersonal World of the Infant*. New York: Basic Books.

Stolorow, R., Atwood, G., and Brandchaft, B. (1994). Masochism and its treatment. In *The Intersubjective Perspective*, pp. 121–126. Northvale, NJ: Jason Aronson.

Sue, S. (1998). In search of cultural competence in psychotherapy and counseling. *American Psychologist* 53(4):440–448.

Sue, S., and Zane, N. (1987). The role of culture and cultural techniques in psychotherapy. *American Psychologist* 42(1):37–45.

Sullivan, H. (1953). *The Interpersonal Theory of Psychiatry*. New York: Norton.

———— (1954). *The Psychiatric Interview*. New York: Norton.

———— (1956). *Clinical Studies in Psychiatry*. New York: Norton.

Super, C.M., and Harkness, S. (1986). The developmental niche: A conceptualization at the interface of child and culture. *International Journal of Behavior and Development* 9:545–569.

Sutherland, J. (1989). *Fairbairn's Journey into the Interior.* London: Free Association Books.

Taketomo, Y. (1989). An American-Japanese transcultural psychoanalysis and the issue of teacher transference. *Journal of the American Academy of Psychoanalysis* 17(3):427–450.

Tedlock, B. (1987). Zuni and Quiche dream sharing and interpretation. In *Dreaming: Anthropological and Psychological Interpretations*, pp. 105–131. New York: Cambridge University Press.

Thompson, C. (1950). *Psychoanalysis: Evolution and Development.* New York: Da Capo, 1984.

Ticho, G. (1971). Cultural aspects of transference and countertransference. *Bulletin of the Menninger Clinic* 35(5):313–334.

Triandis, H. (1995). *Individualism and Collectivism.* Boulder, CO: Westview.

Tronick, E., Morelli, G., and Winn, S. (1987). Multiple caretaking of Efe (Pygmy) infants. *American Anthropologist* 89:96–106.

Tsui, P., and Schultz, G. (1985). Failure of rapport: why psychotherapeutic engagement fails in the treatment of Asian clients. *American Journal of Orthopsychiatry* 55(4):561–569.

Varghese, F. T. (1983). The racially different psychiatrist—implications for psychotherapy. *Australian and New Zealand Journal of Psychiatry* 17:329–333.

Varma, V. K. (1988). Culture, personality and psychotherapy. *International Journal of Social Psychiatry* 34(2):142–149.

Wallerstein, R. (1995). *The Talking Cures: The Psychoanalyses and the Psychotherapies.* New Haven: Yale University Press.

Warren, K. (1995). Each mind is a world: dilemmas of feeling and intention in a Kaqchikel Maya community. In *Other Intentions: Cultural Contexts and the Attributions of Inner States*, ed. L. Rosen, pp. 47–67. Santa Fe: School of American Research Press.

Weber, M. (1963). "Objectivity" in social science and science policy. In *The Philosophy of the Social Sciences*, ed. M. Natanson, pp. 335–418. New York: Random House.

Welles, J. K. (1993). *Counterfeit analyses: maintaining the illusion of knowing.* Paper presented at the APA Division 39 Spring meeting, New York.

White, G., and Kirkpatrick, J., eds. (1985). *Person, Self and Experience: Exploring Pacific Ethnopsychologies.* Berkeley: University of California Press.

White, G., and Lutz, C. (1992). Introduction. In *New Directions in Psychological Anthropology*, ed. T. Schwartz, G. White, and C. Lutz, pp. 1–17. New York: Cambridge University Press.

Wilce, J. (1995). "I can't tell you all my troubles": conflict, resistance, and metacommunication in Bangladeshi illness interactions. *American Ethnologist* 22(4):927–952.

Williams, A. (1996). Skin color in psychotherapy. In *Reaching Across Boundaries of Culture and Class*, ed. R. Perez Foster, M. Moskowitz, and R. A. Javier, pp. 211–224. Northvale, NJ: Jason Aronson.

Winnicott, D. W. (1960a). Ego distortions in terms of true and false self. In *The Maturational Processes and the Facilitating Environment*, pp. 140–152. Madison, CT: International Universities Press.

——— (1960b). The theory of the parent–infant relationship. In *Essential Papers on Object Relations*, ed. P. Buckley, pp. 233–253. New York: New York University Press.

——— (1971). *Playing and Reality.* London: Tavistock.

Wohl, J. (1989). Cross-cultural psychotherapy. In *Counseling across Cultures*, ed. P. Pedersen, J. Draguns, W. Lonner, and J. Trimble, pp. 79–114. Honolulu: University of Hawaii Press.

Young, L. (1994). *Crosstalk and Culture in Sino-American Communication.* New York: Cambridge University Press.

Index

ABOUT THE AUTHOR

Karen Seeley, M.S.W., Ph.D., is an adjunct professor of anthropology at Columbia University, an adjunct professor of psychology at Barnard College, and a staff psychotherapist at Barnard College's Counseling and Psychological Services. She received a master's degree in comparative human development from the Harvard Graduate School of Education, a master's degree in social work from the New York University School of Social Work, and a doctorate from the University of Pennsylvania Graduate School of Education, where she specialized in cultural psychology. Dr. Seeley is in the private practice of psychotherapy in New York City.